INTRODUCTION TO ET
A READER

Philip Q. Yang

California Polytechnic State University

San Luis Obispo

KENDALL/HUNT PUBLISHING COMPANY
4050 Westmark Drive   Dubuque, Iowa 52002

Copyright © 1999 by Kendall/Hunt Publishing Company

ISBN 0-7872-5957-X

Printed in the United States of America
10 9 8 7 6 5 4 3 2

For My Students

Table of Contents

Preface   ix

Chapter 1 Introduction
1. The History, Development, and Future of Ethnic Studies   2
   Evelyn Hu-DeHart
2. Statement of the National Association for Ethnic Studies   11
   National Association for Ethnic Studies

Chapter 2 Ethnic Identity
1. Ethnicity as Kin Selection: The Biology of Nepotism   15
   Pierre van den Berghe
2. Constructing Ethnicity: Creating and Recreating Ethnic Identity
   and Culture   22
   Joane Nagel
3. "Soulmaning": Using Race for Political and Economic Gain   53
   Luther Wright, Jr.
4. "I'm Just Who I am': Race Is No Longer Black or White. So, What Does   57
   This Mean for America?"
   Jack E. White
5. A Black Spy in White America   62
   Danzy Senna
6. What Am I?   64
   Laura Hymson
7. What Are You?   66
   Ryan Trammel

Chapter 3 Ethnic Stratification
1. A Theory of the Origin of Ethnic Stratification   70
   Donald Noel
2. The "Giddy Multitude": The Hidden Origins of Slavery   89
   Ronald Takaki

Chapter 4 Ethnic Adaptation
1. Assimilation in America: Theory and Reality   98
   Milton M. Gordon
2. An Alternative Perspective for Studying American Ethnicity   117
   Andrew Greeley

3. Colonized and Immigrant Minorities   128
    Robert Blauner
4. The Prodigal Daughter   132
    Terry Hong

Chapter 5 Ethnic Differences in Socioeconomic Achievement
1. Ethnic Differences in IQ and Ethnic Inequalities   136
    Richard Herrstein and Charles Murray
2. Culture   138
    Thomas Sowell
3. Education and Ethnic Mobility   143
    Stephen Steinberg
4. Making It in America   147
    Alejandro Portes and Rubén G. Rumbaut

Chapter 6 Racism
1. Verbal Race Wars   156
    Dexter Lopina and Stanley Vickers
2. The police and the Black Male   158
    Elijah Anderson
3. What Color Are You?   163
    Melissa Eastham
4. The Ages of Intolerance   165
    Jose Estorga

Chapter 7 Ethnic Segregation
1. Changes in the Segregation of Whites from Blacks during the 1980s:
    Small Steps toward a More Integrated Society   168
    Reynolds Farley and William Frey
2. Public Schools in the United States: Still Separate, Still Unequal 170
    Applied Research Center
3. Recent Changes in School Desegregation   174
    Jeanne Weiler

Chapter 8 Ethnic Conflict
1. Blacks, Jews Take New Steps to Heal Divisions   182
    Andrew Ford
2. Black, Cuban Racial Chasm Splits Miami   186
    Mike Clary

3. Korean/African-American Conflicts   189
    Pyong Gap Min

Chapter 9 Race, Class, and Gender
    1. Conceptualizing Race, Class, and Gender   194
        Margaret Anderson and Patricia Hill Collins

Chapter 10 Controversial Issues in Ethnic Studies
    1. Affirming Affirmative Action   198
        Jesse Jackson
    2. What to Do About Affirmative Action   203
        Arch Puddington
    3. Mend It, Don't End it   216
        Bill Clinton
    4. Bashing Illegals in California   224
        Elizabeth Kadetsky
    5. Securing Our Nation's Borders   228
        Pete Wilson
    6. Text of Proposition 187 – The Save Our State Initiative   231
    7. Text of Proposition 209 – The California Civil Rights Initiative 237
    8. Text of Proposition 227 – The English Language Education for
        Children in Public Schools Initiative   238

Preface

This book is a product of my years of teaching Introduction to Ethnic Studies at California Polytechnic State University (Cal Poly), San Luis Obispo. Complementary to another introductory ethnic studies course that highlights the experiences of various ethnic or racial groups, Introduction to Ethnic Studies at Cal Poly is designed as a course that focuses on "comparative approaches involved in the interdisciplinary study of United States and international ethnic groups." When I began to teach this thematic course in 1995, I found neither any textbook nor any anthology suitable for the course. I was compelled to assemble a reader for my students. Over the years, the reader has undergone many revisions in content, selection, and length. When Kendall/Hunt Publishing Company learned the potential market of this reader, they immediately offered to publish it. After some thoughts, I consented. I thought that the publication of this collection could benefit many students who take Introduction to Ethnic Studies or similar courses in more than 800 ethnic studies programs nationwide. Moreover, the production of the book can invite further endeavors to improve it.

Introduction to Ethnic Studies: A Reader is a companion to my book *Ethnic Studies: Issues and Approaches* forthcoming by the State University of New York Press. While the latter is a scholarly book/textbook that systematically surveys the history of ethnic studies in the United States, its methodologies, its major issues and theoretical approaches, and current controversies in the field, it contains no original writings of different authors. The primary purpose of this reader is to provide students with first-hand reading materials on main issues and approaches in ethnic studies. The selections can enhance students' ability to critically assess the literature in ethnic studies, and the stories or empirical cases can intrigue students and enliven class discussions. Both books together should better serve students enrolled in Introduction to Ethnic Studies or the like.

In selecting materials for this compilation, I have sought to strike a balance between classic selections and the latest in the field, between social science writings and humanistic works, and between theoretical selections and empirical pieces or stories. In addition, to facilitate class discussions I have included the original texts of several contentious ballot measures passed by California voters in the past several years including Propositions 187, 209, and 227. In order not to bore students, I have also opted to cull shorter pieces or curtail long ones.

This book is organized into ten chapters. Chapter 1 aims at providing information about the history and the field of ethnic studies. Chapters 2 to 9 address main issues in ethnic studies such as ethnic identity; ethnic stratification; ethnic adaptation; ethnic differences in socioeconomic achievement; racism; ethnic segregation; ethnic conflict; and race, class, and gender. The readings represent influential approaches to the issues addressed and present some empirical evidence. The last chapter highlights current controversies in ethnic studies that demand social actions, such as affirmative action, illegal immigration, and bilingual education. To guide students in organizing the analytical frameworks or perspectives of the readings, I have included, in the beginning of each chapter, a synopsis of the selections with an emphasis on their approaches to the key issue(s) of the chapter.

Instructors who teach Introduction to Ethnic Studies or comparable courses are encouraged to modify the readings according to their specialties, their preferences, and their availability of time. For example, humanities-oriented teachers may opt to add stories, poems, and personal narratives of their choosing. Instructors familiar with quantitative methodologies may increase the amount of quantitative evidence. Topics could be added or deleted depending upon whether a school is run on a quarter system or a semester system.

I own the greatest debt to the students who have taken my Introduction to Ethnic Studies course at Cal Poly San Luis Obispo over the years. It was them who motivated me to start and to keep revising this collections. It was them who collectively contributed to searching for intriguing articles for this reader. It was them who gave me feedback to the suitability and the quality of the selections. It is to them that I dedicate this book.

This book might not have taken shape without the encouragement of Dr. Robert Gish, Director of the Ethnic Studies Department at Cal Poly. In particular, his suggestion of turning it into a companion to my SUNY Press book nudged me closer toward the direction of publishing this reader.

I am indebted to many professionals at Kendall/Hunt Publishing Company for their indispensable assistance in the publication of this book.

Last but not least, my gratitude goes to my wife Jianling Li and my daughter MingYang for their support and for just being there.

CHAPTER 1

Introduction

When and under what conditions did ethnic studies as a discipline emerge in the United States? How has it developed over time? What is the current status of ethnic studies? What is ethnic studies about? What are the basic approaches of ethnic studies? The readings in this introductory chapter attempt to answer these questions.

The article by Evelyn Hu-DeHart provides an overview about the history, current status, and future of ethnic studies as a discipline in America. It also discusses what ethnic studies is, how it differs from "international area studies," and what the methodologies of ethnic studies are. The statement of the National Association for Ethnic Studies further sheds light on how ethnic studies is presently defined and demarcated.

1. The History, Development, and Future of Ethnic Studies
   Evelyn Hu-DeHart

2. Statement of the National Association for Ethnic Studies
   National Association for Ethnic Studies

Article 1.1

The History, Development, and Future of Ethnic Studies

Evelyn Hu-DeHart

Inspired by the civil rights movement and buoyed by the energy of the antiwar movement, a generation of American college students invaded administrative offices 25 years ago, demanding fundamental changes in higher education. The occupation of administrative offices by students of color and their white supporters startled and terrified presidents, deans, and professors. The faculty and administration were almost exclusively white and predominantly male—and the student body was predominantly white and primarily male. The curriculum had been fairly static since the first decades of the century, and multiculturalism had not evolved.

Beginning in 1968 at San Francisco State University and at the Berkeley and Santa Barbara campuses of the University of California, the movement spread to many other schools throughout the nation. Students of color demanded better access to higher education, changes in the curriculum, the recruitment of more professors of color, and the creation of ethnic studies programs. These programs were the beginning of multicultural curriculum reform in higher education.

From their origins in California, ethnic studies programs and departments have survived and proliferated throughout the United States.[1] After serious cut-backs during the budgetary crises of the 1970s and 1980s, they are back bigger and stronger than ever. Ethnic studies programs have been revitalized, reorganized, and reconceptualized. Indeed, they are increasingly becoming institutionalized. The field of ethnic studies has produced a prodigious amount of new scholarship, much of which is good and innovative. However, as is true in all disciplines, some of the work is weak. The perspectives of ethnic studies are intended not only to increase our knowledge base but eventually to transform the disciplines. Their influence is being widely felt and hotly debated.

Today there are more than 700 ethnic studies programs and departments in the United States.[2] They are represented by five established professional associations: the National Council of Black Studies, The National Association of Chicano Studies, the Asian-American Studies Association, The American Indian Studies Association, and the National Association of Ethnic Studies. The Association of Puerto Rican Studies was formed in 1992.

A disproportionate number of ethnic studies programs are located in public colleges and universities because these institutions are more susceptible to public pressure than are private schools. There are more ethnic studies programs in the West because of that region's fast-growing and ethnically diverse population. The biggest and most powerful programs are found in four public research universities in the West:

1. The Department of Ethnic Studies at the University of California, Berkeley, has programs in Asian-American, Chicano, and Native-American studies and offers the nation's only Ph.D. in ethnic studies.
2. The Department of Ethnic Studies at the University of California, San Diego, was created in 1990. It takes a comparative approach and has no ethnic-specific programs.
3. The Department of American Ethnic Studies at the University of Washington, Seattle, was created in 1985 by bringing together programs in African American, Asian American, and Chicago studies. → Chicano
4. The Center for Studies of Ethnicity and Race in America at the University of Colorado, Boulder, was created in 1987 by consolidating existing programs in black studies and Chicano studies and adding new programs in Asian-American and American Indian studies.

Aside from the West, Bowling Green State University in Ohio has one of the oldest ethnic studies departments, which was founded in 1979.

During the decades in which ethnic studies programs were established and grew strong, American society underwent dramatic changes that continue to this day. The civil rights movement might have removed the last vestiges of legal apartheid in the United States. However, other ways have been invented to deny equal opportunity to the historically marginalized communities of color. In the 25 years since the issuance of the Kerner Commission Report, which spoke of two Americas—one rich, one poor; one white, one black—the gulf that divides the nation has grown wider than ever. Today 1% of the population of the U.S. has "gained control" of more of the nation's wealth than the bottom 90%. This situation parallels the stark and painful inequality in much of the Third World.[3]

Significant demographic changes have also taken place in the United States in the last 25 years. Since 1965, when U.S. immigration laws eliminated the "national origins" quotas that favored Europeans, immigrants from Asia, Latin America, and the Caribbean have for the first time outnumbered white European immigrants to the U.S. The country's political and military interventions since World War II have also boosted immigration from Asia, Central America, and the Caribbean. From 1965 to the 1990s, non-Europeans have composed over 80% of all immigrants—almost nine million in a surge during the 1980s. This new wave of immigration accounts for the doubling of Asian-Americans in the U.S. population and the increase of Latinos by 60%.[4]

As a result of these immigration patterns, the U.S. population is rapidly becoming "colored" and increasingly more diverse—in race, ethnicity, religion, language, music, art, literature, and other cultural expressions. In fact, with more than half of its population already highly diversified, California provides a glimpse of the nation's future. It will be an oxymoronic "majority minority" state by 2050. The relatively high birthrate of minority

Americans, as well as their lower age distribution, will mean that ever increasing numbers of people of color will fill our classrooms and enter our work force.

In order to bring about a truly pluralistic democracy, our education system at all levels not only must reflect the nation's diversity in its student body, faculty, and curriculum, but also must seek to achieve comparable educational outcomes for all groups in society. The education reforms known collectively as "multiculturalism"—one example of which is the integration of ethnic studies into the college curriculum—have as major goals the establishment of democratic pluralism and the achievement of educational equity.

The Nature of Ethnic Studies

What is ethnic studies? First, the field is distinct from global or international studies, particularly those programs known generally, as "area studies," with which ethnic studies is often compared and confused. Area studies programs arose out of American imperialism in the Third World and bear names such as African studies, Asian studies, and Latin American studies. These programs were designed to focus on U.S./Third World relations and to train specialists to uphold U.S. hegemony in regions in which the U.S. had heavy economic and political investments. Area studies scholars have become far more critical of U.S./Third World relations since the antiwar movement of the 1960s, and many have adopted third World perspectives. However, they are still predominantly white male scholars entrenched in established departments, subscribing to and benefiting from traditional patterns of distributing power and rewards in the academy.[5]

Ethnic studies programs, which grew out of student and community grassroots movements, challenge the prevailing academic power structure and the Eurocentric curricula of our colleges and universities. These insurgent programs had a subversive agenda from the outset; hence they were suspect and regarded as illegitimate even as they were grudgingly allowed into the academy. Definitions of ethnic studies vary from campus to campus and change over time. What the programs have in common is a specific or comparative focus on groups viewed as "minorities" in American society. European immigrants have dominated America and defined the national identity as white and Western. Groups of color have a shared history of having been viewed as distinct from the European immigrants and their descendants. They are the "unmeltable ethnics," or ethnics without options regarding whether to invoke their ethnicity.[6]

A culturally nationalistic vantage point characterized almost all of the early ethnic studies programs. This perspective still has enormous resonance in the Afrocentrism of some black studies programs. Most ethnic studies scholars today adopt a relational and comparative approach, poking at questions of power through the prisms of race, class, and gender. One definition of the academic purpose of ethnic studies can be found in the 1990 proposal to create a Department of Ethnic Studies at the University of California, San Diego:

> Focusing on immigration, slavery, and confinement, those three processes that combined to create in the United States a nation of nations, Ethnic Studies intensively examines the histories, languages and cultures of America's racial and ethnic groups

in and of themselves, their relationships to each other, and particularly, in structural contexts of power.[7]

To most scholars in the field, it is the role of ethnic studies to pose a fundamental challenge to the dominant paradigms of academic disciplines. While he was specifically addressing the goals of Puerto Rican Studies, Frank Bonilla, founder and director of Hunter College's Centro de Estudios Puertorriqueños, expressed guiding principles applicable to all ethnic studies:

> We have set out to contest effectively those visions of the world that assume or take for granted the inevitability and indefinite duration of the class and colonial oppression that has marked Puerto Rico's history. All the disciplines that we are most directly drawing upon—history, economics, sociology, anthropology, literature, psychology, pedagogy—as they are practiced in the United States are deeply implicated in the construction of that vision of Puerto Ricans as an inferior, submissive people, trapped on the underside of relations from which there is no foreseeable exit.[8]

In short, the field of ethnic studies provides a "liberating educational process"[9] that challenges Western imperialism and Eurocentrism, along with their claims to objectivity and universalism. Ethnic studies scholars recognize the importance of perspective, believing that "perspectives...are always partial and situated in relationship to power."[10] Putting it concretely, "It is both practically and theoretically incorrect to use the experience of white ethnics as a guide to comprehend those of nonwhite, or so-called 'racial' minorities."[11]

As an approach to knowledge, ethnic studies is interdisciplinary—and it is more than just a grab bag of unrelated applications of separate discipline-based methodologies. Ethnic studies scholarship focuses on the central roles that race and ethnicity play in the construction of American history, culture, and society. Johnnella Butler, head of the Department of American Ethnic Studies at the University of Washington, Seattle, writes, "Its interdisciplinary nature and simultaneous attention to race, ethnicity, gender, and class should provide the scholarship and teaching necessary to illuminate it as a specific field of study."[12] Butler is a strong proponent of the comparative approach to ethnic studies, and she urges the examination of connections between groups and experiences. She proposes a "matrix model," described as "looking at the matrix of race, class, ethnicity, and gender...within the context of cultural, political, social, and economic expression."[13]

Ethnic studies seeks to recover and reconstruct the histories of those Americans whom history has neglected; to identify and credit their contributions to the making of U.S. Society and culture; to chronicle protest and resistance; and to establish alternative values and visions, institutions and cultures. Ethnic studies scholarship has become a new discipline in and of itself. It is continuously defining and clarifying its own unique methodology and epistemology.

CURRENT DEBATES

Ethnic studies is not totally stabilized, institutionalized, harmonious, or monolithic. It is in a state of transition structurally, intellectually, and ideologically. There is little uniformity among the approximately 700 ethnic-specific programs and departments in the United States. In part, the discussions within ethnic studies are no different from the ongoing debates among biologists, anthropologists, and historians as their fields grow and change. While discussions among ethnic studies practitioners are not usually vituperative or destructive, they are often heated and reflect the state of development of a young discipline. The following comments by no means exhaust the list of issues but should convey some sense of the concerns in the field. This discussion should also suggest the directions that the field of ethnic studies will probably take as it moves into the 21st century.

The key organizational issue seems to be the structure and location of ethnic studies within the academy. Should ethnic studies be an interdisciplinary program that follows the model of area studies, drawing faculty from established disciplines? Or should ethnic studies push for autonomy and full departmental status in view of the fact that the field has developed as a discipline? Should ethnic studies now concentrate on establishing intellectual credentials and credibility, while loosening or severing ties, forged in the early days, with minority student services?

As a program relying on departments for faculty members and courses, ethnic studies has no control over faculty resources and minimal influence on course offerings. Thus it has little power to define itself intellectually and academically. It becomes nearly impossible to build a sound, coherent, and intellectually challenging program through a rather haphazard sampling of whatever courses may be available through a number of different departments.

The unfortunate result of such efforts, well-intentioned though they may be, is that they fuel the argument of skeptics and critics that ethnic studies programs lack rigor and legitimacy. Hence in practice such programs at best function as mere coordinating bodies, organizing a set of loosely related courses around an ethnic-specific or comparative theme. They must rely on the good will, sympathy toward their mission, and positive attitude of traditional departments. Most often, the relationship between ethnic studies programs and departments is tenuous and uneasy, if not outrightly hostile.

The relationship between ethnic studies programs and traditional academic departments becomes unmanageable because it raises issues of turf protection, competition for scarce resources, and racism on the part of traditional scholars. Traditional scholars find it difficult to shake off their preconceptions about the illegitimacy and inferiority of ethnic studies programs and, by extension, ethnic studies scholars. Ethnic studies programs suffer disproportionately because they are the weaker member of the partnership. During periods of financial constraints, ethnic studies programs can easily be cut back or disbanded. This happened to many of them in the 1970s.

Departments, on the other hand, control budgets, hire their own faculty members, and, most important, determine the course of study. Hence they define the field, setting standards for pedagogy, research, and publication. In short, they have status and, at least structurally, enjoy equality with other disciplines. Departments can also readily create and sponsor graduate programs. Not surprisingly, there is little dispute within ethnic studies about the theoretical desirability of establishing departments rather than programs.

But political expediency and practical financial matters often dictate the less ideal course of action. In public institutions, a program can be created by administrative fiat, whereas the creation of a new department requires extensive review by the faculty and by other oversight bodies. This is a long, drawn-out process that can become contentious. A program is still the most common model for ethnic studies because it is the easiest and least costly way to accommodate a new discipline. Tight budgets and programs, retrenchment are likely to increase in the mid-1990s because of the limited resources that most colleges and universities will have.

On those campuses where administrators have yielded to the department model, ethnic studies departments usually have few faculty members, and most of them are untenured, which reduces them to a marginal status within the academy. Nevertheless, seeing it as an easy way to make a positive statement of their commitment to diversity, administrators are often eager to establish some kind of ethnic studies presence on their campuses. They also know that, if they can go the extra mile and create an ethnic studies department with its own faculty lines, it will be the fastest route to diversifying the faculty. Ethnic studies scholars and supporters, having been stranded on the margins for so long, see any movement toward the inside as acceptable—hence their tendency to settle for less.

Undeniably, the field of ethnic studies is being institutionalized. In addition to the creation of ethnic studies programs or departments, there is a general push toward multiculturalism on the nation's college campuses. Curriculum reform movements are striving to integrate ethnic studies perspectives and scholarship into the mainstream curriculum. This goal entails more than hiring ethnic studies scholars in traditional departments such as history, sociology, psychology, political science, and literature. Ethnic studies scholars must be encouraged to integrate their discipline's scholarship and perspectives into other university courses. A current debate among students and faculty members on many campuses concerns the desirability of requiring an ethnic studies course as part of the core or general undergraduate education program.

About five years ago campuses began offering faculty members voluntary inservice training workshops typically described as "curriculum integration projects." Now that organizations such as the Ford Foundation have added their support to these endeavors, the workshops have become more ambitious and were recently redesignated as "curriculum transformation" programs.[14] This is good news for ethnic studies. With institutionalization and widespread influence come respect and legitimacy.

In spite of the good news about ethnic studies, these developments have created some uneasiness. Does the push for multiculturalism on campuses threaten to swallow up or co-opt ethnic studies? Will the fading argument be revived that, once the campus is integrated, ethnic studies will no longer be necessary? Even as some applaud the inevitable spillover of ethnic studies into the rest of the curriculum, they also note the tension between that field and traditional fields, "as people try to locate the boundaries between the two."[15]

The dispute over boundaries raises a larger issue that will be even more hotly debated in the future. In 1988 Jesse Vasquez, head of the Puerto Rican Studies Department at Queens College, noted that "even traditional academic departments, formerly resolute in their refusal to include ethnic studies courses in their curriculum, now cross-list, and in many in-

stances generate their own version of ethnic studies courses in direct competition with existing ethnic studies programs." Vasquez also warned that these multicultural curricular reforms may have "effectively managed to co-opt some of the more socially and politically
palatable aspects of the ethnic studies movement of the late 1960s and early 1970s." He
went on to say that

> these latest curricular trends seem to be moving us away from the political and social
> urgency intended by the founders of ethnic studies and toward the kind of program
> design [that] conforms to and is consistent with the traditional academic struc-
> tures…Certainly, the struggle to legitimize these programs academically has taken
> the edge and toughness out of the heart of some of our ethnic studies curriculum.[16]

The question is, Does the drive for legitimacy and institutionalization entail tradeoffs for
ethnic studies that may, ironically, weaken the field in the long run? Should ethnic studies be
"seduced and lulled" into believing that institutionalization translates into full acceptance,
and does that acceptance signal a change in traditional faculty attitudes, behavior, and values? Vasquez does not think so. Neither does Epifanio San Juan, Jr. Trained at Harvard in
Western Literature, San Juan has recently become one of the most incisive and vociferous
critics of U.S. racial politics as manifested through issues of multiculturalism and ethnic
studies. He is concerned that the "gradual academization" of ethnic studies will force it into
the dominant European orthodoxy, which emphasizes ethnicity to the exclusion of race.
Such an approach will" systematically [erase] from the historical frame of reference any
perception of race and racism as causal factors in the making of the political and economic
structure of the United States."[17]

If race and racism should remain the analytical core of ethnic studies, when would the
total retreat of ethnic studies into the academy not be a contradiction? How could the field
separate itself from the ongoing, real-life struggles of people of color in the U.S. today?
That is precisely the dilemma that noted ethnic studies scholars such as Henry Louis Gates,
Jr., head of the Black Studies Department at Harvard, point out. His solution, in describing a
black studies agenda for the 21st century, is "an emphasis upon cultural studies and public
policy, as two broad and fruitful rubrics under which to organize our discipline."[18] San Juan
also seeks to capture the "activist impulse" that propelled the creation of ethnic studies in
the first place. He and other scholars characterize this challenge as the integration of theory
(or critique) and praxis. Others put it even more simply and directly: the challenge is to rec-
oncile the academic goal of ethnic studies—the production of knowledge—with its original
commitment to liberating and empowering the communities of color. San Juan wonders if
ethnic studies will return to its "inaugural vision" of being a part of the "wide-ranging popular movements for justice and equality, for thoroughgoing social transformation." Or will it
settle for being just another respected academic unit? These are the questions, challenges,
and opportunities that the field of ethnic studies faces as we enter a new century.

Notes

1. There are several accounts of the founding and histories of various ethnic studies programs. See, for example, Rudolfo Acuna, *Occupied America*, 3rd ed. (Harper & Row, 1988). The *Amerasia Journal* devoted an entire issue (vol. 15, no.1, 1989) to the struggles connected with the founding of Asian American studies. For a brief history of black studies, see Darlene Clark Hine," The Black Studies Movement: Afrocentric-Traditionalist-Feminist Paradigms for the Next Stage," *Black Scholar*, Summer 1992, pp. 11–19.

2. Johnnella E. Butler, "Ethnic Studies: A Matrix Model for the Major," *Liberal Education*, March/April 1991, p. 30. I am including in my discussion of ethnic studies only those programs that focus on people of color. Thus I will not discuss women's studies, even though that field was born at the same time as ethnic studies and grew out of similar dynamics, generated in this case by the women's movement. The field of women's studies remains dominated by white, middle-class women academicians and students.

3. Salim Mukwakil, "L.A. Lessons Go Unlearned," *In these Times*, 27 May–9 June 1992, p.3; and Sylvia Nasar, "The 1980s: A Very Good Time for the Very Rich," *New York Times*, 5 March1992, p. A-1.

4. The national media have been publishing numerous analyses of the 1990s census data as they have become available. A good recent analysis is the cover story by Margaret Usdansky, "'Diverse' Fits Nation Better than 'Normal,'" *USA Today*, 29–31 May 1992, p. 1.

5. For discussions comparing and contrasting area studies and ethnic studies, see the articles by Shirley Hune, Evelyn Hu-DeHart, Gary K. Okhiro, and Sucheta Mazumdar in Shirley Hune et al., eds., *Asian Americans: Comparative and Global Perspectives* (Pullman: Washington State University Press, 1991).

6. Mary C. Waters, *Ethnic Options: Choosing Identities in America* (Berkeley: University of California Press, 1990).

7. "Proposal for the Creation of a Department of Ethnic Studies at the University of California, San Diego," unpublished document, 25 January 1990.

8. Quoted in Jesse Vasquez, "The Co-opting of Ethnic Studies in the American University: A Critical View," *Explorations in Ethnic Studies*, January 1988, p. 25.

9. Ibid.

10. "Proposal for the Creation of a Department." pp. 5–6.

11.   E. Antoinette Charfauros, "New Ethnic Studies in Two American Universities: A Preliminary Discussion," unpublished paper, 1 July 1992, p. 20.

12.   Butler, p. 28.

13.   Ibid., p. 29.

14.   For example, Johnnella Butler and Berry Schmitz conduct "curriculum transformation seminars" at the University of Washington, Seattle. The seminars are funded by the Ford Foundation for the purpose of "incorporating cultural pluralism into the undergraduate curriculum." See also Johnnella Butler and John C. Walter, eds., *Transforming the Curriculum: Ethnic Studies and Women's Studies* (Albany: State University of New York Press, 1991).

15.   Clayborne Carson of Stanford University, quoted in Denise Magner, "Push for Diversity in Traditional Department Raises Questions About the Future of Ethnic Studies," *Chronicle of Higher Education*, 1 May 1991, p. A–11.

16.   Vasquez, pp. 23–24.

17.   E. San Juan, Jr., "Multiculturalism Versus Hegemony: Ethnic Studies, Asian Americans, and U.S. Racial Politics," unpublished paper.

18.   Quoted in San Juan.

Article 1.2

Statement of the National Association for Ethnic Studies

National Association for Ethnic Studies

The National Association for Ethnic Studies was founded in 1982. It provides an interdisciplinary forum for scholars and activists concerned with the national and international dimensions of ethnicity. The association welcomes scholars and teachers at all educational levels, students, libraries, civic and governmental organizations, and all persons interested in ethnicity, ethnic groups, intergroup relations, and the cultural life of ethnic minorities. As a non-profit corporation, NAES provides a vehicle for interested members and donors to promote responsible scholarship and advocacy in the diverse fields of enquiry which constitute ethnic studies.

The National Association for Ethnic Studies has as its basic purpose the promotion of activities and scholarship in the field of ethnic studies. The Executive Council includes scholars and professionals from several disciplines who are available to serve as consultants.

The Association is open to any person or institution. The Association serves as a forum to its members for promoting research, study, curriculum design, and publications.

Reprinted by permission of the National Association for Ethnic Studies, Inc.

CHAPTER 2

Ethnic Identity

Ethnic identity is a central issue in ethnic studies. This chapter focuses on theories of ethnic identity and the identity of mixed-race people.

The first three selections of this chapter represent the three most influential approaches to the nature and basis of ethnic identity: (1) primordialism, which views ethnic identity or affiliation as ascribed, fixed, and biologically defined; (2) constructionism, which underscores the social construction, mutability, and social determination of ethnic identity; and (3) instrumentalism, which sees ethnic identity as a social instrument for gaining economic, political, and social resources. Pierre van den Berghe's view in this particular selection tilts toward the traditional primordialist approach, though elsewhere he made attempts to integrate some competing theories. Joane Nagel's article clearly shows the constructionist paradigm, which emerged in the 1950s and 1960s and has gained momentum in the past two decades. The enlightening cases of the Malone brothers and Mark Stebbins presented in Luther Wright's article reflect the instrumentalist perspective.

Along with the growth of interracial marriages and their resulting multiracial offsprings, the identity of mixed-race people has captivated increasing attention. The story of Tiger Woods reported by Jack White spotlights Woods's self-identity as a "Cablinasian" in lieu of the initial media label of "African American" and discusses the implications of racial blending for America's future race relations. The article also touches upon the social construction and determination of racial identity or categorization of mixed-race people. The engrossing autobiographic essay of novelist Danzy Senna suggests that the identity of the mixed-race is largely shaped by their surrounding environment and experience and that the contradiction between self-identity and other-identity could expose one to racist confession, confusion, and pain. Laura Hymson's poem pinpoints a search of mixed-race people for identity and for interracial harmony. In a similar vein, Ryan Trammel's poem reveals a critical shift of his view about being multiracial from a burden and shame to an asset and pride.

1. Ethnicity as Kin Selection: The Biology of Nepotism
   Pierre van den Berghe

2. Constructing Ethnicity: Creating and Recreating Ethnic Identity and Culture
   Joane Nagel

3. "Soulmaning": Using Race for Political and Economic Gain
   Luther Wright, Jr.

4. "I'm Just Who I am': Race Is No Longer Black or White. So, What Does This
    Mean for America?"
    Jack E. White

5. A Black Spy in White America
    Danzy Senna

6. What Am I?
    Laura Hymson

7. What Are You?
    Ryan Trammel

Ethnicity as Kin Selection: The Biology of Nepotism

Pierre van den Berghe

The notion that ethnicity has something to do with kinship or "blood" is not new. Indeed, descent seems to be, implicitly and very often explicitly, the essential element of the definition of those groups of "significant others" that go under a wide variety of labels: tribe, band, horde, deme, ethnic group, race, nation and nationality. This is clearly the case in the Western tradition where the ideology of nationalism is replete with the rhetoric of kinship: fellow ethnics refer to each other as brothers and sisters: soldiers are said to die for the *mére patrie* or the *Vaterland*, depending on the gender ascribed by language to the collective parent: mystical notions of blood are said to be shared by members of one nation and to differentiate them from other groups.

True, the legacy of two world wars and of virulent racism in Nazi Germany somewhat dampened nationalist fervor in some intellectual circles in Europe and America during the 1950s and early 1960s. No sooner did intellectuals pronounce nationalism dead or dying in the "advanced" industrial countries, however, than it resurfaced within long-established states in the form of multitudinous movements for regional autonomy, ethnic separatism, racial pride, cultural identity and the like.

Nor is the irrepressible nature of ethnic sentiments a uniquely Western perversion. The most common origin myth of "primitive" societies ascribes the birth of the nation to an ancestral couple, divinely created or descended. In the simplest form of the myth, the ancestral couple is thought of as the progenitors of the entire society. In stratified societies, the royal family often attempts to monopolize divine ancestry, but then it quickly makes up for it by claiming paternity over its subjects.

For the followers of the monotheistic religions of Judaism, Christianity and Islam, the Book of Genesis serves as origin myth, and Adam and Eve as the ancestral couple. More specifically, Muslims and Jews see themselves as descendants of Abraham. Those groups have now become so large and so diverse that these putative ancestors are no longer very meaningful to many contemporary followers of these religions, but the Biblical origin myths are in fact quite similar to those of other traditions. For example, the Yoruba of Southwestern Nigeria place their own origin (which in typical ethnocentric manner, they identify with the origin of mankind) in their sacred city of the Ile Ife. The earth was created at Ile Ife by Oduduwa, one of the main divinities of the Yoruba pantheon, on instructions from Olorun the supreme deity. Oduduwa came down to the earth he created, sired sixteen sons who became the founders of the various Yoruba kingdoms and the ancestors of all the Yoruba people (Bascome, 1969).

The Navajo, an indigenous American group inhabiting the southwestern United States, have a complex myth in which Changing Woman, the principal figure among the supernatural Holy People, was magically impregnated by the rays of the Sun and by water from a waterfall and gave birth to twin sons, Hero Twins, who first dwelt with their father, the Sun. Holy People later descended to earth where they created Earth Surface People, the ancestors of the Navajos, and taught them culture, i.e. the Navajo way of life (Kluckhohn and Leighton, 1958).

The Pathan, stateless agriculturalists and pastoralists of Afghanistan and Pakistan, clearly define their ethnicity in terms of descent in patrilineal line from a common ancestor, Qais, who lived some 20 to 25 generations ago, and was a contemporary of Prophet Mohammed from whom he embraced the Muslim faith. A Pathan thus a descendant of Qais in the male line who is Muslim and conforms to Pathan customs (Fredrik Barth, 1959, 1969).

Even a large centralized state like Japan has a traditional nationalist myth whereby all Japanese are descended from the same common ancestor of whom the Imperial Family represent the line of direct descent, and all the other families of Japan represent collateral branches formed by younger sons of earlier generations. The entire nation is, thus, one single vast lineage (Ronald Dore, 1958). In the words of a Hozumi Nobushige, a Japanese writing in 1898, "The Emperor embodies the Spirit of the Original Ancestor of our race....In submitting to the Emperor of a line which has persisted through the ages, we subjects are submitting to the Spirit of the Joint Parent of our Race, the Ancestor of our ancestors." [Quoted by Dore (1958, p. 94).] This "blood ideology," as Hayashida (1976) called it, has been the essential defining element of Japanese nationhood for centuries.

Examples could be multiplied, but these few illustrations from widely scattered parts of the world will suffice. Ethnicity is common descent, either real or putative, but, even when putative, the myth has to be validated by several generations of common historical experience.

When most of the world's "traditional" societies became incorporated in the colonial empires of European or neo-European countries, ideologues and social scientists of both right and left believed that ethnic sentiments would become increasingly vestigial, and that "modernity" (or "socialist internationalism" in the communist societies) would engulf petty particularisms, giving rise to ever wider and more rational bases of solidarity based on market forces, proletarian consciousness, Third World brotherhood or whatever.

Few, if any, of these expectations came to pass. When imperial rule was securely established, it often managed to suppress emergent nationalisms by violence, but no sooner did these imperial systems collapse in the aftermath of war or revolution than did ethnic sentiments burst forth. Ironically, the only large empire to have emerged relatively intact from the postimperial turmoil of the two world wars is that of the Czars. Even the new successor states to the European colonial empires have been rent by ethnic dissidence: Nigeria, Zaïre, India, Pakistan and Malaysia—to name but a few. Nor were the smaller imperial systems spared the threat of ethnic separatism when the traditional system of rule collapsed, as witnessed by the events of the 1970s in Ethiopia and Iran. Even centuries of centralized despotism cannot suppress ethnic sentiment.

The position that ethnicity is a deeply rooted affiliation is often labeled "primordialist" in social science. Articulated by Max Weber (1968, first published in 1922), and later by Geertz (1967) and Shils (1957), the primordialist position was under severe attack in the 1950s and 1960s when most social scientists treated ethnicity as one affiliation among many—highly changeable and responsive to circumstances. The Marxists viewed ethnicity as an epiphenomenon, a remnant of precapitalist modes of production, a false consciousness masking class interests, a mystification of ruling classes to prevent the growth of class consciousness (Cox, 1948). To functionalists and other non-Marxists, ethnicity was also a premodern phenomenon, a residue of particularism and ascription incompatible with the trend toward achievement, universalism and nationality supposedly exhibited by industrial societies (Deutsch, 1966).

All the bad things said of ethnicity were of course ascribed a *fortiori* to race. Sentiments of group-belonging, based on physical attributes, were held to be even more wrong-headed and heinous than group membership based upon cultural attributes, such as language, religion and other customs—the usual diacritica of ethnicity (Comas, 1982; Glazer, 1975; Gossett, 1963; Hoffstadter, 1959; Leo Kuper, 1975, Levi-Strauss, 1952; van den Berghe, 1965). Only recently, with the revival of ethnicity, is the "primordialist" position once more being stated (Francis, 1976; Keyes, 1976).

The conventional primordialist position on ethnicity was vulnerable on two scores:

1. It generally stopped at asserting the fundamental nature of ethnic sentiment without suggesting any explanation of why that should be the case. As a theoretical underpinning, the primordialists had nothing better to fall back on than the nebulous, romantic, indeed sometimes racist ideologies of nationalists to which the primordialists pointed as illustrations of their contention. what kind of mysterious and suspicious force was this "voice of the blood" that moved people to tribalism, racism and ethnic intolerance?
2. If ethnicity was primordial, then was it not also ineluctable and immutable? Yet, patently, ethnic sentiments waxed and waned according to circumstances. Ethnicity could be consciously manipulated for personal gain. Ethnic boundaries between groups are sometimes quite fluid. Smaller groups often merge into larger ones and vice-versa. New ethnic groups constantly arise and disappear, and individuals may choose to assert ethnic identities or not as their interests of fancies dictate. How is all this circumstantial fluidity reconcilable with the primordialist position?

In contrast to the primordialist view of ethnicity, there came to be formulated the "instrumentalist" or "circumstantialist" position that held ethnicity to be something manipulable, variable, situationally expressed, subjectively defined and only one possible type of affiliation among many (Brass, 1974, 1976). One of the leading exponents of this position is Fredrik Barth, who in his classical introduction to *Ethnic Groups and Boundaries* (1969), explicitly defines ethnicity in subjective terms. Ethnicity is whatever the natives say it is. It

is the natives' perceptions of reality that create and define ethnic boundaries and ethnic relations. It just happens that the Pathans whom Barth studied so extensively define their ethnicity in terms of descent from a common ancestor; that ethnographic fact does not invalidate
Barth's position. Indeed, nothing can, if the analytical categories used in social science must
always be defined by the natives who, in turn, are, by definition, always right! The problem
for those of us who try to formulate scientific propositions, is that natives do not always
agree with each other, even *within* cultures, and that therefore a science of human behavior
based exclusively on native opinion tends to be shaky.

As most controversies based on a simple-minded antimony, the primordialist-instrumen-
talist debate serves little purpose other than to help Ph.D. candidates organize their examination answers. It is one of the main aims of this book to show that both positions are
correct, although not necessarily in the way the protagonists envisaged, and that the two
views complement each other. In Chapter 3, we shall see that ethnicity is indeed situationally variable, according to a multiplicity of ecological conditions. And, in Chapter 4, we shall
examine the many ways in which ethnicity is manipulated in power relationships. Before I
turn to the ecology and politics of ethnicity, and thereby vindicate the instrumentalists,
however, a theoretical basis for the primordialist position must be developed. Briefly, I suggest that there now exists a theoretical paradigm of great scope and explanatory power—
evolutionary biology—that sheds a new light on phenomena of ethnocentrism and racism.
In so doing, I am fully cognizant of the protest that such an endeavor will elicit.

My basic argument is quite simple: ethnic and racial sentiments are extensions of kinship
sentiments. Ethnocentrism and racism are thus extended forms of nepotism—the propensity
to favor kin over nonkin. There exists a general behavioral predisposition, in our species as
in many others, to react favorable toward other organisms to the extent that these organisms
are biologically related to the actor. The closer the relationship is, the stronger the preferential behavior.

Why should parents sacrifice themselves for their children? Why do uncles employ
nephews rather than strangers in their business? Why do inheritance laws provide for passing property on along lines of kinship? Why, in short, do people, and indeed other animals
as well, behave nepotistically. To many, these questions appear so intuitively obvious as to
require no explanation. We favor kin because they *are* kin. This is no answer of course, but a
mere restatement of the problem. Besides, we do not *always* favor kin. Profligate sons are
sometimes disinherited, incompetent nephews not hired and so on. Yet, on the whole we are
nepotists, and when we are not, it is for some good reason. Nepotism, we intuitively feel is
the natural order of things. Where we feel nepotism would interfere with efficiency, equity
or some other goals, we institute explicit safeguards against it and, even then, we expect it to
creep in again surreptitiously.

But why? A convincing answer was hinted at by the British biologists R. A. Risher (1958,
first published in 1930) and J.B.S. Haldane (1932) but elaborated on only about 15 years
ago by W.D. Hamilton (1964) and J. Maynard Smith (1964). The theorem of "altruism",
"kin selection" or "inclusive fitness," as biologists often refer to nepotism, was increasingly
discovered to be the keystone of animal sociality. Soon, a theoretical synthesis of population

genetics, ecosystem theory and ethology gave birth to the new discipline of "sociobiology" as E.O. Wilson labeled it in his magisterial compendium on animal behavior (1975, ably summarized in Barash, 1977).

The problem that posed itself to biologists was the seemingly self-sacrificial behavior of some animals under some conditions, e.g. the emission of alarm calls to warn conspecifics, the mimicking of injuries to distract predators, or seeming restrains on reproduction under adverse ecological conditions. Wynne-Edwards (1962) answered the problem in terms of group selection. Altruists behave in such a way for the good of their social group; groups that produce altruists have a competitive advantage over those that do not. However, there is one big drawback to the group selectionist argument. Altruism, by biological definition, is behavior that enhances the fitness (i.e. the reproductive success) of others at the cost of reducing the fitness of the altruist. If the altruists do indeed reduce their fitness by behaving altruistically, then genes fostering altruism would be selected against. How can an animal population sustain altruistic genes that reduce the reproductive success of their carriers through enhanced predation, induced sterility (as in the worker castes of social insects) or some other cause?

The answer is so disarmingly simple and convincing that even Wynne-Edwards has recently recanted his group selectionist argument. Seeming altruism is, in fact, the ultimate in genetic selfishness. Beneficent behavior is the product of a simple fitness calculus (presumably an unconscious one in most animals, though often a partially conscious one in humans) that takes two factors into account: the cost-benefit ratio of the transaction between altruist and recipient, and the coefficient of relatedness r between altruist and recipient. Simply put, an altruistic transaction can be expected if, and only if, the cost-benefit ratio of the transaction is smaller than the coefficient of relatedness between the two actors.

The coefficient of relatedness between any two organisms is the proportion of genes they share through common descent. It can range from a value of one (for organisms that reproduce asexually, e.g. through cell division) to zero (between unrelated organisms). In sexually reproducing organisms, parents and offspring and full siblings share one-half of their genes; half-siblings, grandparents and grandchildren, uncles-aunts and nephews-nieces share one-fourth; first cousins, one-eighth, and so on.

Reproduction, in the last analysis, is passing on one's genes. This can be done directly through one's own reproduction or indirectly through the reproduction of related organisms. The fitness of an organism is, by definition, its reproductive success. The *inclusive* fitness of an organism is the sum of its own reproductive success plus that of related organisms discounted for their coefficient of relatedness. Thus, it takes two children to reproduce the genetic equivalent of ego; but the same effect can be achieved through four nephews or eight first cousins.

As brilliantly argued by Richard Dawkins (1976), the ultimate unit of replication is the gene, not the organism. Bodies are, in Dawkins' words, mere mortal and expendable "survival machines" for potentially immortal genes. Such genes, therefore, as predispose their carrying organisms to behave nepotistically will be selected for, because, by favoring nepotism, they enhance their own replication. Nepotistic organisms foster the fitness of relatives who have a high probability of carrying the same gene or genes for nepotism. Nepotism genes, therefore, will spread faster than genes that program their carriers to care only for their own direct survival and reproduction—genes, for instance, that would program organisms to eat their siblings when hungry. This phenomenon of fostering inclusive fitness through *kin selection* or nepotism has been conclusively shown (mostly by studies of social insets, but also, increasingly, of vertebrates) to be the basis of much animal sociality (E.O. Wilson, 1975; Daly and Wilson, 1978).

Animal societies, from social insets to higher vertebrates, are held together primarily by cooperating kin who thereby enhance each other's fitness. This seeming "altruism" is thus the ultimate genic selfishness of maximizing one's *inclusive* fitness. An individual will only behave "altruistically" (i.e. in such a way as to reduce its own direct fitness) if, by doing so, the increment of fitness of a relative more than makes up for the loss to ego. For instance, my full sister shares half of her genes with me; she must, therefore, get more than twice as much out of my beneficent act to her than what that act costs me. For a half-sister or a niece, who only shares one-fourth of her genes with me, the benefit-cost ratio of the transaction would have to be better than four to one—and so on, according to the coefficient of relatedness between giver and receiver. The biological golden rule is "give unto others as they are related unto you."

· · ·

Let us summarize the argument so far. Humans, like other social animals, are biologically selected to be nepotistic because, by favoring kin, they maximize their inclusive fitness. Until the last few thousand years, hominids interacted in relatively small groups of a few score to a couple of hundred individuals who tended to mate with each other and, therefore, to form rather tightly knit groups of close and distant kinsmen. Physical boundaries of territory and social boundaries of inbreeding separated these small human societies from each other. Within the group, there was a large measure of peace and cooperation between kinsmen and in-laws (frequently both kinds of relationship overlapped). Relations between groups were characterized at best by mistrust and avoidance—but frequently by open conflict over scarce resources. These solidary groups were, in fact, primordial ethnies.

Such was the evolutionary origin of ethnicity; an extended kin group. With the progressive growth in the size of human societies, the boundaries of the ethny became wider; the bonds of kinship were correspondingly diluted, and indeed sometimes became fictive, and ethnicity became increasingly manipulated and perverted to other ends, including domination and exploitation. The urge, however, to continue to define a collectively larger than the immediate circle of kinsmen on the basis of biological descent continues to be present even in the most industrialized mass societies of today. A wide variety of ethnic markers are used to define such collectivities of descent, but their choice is not capricious. Those markers will be stressed that are, in fact, objectively reliable predictors of common descent, given the environment in which the discriminating group finds itself. Sometimes, but rather rarely, race is the paramount criterion; more commonly, cultural characteristics, especially language, do a much better job of defining ethnic boundaries.

So far, we have suggested the *raison d'être* of ethnicity—the reason for its persistence and for its seeming imperviousness to rationality. Ethnic (and racial) sentiments often seem irrational because they have an underlying driving force of their own, which is ultimately the blunt, purposeless natural selection of genes that are reproductively successful. Genes favoring nepotistic behavior have a selective advantage. It does not matter whether their carrying organisms are aware of being nepotistic or even that they consciously know their relatives. Organisms must only behave *as if they knew*. It happens that, in humans, they often know in a conscious way, though they are sometimes mistaken.

The phenomenon of ethnicity in humans, however, is not in principle different from the phenomenon of boundary maintenance between animal societies. Other animals maintain clear boundaries between themselves and other species, most importantly barriers to matings between closely related species that are the very mechanism making for speciation in the first instance (Mayr, 1963). But humans are not even unique in maintaining societal boundaries *within* the species. Thousands of species of eusocial insects keep different colonies of the same species quite distinct from each other, often using pheromones (smell signals) to recognize each other (E.O. Wilson, 1971). Among mammals, man included, the boundaries between societies are, on the whole much *less* rigid than among the eusocial insects but nevertheless, societal boundaries between groups of conspecifics are clearly marked and defended.

We conventionally restrict the meaning of ethnicity to humans, but we would not be unduly extending the meaning of the term by applying it to troops of macaques, prides of lions or packs of wolves. These other animal societies too are held together by kin selection and must compete with other societies of conspecifics for scarce resources (E.O. Wilson, 1975). In principle, the problems of boundary maintenance are the same for humans and other animals, despite the vastly greater order of complexity of human societies.

Like many other species, man too lives in an environment that includes other societies of his species. Interethnic relations, therefore, must be analyzed not only within the genetic context of kin selection but also, and equally importantly, within an *ecological* context. This is the subject of the next chapter.

Article 2.2

Constructing Ethnicity: Creating and Recreating Ethnic Identity and Culture*

Joane Nagel

Identity and culture are two of the basic building blocks of ethnicity. Through the construction of identity and culture, individuals and groups attempt to address the problematics of ethnic boundaries and meaning. Ethnicity is best understood as a dynamic, constantly evolving property of both individual identity and group organization. The construction of ethnic identity and culture is the result of both structure and agency—a dialectic played out by ethnic groups and the larger society. Ethnicity is the product of actions undertaken by ethnic groups as they shape and reshape their self-definition and culture; however, ethnicity is also constructed by external social, economic, and political processes and actors as they shape and reshape ethnic categories and definitions. This paper specifies several ways ethnic identity and culture are created and recreated in modern societies. Particular attention is paid to processes of ethnic identity formation and transformation, and to the purposes served by the production of culture—namely, the creation of collective meaning, the construction of community through mythology and history, and the creation of symbolic bases for ethnic mobilization.

Introduction

Contrary to expectations implicit in the image of the "melting pot" that ethnic distinctions could be eliminated in U.S. society, the resurgence of ethnic nationalism in the United States and around the world has prompted social scientists to rethink models of ethnicity rooted in assumptions about the inevitability of assimilation.[1] Instead, the resiliency of cultural, linguistic, and religious differences among populations has led to a search for a more accurate, less evolutionary means of understanding not only the resurgence of ancient differences among peoples, but also the actual emergence of historically new ethnic groups.[2] The result has been the development of a model of ethnicity that stresses the fluid, situational, volition-

*I wish to thank Richard Alba, Stephen Cornell, Jim Holstein, Carol A.B. Warren, and Norman Yetman for their helpful comments on an earlier version of this paper.

al, and dynamic character of ethnic identification, organization, and action—a model that emphasizes the socially "constructed" aspects of ethnicity, i.e., the ways in which ethnic boundaries, identities, and cultures, are negotiated, defined, and produced through social interaction inside and outside ethnic communities.[3]

According to this constructionist view, the origin, content, and form of ethnicity reflect the creative choices of individuals and groups as they define themselves and others in ethnic ways. Through the actions and designations of ethnic groups, their antagonists, political authorities, and economic interest groups, ethnic boundaries are erected dividing some populations and unifying others (see Barth 1969; Moerman 1965, 1974). Ethnicity is constructed out of the material of language, religion, culture, appearance, ancestry, or regionality. The location and meaning of particular ethnic boundaries are continuously negotiated, revised, and revitalized, both by ethnic group members themselves as well as by outside observers.

To assert that ethnicity is socially constructed is not to deny the historical basis of ethnic conflict and mobilization.[4] However, a constructionist view of ethnicity poses questions where an historical view begs them. For instance, to argue that the Arab-Israeli conflict is simply historical antagonism, built on centuries of distrust and contention, asserts a certain truth, but it answers no questions about regional or historical variations in the bases or extent of the conflict, or about the processes through which it might be ameliorated. In fact, scholars have asserted that both Israeli and Palestinian ethnic identities are themselves fairly recent constructions, arising out of the geopolitics of World War II and the Cold War, and researchers have documented the various competing meanings of the Arab-Israeli conflict in American Political culture.[5]

Similarly, to view black-white antagonism in contemporary American society simply as based in history—albeit a powerful and divisive history—is to overlook the contemporary demographic, political, social, and economic processes that prop up this ethnic boundary, reconstructing it, and producing tension along its borders and within the two bounded ethnic groups.[6] For instance, Lemann's (1991) study of the post-World War II demographic shift of African-Americans from rural to urban areas and from the South to the North reveals a reconfiguration of the black-white ethnic boundary in northern and southern cities. this migration magnified urban ethnic segregation, stratified black society, increased interethnic tensions, promoted ethnic movements among both blacks and whites, and produced a black urban underclass. All of these changes reflect the dynamic, constructed character of black ethnicity in U.S. society.[7]

Since ethnicity is not simply an historical legacy of migration or conquest, but is constantly undergoing redefinition and reconstruction, our understanding of such ethnic processes as ethnic conflict, mobilization, resurgence, and change might profit from a reconsideration of some of the core concepts we use to think about ethnicity. This paper examines two of the basic building blocks of ethnicity: identity and culture. Identity and culture are fundamental to the central projects of ethnicity: the construction of boundaries and the production of meaning. In this paper, I attempt to answer several questions about the construction of identity and culture: Where are the processes by which ethnic identity is created or destroyed, strengthened or weakened? To what extent is ethnic identity the result of internal processes, and to what extent is ethnicity externally defined and motivated? What are the processes that motivate ethnic boundary construction? What is the relationship between culture and ethnic identity? How is culture formed and transformed? What social purposes are served by the construction of culture? Rather than casting identity and culture as prior, fixed aspects of ethnic organization, here they are analyzed, as emergent, problematic features of ethnicity. By specifying several mechanisms by which groups reinvent themselves—who they are and what their ethnicity means—I hope to clarify and organize the grouping literature documenting the shifting, volitional, situational nature of ethnicity. Next I examine the construction of ethnic identity, followed by a discussion of the construction of culture.

Constructing Ethnic Identity

Ethnic identity is most closely associated with the issue of boundaries. Ethnic boundaries determine who is a member and who is not and designate which ethnic categories are available for individual identification at a particular time and place. Debates over the placement of ethnic boundaries and the social worth of ethnic groups are central mechanisms in ethnic construction. Ethnicity is created and recreated as various groups and interests put forth competing visions of the ethnic composition of society and argue over which rewards or sanctions should be attached to which ethnicities.

Recent research has pointed to an interesting ethnic paradox in the United States. Despite many indications of weakening ethnic boundaries in the white American population (due to intermarriage, language loss, religious conversion or declining participation), a number of studies have shown a maintenance or increase in ethnic identification among whites (Alba 1990; Waters 1990; Kivisto 1989; Bakalian 1993; Kelly 1993, 1994). This contradictory dualism is partly due to what Gans terms "symbolic ethnicity," which is "characterized by a nostalgic allegiance to the culture of the immigrant generation, or that of the old country; a love for and pride in a tradition that can be felt without having to be incorporated in everyday behavior" (1979:205). Bakalian (1991) provides the example of Armenian-Americans:

> For American-born generations, Armenian identity is a preference and Armenianness is a *state of mind*....One can say he or she is an Armenian without speaking Armenian, marrying an Armenian, doing business with Armenians, belonging to an Armenian church, joining Armenian voluntary associations, or participating in the events and activities sponsored by such organizations (Bakalian 1991:13).

This simultaneous decrease and increase in ethnicity raises the interesting question: How can people behave in ways which disregard ethnic boundaries while at the same time claim an ethnic identity? The answer is found by examining ethnic construction processes—in particular, the ways in which individuals and groups create and recreate their personal and collective histories, the membership boundaries of their group, and the content and meaning of their ethnicity.

Negotiating Ethnic Boundaries

While ethnicity is commonly viewed as biological in the United States (with its history of an obdurate ethnic boundary based on color), research has shown people's conception of themselves along ethnic lines, especially their ethnic identity, to be situational and change-able (see especially Waters 1990, Chapter Two). Barth (1969) first convincingly articulated the notion of ethnicity as mutable, arguing that ethnicity is the product of social ascriptions, a kind of labeling process engaged in by oneself and others. According to this perspective, one's ethnic identity is a composite of the view one has of oneself as well as the views held by others about one's ethnic identity. As the individual (or group) moves through daily life, ethnicity can change according to variations in the situations and audiences encountered.

Ethnic identity, then, is the result of a dialectical process involving internal and external opinions and processes, as well as the individual's self-identification and outsiders' ethnic designations—i.e., what *you* think your ethnicity is, versus what *they* think your ethnicity is. Since ethnicity changes situationally, the individual carries a portfolio of ethnic identities that are more or less salient in various situations and vis-a-vis various audiences. As audiences change, the socially-defined array of ethnic choices open to the individual changes. This produces a "layering" (McBeth 1989) of ethnic identities which combines with the as-criptive character of ethnicity to reveal the negotiated, problematic nature of ethnic identity. Ethnic boundaries, and thus identities, are constructed by both the individual and group as well as by outside agents and organizations.

Examples can be found in patterns of ethnic identification in many U.S. ethnic communi-ties.[8] For instance, Cornell (1988) and McBeth (1989) discuss various levels of identity available to Native Americans: *subtribal* (clan, lineage, traditional), *tribal* (ethnographic or linguistic, reservation-based, official), *regional* (Oklahoma, California, Alaska, Plains), *supratribal* or *pan-Indian* (Native American, Indian, American Indian). Which of these iden-tities a native individual employs in social interaction depends partly on where and with whom the interaction occurs. Thus, an American Indian might be a "mixed-blood" on the reservation, from "Pine Ridge" when speaking to someone from another reservation, a "Sioux" or "Lakota" when responding to the U.S. census, and "Native American" when in-teracting with non-Indians.

Pedraza (1992), Padilla (1985, 1986), and Gimenez, Lopez, and Munoz (1992) note a similar layering of Latino or Hispanic ethnic identity, again reflecting both internal and ex-ternal defining processes. An individual of Cuban ancestry may be a Latino vis-à-vis non-Spanish-speaking ethnic groups, a Cuban-American vis-à-vis other Spanish-speaking groups, a Marielito vis-à-vis other Cubans, and white vis-à-vis African Americans.[9] The chosen ethnic identity is determined by the individual's perception of its meaning to differ-ent audiences, its salience in different social contexts, and its utility in different settings. For instance, intra-Cuban distinctions of class and immigration cohort may not be widely under-stood outside of the Cuban community since a Marielito is a "Cuban" or "Hispanic" to most Anglo-Americans. To a Cuban, however, immigration cohorts represent important political "vintages," distinguishing those whose lives have been shaped by decades of Cuban revolu-tionary social changes from those whose life experiences have been as exiles in the United

States. Others' lack of appreciation for such ethnic differences tends to make certain ethnic identity choices useless and socially meaningless except in very specific situations. It underlines the importance of external validation of individual or group ethnic boundaries.

Espiritu (1992) also observes a layering of Asian-American identity. While the larger "Asian" pan-ethnic identity represents one level of identification, especially vis-à-vis non-Asians, national origin (e.g., Japanese, Chinese, Vietnamese) remains an important basis of identification and organization both vis-à-vis other Asians as well as in the larger society. Like Padilla (1985, 1986), Espiritu finds that individuals choose from an array of pan-ethnic and nationality-based identities, depending on the perceived strategic utility and symbolic appropriateness of the identities in different settings and audiences. She notes the larger Asian-American pan-ethnic boundary is often the basis for identification where large group size is perceived as an advantage in acquiring resources or political power. However she also observes that Asian-American pan-ethnicity tends to be transient, often giving way to smaller, culturally distinct nationality-based Asian ethnicities.

Waters (1991) describes similar situational levels of ethnic identification among African Americans. She reports that dark-skinned Caribbean immigrants acknowledge and emphasize color and ancestry similarities with African Americans at some times; at other times Carribeans culturally distinguish themselves from native-born blacks. Keith and Herring (1991) discuss the skin tone distinctions that exist among African Americans, with the advantages and higher social status that accrue to those who are lighter skinned. This color consciousness appears to be embraced by blacks as well as whites, and thus demarcates an internal as well as external ethnic boundary.

White Americans also make ethnic distinctions in various settings, vis-à-vis various audiences. They sometimes emphasize one of their several European ancestries (Waters 1990; Alba 1990); they sometimes invoke Native American lineage (Beale 1957; Quinn 1990); they sometimes identify themselves as "white," or simply assert an "American" identity (Lieberson 1985). The calculations involved in white ethnic choices appear different from those of other ethnic groups, since resources targeted for minority populations are generally not available to whites, and may not directly motivate individuals to specify an ethnicity based on European ancestry or "white"-ness. In these cases, white ethnicity can take the form of a "reverse discrimination" countermovement or "backlash" against the perceived advantages of non-whites (Burstein 1991). In other cases, white ethnicity is more symbolic (Gans 1979), representing less a rational choice based on material interests than a personal option exercised for social, emotional, or spiritual reasons (Waters 1990; Fischer 1986).

External Forces Shaping Ethnic Boundaries

The notion that ethnicity is simply a personal choice runs the risk of emphasizing agency at the expense of structure. In fact, ethnic identity is both optional and mandatory, as individual choices are circumscribed by the ethnic categories available at a particular time and place. That is, while an individual can choose from among a set of ethnic identities, that set is generally limited to socially and politically defined ethnic categories with varying degrees of stigma or advantage attached to them. In some cases, the array of available ethnicities can be quite restricted and constraining.

For instance, white Americans have considerable latitude in choosing ethnic identities based on ancestry. Since many whites have mixed ancestries, they have the choice to select from among multiple ancestries, or to ignore ancestry in favor of an "American" or "unhyphenated white" ethnic identity (Lieberson 1985). Americans of African ancestry, on the other hands, are confronted with essentially one ethnic option—black. And while blacks may make intra-racial distinctions based on ancestry or skin tone, the power of race as a socially defining status in U.S. society makes these internal differences rather unimportant in interracial settings in comparison to the fundamental black/white color boundary.[10]

The differences between the ethnic options available to blacks and whites in the United States reveal the limits of individual choice and underline the importance of external ascriptions in restricting available ethnicities. Thus, the extent to which ethnicity can be freely constructed by individuals or groups is quite narrow when compulsory ethnic categories are imposed by others. Such limits on ethnic identification can be official or unofficial. In either case, externally enforced ethnic boundaries can be powerful determinants of both the content and meaning of particular ethnicities. For instance, Feagin's (1991, 1992) research on the day-to-day racism experienced by middle-class black Americans demonstrates the potency of *informal* social ascription. Despite the economic success of middle-class African Americans, their reports of hostility, suspicion, and humiliation in public and private interactions with non-blacks illustrate the power of informal meanings and stereotypes to shape interethnic relations (see also Whitaker 1993).

If informal ethnic meanings and transactions can shape the everyday experiences of minority groups, formal ethnic labels and policies are even more powerful sources of identity and social experience. Official ethnic categories and meanings are generally political. As the state has become the dominant institution in society, political policies regulating ethnicity increasingly shape ethnic boundaries and influence patterns of ethnic identification. There are several ways that ethnicity is "politically constructed," i.e., the ways in which ethnic boundaries, identities, cultures, are negotiated, defined, and produced by political policies and institutions (J. Nagel 1986): by immigration policies, by ethnically-linked resource policies, and by political access that is structured along ethnic lines.

Immigration and the production of ethnic diversity. Governments routinely reshape their internal ethnic maps by their immigration policies. Immigration is a major engine of new ethnic group production as today's immigrant groups become tomorrow's ethnic groups (Hein 1994). Around the world, immigrant populations congregate in both urban and rural communities to form ethnic enclaves and neighborhoods, to fill labor market niches, sometimes providing needed labor, sometimes competing with native-born workers, to specialize in particular commodity markets, and as "middlemen."[11] Whether by accident or design, whether motivated by economics, politics, or kinship, immigrant groups are inevitably woven into the fabric of ethnic diversity in most of the world's states.

It is also through immigration that both domestic and foreign policies can reshape ethnic boundaries. The growing ethnic diversity and conflict in France and Britain are direct legacies of both their success and failures at colonial empire-building. In many other European states, such as Sweden and Germany, economic rather than political policies, in particular the importation of guest workers to fill labor shortages, encouraged immigration. The result has been the creation of permanent ethnic minority populations. In the United States, various Cold War policies and conflicts (e.g., in Southeast Asia and Central America) resulted in immigration flows that make Asians and Latin Americans the two fastest growing minority populations in the United States (U.S. Census 1991). Political policies designed to house, employ, or otherwise regulate or assist immigrant populations can influence the composition, location, and class position of these new ethnic subpopulations.[12] Thus the politics of immigration are an important mechanism in the political construction of ethnicity.

Resource competition and ethnic group formation. Immigration is not the only area in which politics and ethnicity are interwoven. Official ethnic categories are routinely used by governments worldwide in census-taking (Horowitz 1985), and acknowledgment of the ethnic composition of populations is a regular feature of national constitutions (Maarseveen and van der Tan 1978; Rhoodie 1983). Such designations can serve to reinforce or reconstruct ethnic boundaries by providing incentives for ethnic group formation and mobilization or by designating particular ethnic subpopulations as targets for special treatment. The political recognition of a particular ethnic group can not only reshape the designated group's self-awareness and organization, but can also increase identification and mobilization among ethnic groups not officially recognized, and thus promote new ethnic group formation. This is especially likely when official designations are thought to advantage or disadvantage a group in some way.

For instance, in India, the provision of constitutionally guaranteed parliamentary representation and civil service posts for members of the "Scheduled Castes" or "Untouchables" contributed to the emergence of collective identity and the political mobilization of Untouchables from different language and regional backgrounds; one result was the formation of an Untouchable political party, the Republican Party (Nayar 1966; Rudolph and Rudolph 1967). This affirmative action program produced a backlash and a Hindu revival movement, mainly among upper caste Indians who judged Untouchables to have unfair political and economic advantages (Desai 1992). Such backlashes are common around the world. In Malaysia, constitutional provisions granting political advantages to majority Malays prompted numerous protests from non-Malays—mainly Chinese and Indians (Means 1976). In many of the new republics of the former Soviet Union, nationalist mobilizations are built as much on a backlash against Russia and local Russians (who comprise a significant part of the population in most republics) than on a strong historic pattern of national identity.[13] In the United States, white ethnic self-awareness was heightened as desegregation and affirmative action programs got under way in the 1960s and 1970s. The result was a white anti-busing movement, and a "legal countermobilization" and cultural backlash against affirmative action (Rubin 1972; Burstein 1991; Faludi 1991). American Indians have also been the targets of white backlashes, mainly against treaty-protected hunting and fishing rights in the Pacific Northwest and the northern Great Lakes region (Adams and La Course 1977); Wright 1977; Kuhlmann forthcoming).

   Official ethnic categories and policies can also strengthen ethnic boundaries by serving as the basis for discrimination and repression, and thus reconstruct the meaning of particular ethnicities. Petonito (1991a, 1991b) outlines the construction of both "loyal American" and "disloyal Japanese" ethnic boundaries during World War II, a process which led to the internment of thousands of Japanese-Americans. Similarly, violence directed toward Iranians and Middle Easterners in the United States increased when American embassy staff were taken hostage during the Iranian revolution in 1980 and attacks against Iraqis and Arab-Americans escalated during the 1991 Gulf War (Applebome, 1991). In the former case, official actions of the Carter administration, such as requiring Iranian nationals in the United States to report for photographing and fingerprinting, contributed to an elevation of ethnic awareness and tended to legitimate the harassment of Iranians. In the latter case, official U.S. military hostilities against Iraq "spread" into U.S. domestic politics, prompting attacks on Arab and Iraqi "targets" living in the United States.
   Political policies and designations have enormous power to shape patterns of ethnic identification when politically controlled resources are distributed along ethnic lines. Roosens (1989) attempts to trace the rise of ethnicity and ethnic movements in the contemporary United States. He argues that the mobilization of ethnic groups in the United States has paralleled the development of the U.S. welfare state and its racial policies:

> There were few advantages in the United States...of the 1930s to define oneself visibly as a member of the Sicilian or Polish immigrant community. When one considers the current North American situation, however, one concludes that ethnic groups emerged so strongly because ethnicity brought people strategic advantages (Roosens 1989:14).

Padilla's (1985, 1986) description of the emergence of a Latino ethnicity among Mexicans and Puerto Ricans in Chicago in response to city programs focused on Hispanics, is consistent with Roosens's analysis. Another example is Espiritu's (1992) account of the emergence of Asian-American ethnic identity as a strategy to counter official policies thought to disadvantage smaller Asian nationality groups. Similarly, the white backlashes described above represent one response to exclusion from what are seen as ethnically-designated rights and resources.
   The observation that ethnic boundaries shift, shaping and reshaping ethnic groups according to strategic calculations of interest, and that ethnicity and ethnic conflict arise out of resource competition, represent major themes in the study of ethnicity (see Banton 1983). Barth and his associates (1969) link ethnic boundaries to resource niches. Where separate niches are exploited by separate ethnic groups (e.g., herders versus horticulturalists), ethnic tranquility prevails; however, niche competition (e.g., for land or water) results in ethnic boundary instability due to conflict or displacement (see also Despres 1975). Examining labor markets, Bonacich (1972) and Olzak (1989, 1992) have shown how informal job competition among different ethnic groups can heighten ethnic antagonism and conflict, strengthening ethnic boundaries as ethnicity comes to be viewed as crucial to employment and economic success. Hannan argues that the pursuit of economic and political advantage underlies the shift in ethnic boundaries upward from smaller to larger identities in modern

states. [14] Thus, in electoral systems, larger ethnic groups mean larger voting blocs; in indus-trial economies regulated by the political sector, and in welfare states, larger ethnic con-stituencies translate into greater influence (see also Lauwagie 1979 and B. Nagel 1986).

This research paints a picture of ethnicity as a rational choice (Hechter 1987a). According to this view, the construction of ethnic boundaries (group formation) or the adoption or pre-sentation of a particular ethnic identity (individual ethnic identification), can be seen as part of a strategy to gain personal or collective political or economic advantage. [15] For instance, Katz (1976) reports the creation of racially restrictive craft unions by white settlers in South Africa in order to gain an edge in labor market competition and create class distance from competing black laborers. Such competitive strategies not only provide ethnic advantages, they stimulate ethnic identity and group formation. An example is "whiteness" which Roediger (1991:13-14) argues emerged as an American ethnicity due to the efforts of work-ing class (especially Irish) whites who sought to distance themselves and their labor from blacks and blackness; by distinguishing their "free labor" from "slave labor," they redefined their work from "white slavery" to "free labor."

Political access and ethnic group formation. The organization of political access along ethnic lines can also promote ethnic identification and ethnic political mobilization. As Brass notes, "the state...is not simply an arena or an instrument of a particular class or ethnic group...the state is itself the greatest prize and resource, over which groups engage in a con-tinuing struggle" (1985:29). Much ethnic conflict around the world arises out of competition among ethnic contenders to control territories and central governments. The civil war in the former republic of Yugoslavia is a clear example of ethnic political competition (Hodson, Sekulic, and Massey forthcoming). [16] The long-standing grievances of the various warring linguistic and religious groups there did not erupt into combat until the Soviet Union lifted the threat of intervention in the late 1980s and opened the door to the possibility of ethno-political competition. The result was an armed scramble for territory based on a fear of dom-ination or exclusion by larger, more powerful ethnic groups.

In the United States, the construction of ethnic identity in response to ethnic rules for po-litical access can be seen in the national debate over affirmative action, in the composition of judicial (judges, juries) and policy-making bodies (committees, boards), and in the en-forcement of laws designed to end discrimination or protect minorities (see Gamson and Modigliani 1987). For example, the redistricting of U.S. congressional districts based on the 1990 census led to ethnic mobilization and litigation as African-American and Latino com-munities, among others sought improved representation in the federal government (Feeney 1992). Similarly, concern based on the importance of ethnic population size for representa-tion and resource allocation led Asian Americans to demand that the Census Bureau desig-nate nine Asian nationality groups as separate "races" in the 1980 and 1990 census (Espiritu 1992; Lee 1993). [17]

Ethnic Authenticity and Ethnic Fraud

Politically-regulated ethnic resource distribution and political access have led to much discussion about just what constitutes legitimate membership in an ethnic group, and about which individuals and groups qualify as disadvantaged minorities. For instance, Hein (1991:1) outlines the debate concerning the extent to which Asian immigrants to the United States should be seen to be ethnic "minorities" with an "historical pattern of discrimination," and thus eligible for affirmative action remedies. In universities, concerned with admissions practices, financial aid allocation, and non-discriminatory employment and representation, the question of which ethnic groups fulfill affirmative action goals is often answered by committees charged with defining who is and is not an official minority group (see Simmons 1982).

Discussions about group eligibility are often translated into controversies surrounding individual need, individual ethnicity, and ethnic proof. The multi-ethnic ancestry of many Americans combines with ethnically-designated resources to make choosing an ethnicity sometimes a financial decision. In some instances, individuals respond to shifting ethnic incentive structures (Friedman and McAdam 1987, 1992) by asserting minority status or even changing their ethnicity. Ethnic switching (Barth 1969) to gain advantage can be contentious when resources are limited. In many cases, particularly those involving individuals of mixed ancestry, the designation of a resource-endowed ethnicity for public or official purposes can elicit suspicion and challenge. For instance, Snipp (1993) reports concern among Native American educators about "ethnic fraud" in the allocation of jobs and resources designated for American Indian students; this concern was reflected in the inclusion of ethnic fraud among the topics of discussion at a recent national conference on minority education.

Indeed, questions of who is Indian or Latino or black[19] are often raised and often are difficult to resolve one way or the other. Even when ancestry can be proven, questions can arise about the cultural depth of the individual's ethnicity (Was he or she raised on a reservation or in the city? Does he or she speak Spanish?), or the individual's social class (Was he or she raised in the inner city or in the suburbs?). Solutions to questions of authenticity are often controversial and difficult to enforce. For instance, the federal government has attempted to set the standards of ethnic proof in the case of American Indian art. The Indian Arts and Crafts Act of 1990 requires that in order for artwork to be labeled as "Indian produced," the producer must be "certified as an Indian artisan by a [federally recognized] Indian tribe" (United States Statutes at Large 1990:4663). By this legal definition, artists of Indian ancestry cannot produce Indian art unless they are enrolled in or certified by officially recognized tribes. The act has thus led a number of Indian artists to seek official tribal status (some have refused to do this) and has also served to exclude some recognized American Indian artists from galleries, museums, and exhibits (Jaimes 1992; *Kansas City Star* 1991).[20] Similar local restrictions on who can sell Indian art and where it can be sold have caused bitter divisions among American Indians and other minority communities in the Southwest (Evans-Pritchard 1987).[21]

In sum, the construction of ethnic boundaries through individual identification, ethnic group formation, informal ascriptions, and official ethnic policies illustrates the ways in which particular ethnic identities are created, emphasized, chosen, or discarded in societies. As the result of processes of negotiation and designation, ethnic boundaries wax and wane. Individual ethnic identification is strongly limited and influenced by external forces that shape the options, feasibility, and attractiveness of various ethnicities.

As we have seen above, research speaks fairly clearly and articulately about how ethnic boundaries are erected and torn down, and the incentives or disincentives for pursuing particular ethnic options. However, the literature is less articulate about the *meaning* of ethnicity to individuals and groups, about the forces that shape and influence the contents of that ethnicity, and about the purposes ethnic meanings serve. This requires a discussion of the construction of culture.

Culture and history are the substance of ethnicity. They are also the basic materials used to construct ethnic meaning. Culture and history are often intertwined in cultural construction activities. Both are part of the "toolkit"—as Swidler (1986) called it—used to create the meaning and interpretative systems seen to be unique to particular ethnic groups (see Tonkin, McDonald, and Chapman 1989). Culture is most closely associated with the issue of meaning. Culture dictates the appropriate and inappropriate content of a particular ethnicity and designates the language, religion, belief system, art, music, dress, traditions, and lifeways that constitute an authentic ethnicity. While the construction of ethnic boundaries is very much a saga of structure and external forces shaping ethnic options, the construction of culture is more a tale of human agency and internal group processes of cultural preservation, renewal, and innovation. The next section explores the ways in which ethnic communities use culture and history to create common meanings, to build solidarity, and to launch social movements.

Constructing Culture

In his now classic treatise on ethnicity, Fredrik Barth (1969) challenged anthropology to move away from its preoccupation with the content of culture, toward a more ecological and structural analysis of ethnicity:

> …ethnic categories provide an organizational *vessel* that may be given varying amounts and forms of content in different socio-cultural systems.…The critical focus of investigation from this point of view becomes the ethnic *boundary* that defines the group, not the cultural stuff that it encloses (Barth 1969:14-15 [emphasis mine]).

Barth's quarrel was not with the analysis of culture, per se, but with its primacy in anthropological thinking. In fact, by modernizing Barth's "vessel" imagery, we have a useful device for examining the construction of ethnic culture: the shopping cart. We can think of ethnic boundary construction as determining the *shape* of the shopping cart (size, number of wheels, composition, etc.); ethnic culture, then, is composed of the things we put into the cart—art, music, dress, religion, norms, beliefs, symbols, myths, customs. It is important that we discard the notion that culture is simply an historical legacy; culture is *not* a shopping cart that comes to us already loaded with a set of historical cultural goods. Rather we construct culture by picking and choosing items from the shelves of the past and the present. As Barth reminds us:

> …when one traces the history of an ethnic group through time, one is *not* simultaneously…tracing the history of "a culture": the elements of the present culture of that group have not sprung from the particular set that constituted the group's culture at a previous time" (Barth 1969:38).

In other words, cultures change; they are borrowed, blended, rediscovered, and reinterpreted. My use of the shopping cart metaphor extends Swidler's (1986) cultural toolkit imagery. Swidler argues that we use the cultural tools in the toolkit in our everyday social labors; I argue that we not only use the tools in the toolkit, but that we also determine its contents—keeping some tools already in the kit, discarding others, adding new ones. However, if culture is best understood as more than mere remnants of the past, then how did it get to its present state—how did the cart get filled, and why? What does culture do?

Culture is constructed in much the same way as ethnic boundaries are built, by the actions of individuals and groups and their interactions with the larger society. Ethnic boundaries function to determine identity options, membership composition and size, and form of ethnic organization. Boundaries answer the question: Who are we? Culture provides the content and meaning of ethnicity; it animates and authenticates ethnic boundaries by providing a history, ideology, symbolic universe, and system of meaning. Culture answers the question: What are we? It is through the construction of culture that ethnic groups fill Barth's vessel—by reinventing the past and inventing the present.

Cultural Construction Techniques

Groups construct their cultures in many ways which involve mainly the *reconstruction* of historical culture, and the *construction* of new culture. Cultural reconstruction techniques include revivals and restorations of historical cultural practices and institutions; new cultural constructions include revisions of current culture and innovations—the creation of new cultural forms. Cultural construction and reconstruction are ongoing group tasks in which new and renovated cultural symbols, activities, and materials are continually being added to and removed from existing cultural repertoires.[22]

Cultural revivals and restorations occur when lost or forgotten cultural forms or practices are excavated and reintroduced, or when lapsed or occasional cultural forms or practices are refurbished and reintegrated into contemporary culture. For example, for many, immigrant and indigenous ethnic groups' native languages have fallen into disuse. Efforts to revitalize language and increase usage are often major cultural reconstruction projects. In Spain, both in Catalonia and the Basque region, declining use of the native tongues (Catalan and Euskera, respectively) due to immigration and/or Castilian Spanish domination, has spurred language education programs and linguistic renewal projects (Johnston 1991; Sullivan 1988). In the United States, the threatened loss of many Native American languages has produced similar language documentation and education programs, as well as the creation of cultural centers, tribal museums, and educational programs to preserve and revive tribal cultural traditions. Study and instruction in cultural history is often a central part of cultural reconstruction.

Cultural revisions and innovations occur when current cultural elements are changed or when new cultural forms or practices are created. As part of U.S. authorities' various historical efforts to destroy Native American cultures by annihilation or assimilation, many Indian communities and groups used cultural revision and innovation to insulate cultural practices when they were outlawed by authorities. Champagne (1989, 1990) reports that the Alaska Tlingits revised traditional potlatch practices, incorporating them into Russian Orthodox or

Protestant ceremonies to conceal the forbidden exchanges. Prucha (1984) reports a form of cultural innovation to protect the use of peyote in American Indian religious rites. The creation of the Native American Church imbedded peyote use in a syncretic, new Indian-Christian religious institution, thus protecting practitioners under the First Amendment of the U.S. constitution. Such cultural camouflage in the form of religious syncretism is reported in many societies, particularly those penetrated by missionaries operating under governmental auspices.[23]

These various cultural construction techniques, and others that will be described below, serve two important collective ends which will be the focus of the remainder of this paper. They aid in the construction of community and they serve as mechanisms of collective mobilization. Cultural constructions assist in the construction of community when they act to define the boundaries of collective identity, establish membership criteria, generate a shared symbolic vocabulary, and define a common purpose. Cultural constructions promote collective mobilization when they serve as a basis for group solidarity, combine into symbolic systems for defining grievances and setting agendas for collective action, and provide a blueprint or repertoire of tactics.

The Cultural Construction of Community

In *Imagined Communities*, Benedict Anderson argues that there is no more evocative a symbol of modern nationalism than the tomb of the unknown soldier. The illustrative power of this icon lies in the fact that such tombs "are either deliberately empty or no one knows who lies inside them" (Anderson 1991:9)—thus, they are open to interpretation and waiting to be filled. The construction of culture supplies the contents for ethnic and national symbolic repositories. Hobsbawm (1983) refers to this symbolic work as "the invention of tradition"—i.e., the construction or reconstruction of rituals, practices, beliefs, customs, and other cultural apparatus. According to Hobsbawm, invented traditions serve three related purposes: a) to establish or symbolize social cohesion or group membership, b) to establish or legitimize institutions, status, and authority relations, or c) to socialize or inculcate beliefs, values, or behaviors (1983:9). By this analysis the invention of tradition is very much akin to what Cohen (1985) calls "the symbolic construction of community."

The construction of history and culture is a major task facing all ethnic groups, particularly those that are newly forming or resurgent. In constructing culture, the past is a resource used by groups in the collective quest for meaning and community (Cohen 1985:99). Trevor-Roper provides an example of the construction of a national culture:

> Today, whenever Scotchmen gather to celebrate their national identity, they assert it openly by certain distinctive national apparatus. They wear the kilt, woven in a tartan whose colour and pattern indicates their 'clan'; and if they indulge in music, their instrument is the bagpipe. This apparatus, to which they ascribe great antiquity, is in fact largely modern....Indeed the whole concept of a distinct Highland culture and tradition is a retrospective invention. Before the later years of the seventeenth century, the Highlanders of Scotland did not form a distinct people. They were simply the overflow of Ireland (Trevor-Roper 1983:15).

Other scholars concur with Trevor-Roper's assertions about the constructed character of Scottish identity and culture (Chapman 1979; Prebble 1963). However, the fictive aspects of Scottish ethnicity in no way lessen the reality of Scottish nationalism in Great Britain, particularly during its heyday during the 1970s and early 1980s. During that time, Scottish and Welsh nationalism combined with the escalating violence in Northern Ireland to represent a major political and economic threat to the integrity of the United Kingdom.[24] Indeed, despite its invented origins, Scottish nationalism contributed to a major devolution of political authority to the British Celtic states (Mercer 1978; Davies 1989; Harvie 1977).

For newly forming ethnic and national groups, the construction of community solidarity and shared meanings out of real or putative common history and ancestry involves both cultural constructions and reconstructions. Smith refers to ethnic and national groups' "deep nostalgia for the past" that results in efforts to uncover or, if necessary, invent an earlier, ethnic "golden age" (1986:174). For instance, Karner (1991) describes the reconstruction of Finnish cultural history (folklore, music, songs) by Swedish-speaking Finnish intellectuals during the mobilization for Finnish independence. Similarly, Kelly (1993) discusses the efforts of Lithuanian-Americans to learn the Lithuanian language and to reproduce Lithuanian foods, songs, dances, and customs illustrating the process whereby people transform a common ancestry (whether by birth or by marriage) into a common ethnicity.[25] And in their homeland, Lithuanians themselves are embarked on a journey of national reconstruction, as decades of Russian influence are swept away in an effort to uncover real and historical Lithuanianness.

The importance of cultural construction for purposes of community building is not limited to the creation of national unity. Cultural construction is especially important to pan-ethnic groups, as they are often composed of subgroups with histories of conflict and animosity. For instance, Padilla (1985) discusses the challenges facing Mexican-Americans and Puerto Ricans in Chicago as they attempt to construct both Latino organizations and an identity underpinned by the assertion of common interests and shared culture—a commonality that is sometimes problematic. Espiritu (1992) also documents the tensions surrounding nationality and cultural differences in the evolution of an Asian-American pan-ethnicity.

One strategy used by polyethnic groups to overcome such differences and build a more unified pan-ethnic community is to blend together cultural material from many component group traditions. About half of the American Indian population lives in urban areas (U.S. Census Bureau 1989). Urban Indians have borrowed from various tribal cultures as well as from non-Indian urban culture to construct supratribal or "Indian" cultural forms such as the powwow, the Indian Center, Indian Christian churches, Indian bowling leagues and softball teams, and Indian popular music groups. In the urban setting, tribal differences and tensions can be submerged in these pan-Indian organizations and activities.[26]

Building a cultural basis for new ethnic and national communities is not only goal prompting cultural reconstruction. Cultural construction is also a method for revitalizing ethnic boundaries and redefining the meaning of ethnicity in existing ethnic populations. The Christmas season celebration of Kwanzaa by African-Americans is an example of the dynamic, creative nature of ethnic culture, and reveals the role scholars play in cultural construction. Created in the 1960s by Professor Maulana Karenga, Kwanzaa is a seven-day cultural holiday which combines African and African-American traditions (Copage 1991).[27] The reconstruction and study of cultural history is also a crucial part of the community construction process and again shows the importance of academic actors and institutions in cultural renewal. Examples can be found in the recent emergence of various ethnic studies programs (e.g., Latino, American Indian, African-American, Asian Studies) established in colleges and universities around the United States during the past three decades (Deloria 1986). Such programs are reflective of a renewed and legitimated interest in ethnicity and cultural diversity. These programs, as well as classes in oral history and ethnic culture, serve as important resources in cultural revivals and restorations.[28]

Cultural Construction and Ethnic Mobilization

Cultural construction can also be placed in the service of ethnic mobilization. Cultural renewal and transformation are important aspects of ethnic movements. Cultural claims, icons, and imagery are used by activists in the mobilization process; cultural symbols and meanings are also produced and transformed as ethnic movements emerge and grow. While there is a large literature on the structural determinants of ethnic mobilization,[29] recent social movement research reflects increased interest in the nature of social movement culture and the interplay between culture and mobilization (see Morris and Mueller 1992). An examination of this literature offers insight into the relationship between culture and ethnic mobilization.

For instance, Snow and his associates argue that social movement organizers and activists use existing culture (rhetorical devices and various techniques of "frame alignment") to make movement goals and tactics seem reasonable, just, and feasible to participants, constituencies, and political officials (Snow et al. 1986; Snow and Benford 1988, 1992). For example, nuclear disarmament movement leaders responded to questions about the hopelessness of opposing a military-industrial complex bent on the production of nuclear weapons by drawing a parallel between the elimination of nuclear weapons and the abolition of slavery—namely, the success of abolitionism was achieved despite an equally daunting opposition (Snow et al. 1986). Thus, by drawing on available cultural themes, the discourse surrounding movement objectives and activism is more likely to recruit members, gain political currency, and achieve movement goals.

Gamson and his associates document the ideational shifts and strategies used by movements, policymakers, and opposition groups to shape debates, define issues, and to paint the most compelling portrait of each side's claims and objectives (Gamson 1988, 1992; Gamson and Modigliani 1987; Gamson and Lasch 1983). For instance, Gamson and Modigliani (1987) argue that the changing culture of affirmative action results from a struggle over the definition of equality, justice, and fairness, as various political actors frame the issues in competing ways, e.g., affirmative action as "remedial action" versus "reverse discrimination." The rhetorics, counter-rhetorics, and rhetorical shifts characterized in this research are common to all social movements, including ethnic movements. They reflect the use of cultural material and representations in a symbolic struggle over rights, resources, and the hearts and minds of constituents, neutral observers, and opponents alike.

The work of Snow and Gamson illustrates the use of existing culture by movement organizers and activists, and shows several forms of cultural reconstruction, where cultural symbols and themes are borrowed and sometimes repackaged to serve movement ends. There is another way in which cultural construction occurs in movements—where protest is a crucible of culture. For instance, Fantasia (1988) describes a "culture of solidarity" that arises out of activism. Cultures of solidarity refer to the emergence of a collective consciousness and shared meanings that result from engaging in a collective action. Ethnic movements often challenge negative hegemonic ethnic images and institutions by redefining the meaning of ethnicity in appealing ways or by using cultural symbols to effectively dramatize grievances and demands.

Examples of the construction and reconstruction of history and culture in order to redefine the meaning of ethnicity can be found in the activities of many of the ethnic groups that mobilized during the civil rights era of the 1960s and 1970s in the United States. During these years, a renewed interest in African culture and history and the development of a culture of black pride—"Black is Beautiful"—accompanied African-American protest actions during the civil rights movement. The creation of new symbolic forms and the abandonment of old, discredited symbols and rhetoric reflected the efforts of African-Americans to create internal solidarity and to challenge the prevailing negative definitions of black American ethnicity. For instance, the evolution of racial nomenclature for African-Americans can be excavated by a retrospective examination of the names of organizations associated with or representing the interests of black Americans: the National Association for the Advancement of Colored People, the United Negro College Fund, the Black Panther Party, and the National Council of African-American Men, Inc. The fluidity of names for other American ethnic groups reflects similar shifts in constructed ethnic definitions and revised meanings associated with evolving collective identities: from Indians to American Indians to Native Americans; from Spanish-Surnamed to Hispanics to Latinos.[30] Such changes in ethnic nomenclature were an important part of the discourse of civil rights protest, as were changes in dress, new symbolic themes in art, literature, and music, and counterhegemonic challenges to prevailing standards of ethnic demeanor and interracial relations.[31]

The expropriation and subversion of negative hegemonic ethnic definitions and institutions is an important way that culture is used in ethnic mobilization around the world. British conceptions of "tribe" and "tribal" shaped many of their colonial policies, such as geographic administrative boundaries, education policies, and hiring practices. These tribal constructions were reshaped by Africans into the anti-colonial ethnic politics of a number of African states (Melson and Wolpe 1981; Young 1976). For instance, Wallerstein (1960) and Iliffe (1979) document the mobilization of various "tribal" unions and associations into nationalist movements for independence in many African countries. In India, similar subversion of colonial cultural constructions designed to facilitate British domination occurred. Cohn (1983) argues that the pomp and ceremony of the British Imperial Assemblage and the Imperial Durbars in nineteenth century India were expropriated by Indian elites, who indigenized and institutionalized this invented tradition, incorporating it into the symbolism and idiom of an independent Indian politics.[32]

This "turning on its head" of cultural symbols and institutions can be seen in the ways ethnic activists use culture in their protest strategies. The tactics used in ethnic movements rely on the presentation, and sometimes the reconstruction, of cultural symbols to demonstrate ethnic unity, to dramatize injustice, or to animate grievances or movement objectives. For instance, Zulaika (1988), Sullivan (1988), and Clark (1984) report the use of various cultural symbols and conventions by Basque nationalist groups, noting, for instance, the central symbolic importance of demands for Basque language rights, although fewer than half of the Basque population speaks the Basque language. The Red Power movement for American Indian rights during the 1960s and 1970s drew its membership from mainly urban Indians from a variety of tribal backgrounds. The movement created a unified pan-Indian cultural front by borrowing cultural forms from many native communities (e.g., the teepee, eagle feathers, the war dance, the drum). Red Power repertoires of contention —as Tilly (1986) called them—also employed a rhetorical and dramaturgical cultural style that reflected movement leaders' sensitivity to the place of the American Indian in American popular culture and history. The American Indian Movement (AIM) was especially skilled in the use of such symbolic dramaturgy, as illustrated in the following description of an AIM-sponsored counter-ceremony in 1976:

> *Custer Battlefield, Mont.* Today, on the wind-buffeted hill...where George Armstrong Custer made his last stand, about 150 Indians from various tribes danced joyously around the monument to the Seventh Cavalry dead. Meanwhile, at the official National parks Service ceremony about 100 yards away, an Army band played...Just as the ceremony got underway, a caravan of Sioux, Cheyenne, and other Indians led by Russell Means, the American Indian Movement leader, strode to the speakers' platform to the pounding of a drum. Oscar Bear Runner, like Mr. Means, a veteran of the 1973 takeover of Wounded Knee, carried a sacred peace pipe (Lichtenstein 1976:II-1).

The above example shows the interplay between pre-existing cultural forms and the new uses to which they are put in ethnic movements. What we see is the National Parks Service's efforts to commemorate the "official story" (Scott 1990), and the American Indian Movement's challenge to this hegemonic interpretation of history. Both groups employed the symbolic paraphernalia available to them, drawn from similar strands of American history and culture, but used in opposing ways. By recasting the material of the past in innovative ways, in the service of new political agendas, ethnic movements reforge their own culture and history and reinvent themselves.

Conclusion

At the beginning of this paper I posed a number of questions about ethnic boundaries and meaning, inquiring into the forces shaping ethnic identity and ethnic group formation, and the uses of history and culture by ethnic groups and movements. My answers have emphasized the interplay between ethnic group actions and the larger social structures with which they interact. Just as ethnic identity results both from the choices of individuals and from the ascriptions of others, ethnic boundaries and meaning are also constructed from within and from without, propped up by internal and external pressures. For ethnic groups, questions of history, membership, and culture are the problematics solved by the construction process. Whether ethnic divisions are built upon visible biological differences among populations or rest upon invisible cultural and ideational distinctions, the boundaries around and the meanings attached to ethnic groups reflect pure social constructions.

Yet questions remain. What is driving groups to construct and reconstruct ethnic identity and culture? What is it about ethnicity that seems to appeal to individuals on so fundamental a level? From what social and psychological domains does the impulse toward ethnic identification originate? Why is ethnicity such a durable basis for group organization around the world? If ethnicity is in part a political construction, why do the goals of some ethnic activists favor equal rights, while others demand autonomy or independence? Other questions remain about the social meaning of ethnicity. How are particular meanings (values, stereotypes, beliefs) attached to different ethnic groups, and by whom? What are the implications of these different meanings for conceptions of social justice, intergroup relations, political policy? Concomitantly, how does ethnic stratification (material and ideational) arise? Can constructionist explanations of ethnicity account for persistent prejudice and discrimination, particularly where race or color are involved? To the extent that the constructionist model emphasizes change, how should we understand intractable racial and ethnic antagonism and stratification?

These questions comprise not only an agenda for future research, they are also warnings. While ethnic boundaries and the meanings attributed to them can be shown to be socially constructed, they must not, therefore, be underestimated as social forces. In fact, the constructionist model constitutes an argument for the durability, indeed the inevitability, of ethnicity in modern societies. As such, it represents a challenge to simple historical, biological or cultural determinist models of human diversity.

Notes

1. The failure of the American melting pot is a qualified one. As Alba and Logan (1991) point out, some groups, particularly whites, have "melted" quite well. Despite the maintenance of a kind of social or symbolic ethnicity among white groups, white ethnicity does not generally involve high levels of ethnic exclusiveness or ethnic group affiliation.

2. An ethnic group can be seen as "new" or "emergent" when ethnic identification, organization, and collective action is constructed around previously nonexistent identities, such as "Latino" or "Asian-American." An ethnic group can be seen as "resurgent" when ethnic identification, organization, or collective action is constructed around formerly quiescent historical identities, such as "Basque" or "Serbian" (see Yancey, Erickson, and Juliani 1976).

3. See Berger and Luckmann (1967) and Spector and Kitsuse (1977) for discussions of the social constructionist model; see Holstein and Miller (1993) for an assessment of the current state of social constructionism.

4. I define ethnic mobilization as the organization of groups along ethnic lines for collective action.

5. See Gerner (1991); Plascov (1981); Gamson (1982). Layne (1989) also describes the construction of a Jordanian national identity in the decades following World War I, and especially during King Hussein's rule beginning in 1953.

6. The use of the term "ethnic group" rather than "race" or "racial group" to describe African Americans is not intended to discount the unique importance of color or race as a basis for discrimination and disadvantage in U.S. society (and elsewhere). However, the arguments about ethnicity I put forth here are meant to apply to all racial and ethnic groups, whether distinguished by color, language, religion, or national ancestry.

7. See Wilson (1987); Burstein (1991); James (1989); Massey (1985); Massey and Denton (1993); Morris (1984).

8. The examples here are drawn from American groups, but the layering of identity is not unique to the United States. Similar levels of ethnic identification have been observed around the world. See Horowitz (1985), Young (1976), and Enloe (1973) for other examples.

9. The racial self-definition of the Hispanics represents an interesting example of the negotiated and constructed character of ethnicity. In 1980 and 1990, nearly half of re-

spondents who identified themselves as "Hispanic" on an ancestry item, reported their race as "other," i.e., they did not choose any of the more than a dozen "races" offered in the Census or Current Population Survey questionnaires (e.g., black, white, American Indian, Japanese, Chinese, Filipino, Vietnamese, etc.) The Census Bureau recoded most of them as "white" (U.S. Bureau of the Census 1980, 1990).

10. Despite the practice of "hypodescent' (Harris 1964) or the "one drop rule" in the classification of African Americans as "black," Davis (1991) shows that throughout U.S. history, there has been considerable controversy and reconstruction of the *meaning* and *boundaries* associated with blackness.

11. See Cohen (1974); Bonacich (1972, 1973); Fernandez-Kelly (1987); Light and Bonacich (1988); Portes and Rumbaut (1990); Sassen (1988, 1991).

12. See Yetman (1983, 1991); Pedraza-Bailey (1985); Horowitz (1985); Light and Bonacich (1988); Whorton (1994).

13. This is more the case in the southern republics, such as Tadzhikistan or Uzbekistan, than in formerly independent republics such as in the Baltics—Latvia, Estonia, Lithuania—where national identities are more historically firmly fixed (see Allworth 1989).

14. Examples are from the town-based Oyo or Ilorin to Yoruba linguistic, regional identity in Nigeria (Laitin 1985); from various regional or linquistic Untouchable groups into an organized national party in India (Nayar 1966); from Chicano or Puerto Rican to Latino or from Cherokee or Apache to Native American in the United States (Padilla 1986; Cornell 1988).

15. See also Hechter 1(1987b, 1991); Hechter and Friedman (1984); Hechter, Friedman, and Appelbaum (1982); Banton (forthcoming).

16. The distinction between "ethnic" and "national" groups is the subject of much definition and debate in the social sciences. I use the terms synonymously, thus "ethnic" group includes religious, linquistic, cultural, and regional groups with claims to political rights, sovereignty, or autonomy. See Connor (1991), Hobsbawm (1990), Smith (1986), and Gellner (1983, 1987) for discussions of nationalism, ethno-nationalism, and ethnicity.

17. On the 1990 census form there were actually 10 Asian nationality groups designated as separate races. They were: Asian Indian, Chinese, Filipino, Guamanian, Hawaiian, Japanese, Korean, Samoan, Vietnamese, and Other Asian or Pacific Islander. Asian American groups were concerned that if the term "Asian" were used in the census race item (Item number 4: "What is this person's race), that many Asian Americans would not mark the choice, and the result would be an undercount of the Asian-American population (Espiritu 1992).

18. In an October 1993 conference sponsored by the American Council on Education in Houston (American Council on Education 1993), Jim Larimore (Assistant Dean and Director of the American Indian Program at Stanford University) and Rick Waters (Assistant Director of Admissions at University of Colorado, Boulder) presented a session, "American Indians Speak Out Against Ethnic Fraud in College Admissions." The session was designed to "identity the problem and its impact on the American Indian community...[and to] discuss effective institutional practices for documenting and monitoring tribal affiliations" (Larimore and Waters 1993).

19. An example is when individuals who are not of African-American ancestry, such as dark-skinned Asians or native-born Africans, are counted as "black" or "minority" for such purposes as demonstrating compliance with affirmative action hiring goals.

20. The entire Indian art authentication process has been criticized as having as its primary purpose, a way of guaranteeing the value of art for mainly non-Indian art owners and purchasers. My thanks to C. Matthew Snipp for bringing this to my attention.

21. The importance and meaning of official recognition as a basis for individual ethnicity, ethnic group formation, and ethnic mobilization is by no means unique to Native Americans or to the United States. Where a particular ethnicity is especially stigmatizing, ethnic conversions (or "passing") often occur. For example, Schermerhorn (1978) reports a common form of ethnic switching in India—religious conversion, when Hindu Untouchables convert to Islam in order to escape untouchability. Also in India, the British colonial preference for Sikh military recruits, led to many Sikh conversions in order to qualify (Nayar 1966). Lelyveld (1985) discusses the phenomenon of individuals officially changing their race under South African apartheid regulations (see also Adam and Moodley 1993). Official recognition or resources tied to particular ethnic groups can prompt not only individual, but also ethnic group formation and mobilization as well. Burstein (1991) documents a white ethnic legal counter-assault against the perceived ethnic advantages of American minority populations. In Canada, the passage of policies favoring the use of the French language in Quebec during the 1970s and 1980s led to ethnic organizational formation and protests among non-French-speaking Canadian ethnic groups, such as those of Italian and Portuguese descent, who feared disadvantage or exclusion under the new language policies (Murray 1977; Lupul 1983).

22. For a detailed discussion of cultural construction, see Nagel (1994).

23. For example, see Whiteman (1985); Salamone (1985); Sanneh (1989); and Taber (1991).

24. Given the location of Britain's North Sea oil holdings off Scotland's coast.

25. An interesting aspect of Lithuanian-American ethnic renewal is what Kelly calls the "ethnic pilgrimage," where Lithuanian-Americans visit Lithuania to learn firsthand

about their ethnic roots and to participate in building the new independent state and nation (Kelly 1994).

26. See Hertzberg (1971); Weibel-Orlando (1991); Steele (1975); Whitehorse (1988); Clark (1988).

27. Tanzanian-born Maulana Karenga is professor and chair of Black Studies at the University of California at Long Beach.

28. The use of historical or anthropological research by ethnic groups engaged in reconstruction projects has its pitfalls. These center on the accuracy and objectivity of such academic work. Recent research "deconstructing" historical and contemporary ethnographies (Wagner 1975; Clifford 1988; Clifford and Marcus 1986; Geertz 1988) has been aimed at revealing the voices and viewpoints of researchers imbedded in "objective" reports of their subjects' social and cultural organization.

29. See Enloe (1973); Hechter (1975); Young (1976); Nagel and Olzak (1982); Brass (1985); Horowitz (1985); Olzak (1992); A. Smith (1992).

30. See Martin (1991), Stein (1989), and T. Smith (1992) for a discussion of shifting nomenclature among African Americans. My thanks to Norm Yetman for raising the issue of evolving nomenclature.

31. See Cleaver (1968); Carmichael and Hamilton (1967); Willhelm (1970); Lister (1968).

32. A less liberating but common cultural construction technique used in ethnic mobilization is the demonization or villification of opposition ethnic groups in civil wars, pogroms, and genocides (e.g., against Armenians in World War I Turkey, against Jews in World War II Germanyk, against Muslims in post-Soviet Yugoslavia).

References

Adam, Heribert, and Kogila Moodley. *The Opening of the Apartheid Mind: Options for the New South Africa*. Berkeley: University of California Press, 1993.

Adams, June, and Richard La Course. "Backlash barrage erupts across U.S." *Yakima Nation Review*, July 18:12, 1977.

Alba, Richard D. Ethnic Identity: The Transformation of White America. New Haven: Yale University Press, 1990.

Alba, Richard D., and John R. Logan. "Variations on two themes: Racial and ethnic patterns in the attainment of suburban residence." *Demography* 28:431–453, 1991.

Allworth, Edward. *Central Asia: 120 Years of Russian Rule*. Durham, NC: Duke University Press, 1989.

American Council on Education. "Educating One-Third of a Nation IV: Making our reality match our rhetoric." Washington, D.C.: American Council on Education, 1993.

Anderson, Benedict. *Imagined Communities: Reflections on the Origin and Spread of Nationalism*. London: Verso, 1991.

Applebome, Peter. "Arab-Americans fear a land war's backlash." *New York Times*, February 20:A1, 1991.

Bakalian, Anny. "From being to feeling Armenian: Assimilation and identity among Armenian-Americans." Paper presented at the annual meeting of the American Sociological Association, Cincinnati, 1991.

———. *Armenian-Americans: From Being to Feeling Armenian*. New Brunswick, NJ: Transaction Books, 1993.

Banton, Michael. *Ethnic and Racial Competition*. Cambridge: Cambridge University Press, 1983.

———. "Rational choice theories." *American Behavioral Scientist*, Forthcoming.

Barth, Fredrik. *Ethnic Groups and Boundaries*. Boston: Little, Brown, 1969.

Beale, Calvin. "American tri-racial isolates: Their status and pertinence to genetic research." *Eugenics Quarterly* 4:187–196, 1957.

Berger, Peter L., and Thomas Luckmann. *The Construction of Reality: A Treatise on the Sociology of Knowledge*. Garden City, NJ: Anchor Books, 1967.

Bonacich, Edna. "A theory of ethnic antagonism: The split labor market." *American Sociological Review* 37:547–559, 1972.

———. "A theory of middleman minorities." *American Sociological Review* 38:583–594, 1973.

Brass, Paul. "Ethnic groups and the state." In *Ethnic Groups and the State*, ed. P. Brass, 1–56. London: Croome-Helm, 1985.

Burstein, Paul. "'Reverse discrimination' cases in the federal courts: Legal mobilization by a countermovement." *Sociological Quarterly* 32:511–528, 1991.

Carmichael, Stokely, and Charles Hamilton. *Black Power: The Politics of Liberation in America*. New York: Vintage, 1967.

Champagne, Duane. *American Indian Societies—Strategies and Conditions of Political and Cultural Survival*, CS Report 32. Cambridge: Cultural Survival, Inc., 1989.

———. "Culture, differentiation, and environment: Social change in Tlingit society." In *Differentiation Theory and Social Change*, eds. J. Alexander and P. Colomy, 88–118. New York: Columbia University Press, 1990.

Chapman, Malcolm. *The Gaelic Vision in Scottish Culture*. London: Croome-Helm, 1979.

Clark, Blue. "Bury my heart in smog: Urban Indians." In *The American Indian Experience. A Profile: 1524 to the Present*, ed. P. Weeks, 278–291. Arlington Heights, Ill.: Forum Press, Inc., 1988.

Clark, Robert. *The Basque Insurgents: ETA, 1952–1980*. Madison: University of Wisconsin Press, 1984.

Cleaver, Eldridge. *Soul on Ice*. New York: McGraw-Hill, 1968.

Clifford, James. *The Predicament of Culture: Twentieth Century Ethnography, Literature, and Art*. Cambridge: Harvard University Press, 1988.

Clifford, James, and George Marcus, eds. *Writing Culture: The Poetics and Politics of Ethnography*. Berkeley: University of California Press, 1986.

Cohen, Abner. *Urban Ethnicity*. New York: Harper and Row, 1974.

Cohen, Anthony P. *The Symbolic Construction of Community*. New York: Tavistock, 1985.

Cohn, Bernard S. "Representing authority in Victorian India." In *The Invention of Tradition*, eds. E. Hobsbawm and T. Ranger, 165–210. Cambridge: Cambridge University Press, 1983.

Connor, Walker. "When is a nation?" *Ethnic and Racial Studies* 13:92–103, 1991.

Copage, Eric V. "The seven days of Kwanzaa." *New York Times*, December 1:18, 1991.

Cornell, Stephen. *The Return of the Native: American Indian Political Resurgence*. New York: Oxford University Press, 1988.

Davies, Charlotte. *Welsh Nationalism in the Twentieth Century: The Ethnic Option and the Modern State*. New York: Prager, 1989.

Davis, James. *Who is Black? One Nation's Definition*. University Park: Pennsylvania State University, 1991.

Deloria, Vine, Jr. "Indian studies—the orphan of academia." *The Wicazo Sa Review* 2:1–7, 1986.

Desai, Manisha. "The demise of secularism and the rise of majority communalism in India." Paper presented at the annual meeting of the Midwest Sociological Society, Kansas City, 1992.

Despres, Leo. "Toward a theory of ethnic phenomena." In *Ethnicity and Resource Competition*, ed. L. Despres, 186–297. The Hague: Mouton, 1975.

Enloe, Cynthia. *Ethnic Conflict and Political Development*. Boston: Little, Brown, 1973.

Espiritu, Yen. *Asian American Panethnicity: Bridging Institutions and Identities*. Philadelphia: Temple University Press, 1992.

Evans-Pritchard, Deirdre. "The Portal Case: Authenticity, tourism, traditions, and the law." *Journal of American Folklore* 100:287–296, 1987.

Faludi, Susan. *Backlash: The Undeclared War Against American Women*. New York: Crown, 1991.

Fantasia, Rick. *Cultures of Solidarity*. Berkeley: University of California Press, 1988.

Feagin, Joe R. "The continuing significance of race: Antiblack discrimination in public places." *American Sociological Review* 56:101–116, 1991.

———. "The continuing significance of racism: Discrimination against black students at white colleges." *Journal of Black Studies* 22:546–578, 1992.

Feeney, Patrick G. "The 1990 census and the politics of apportionment." *Footnotes*. Washington, D.C.: *American Sociological Association* (March):5–6, 1992.

Fernandez-Kelly, Maria Patricia. "Economic restructuring in the United States: The case of Hispanic women in the garment and electronics industries in southern California." Paper presented at the annual meeting of the American Sociological Association, Chicago, 1987.

Fischer, Michael M.J. "Ethnicity and the post-modern arts of memory." In *Writing Culture: The Poetics and Politics of Ethnography*, eds. J. Clifford and G. Marcus, 194–233. Berkeley: University of California Press, 1986.

Friedman, Debra, and Doug McAdam. "Collective identity as a selective incentive." Paper presented at the annual meeting of the American Sociological Association, 1987.

———. "Collective identity and action: Networks, choices, and the life of a social movement." In *Frontiers in Social Movement Theory*, eds. A.D. Morris and C.M. Mueller, 156–173. New Haven: Yale University Press, 1992.

Gamson, William. "The political culture of the Arab-Israeli conflict." *Conflict Management and Peace Sciences* 5:79–93, 1982.

———. "Political discourse and collective action." In *International Social Movements Research*, eds. B. Klandermans, B. Kriesi, and S. Tarrow. Greenwich, Conn.: JAI Press, 1988.

———. "The social psychology of collective action." In *Frontiers in Social Movement Theory*, eds. A.D. Morris and C.M. Mueller 53–76. New Haven: Yale University Press, 1992.

Gamson, William, and Kathryn E. Lasch. "The political culture of welfare policy." In *Evaluating the Welfare State: Social and Political Perspectives*, eds. S.E. Spiro and E. Yuchtman-Yaar, 397–415. New York: Academic Press, 1983.

Gamson, William, and Andre Modigliani. "The changing culture of affirmative action." In *Research in Political Sociology*, ed. R.G. Braungart. Greenwich, conn.: JAI Press, 1987.

Gans, Herbert. "Symbolic ethnicity: The future of ethnic groups and cultures in America." *Ethnic and Racial Studies* 2:1–20, 1979.

Geertz, Clifford. *Works and Lives: The Anthropologist as Author*. Palo Alto: Stanford University Press, 1988.

Gellner, Ernest. *Nations and Nationalism*. London: Basil Blackwell, 1983.

———. *Culture, Identity, and Politics*. Cambridge: Cambridge University Press, 1987.

Gerner, Deborah J. *One Land, Two Peoples: The Conflict over Palestine*. Boulder, Colo.: Westview, 1991.

Gimenez, Marta E., Fred A. Lopez, and Carlos Munoz, Jr. *The Politics of Ethnic Construction: Hispanic, Chicano, Latino?* Beverly Hills: Sage Publications, 1992.

Harris, Marvin. *Patterns of Race in the Americas.* New York: Norton, 1964.

Harvie, Christopher. *Scotland and Nationalism.* London: Allen and Unwin, 1977.

Hechter, Michael. *Internal Colonialism.* Berkeley: University of California Press, 1975.

———. *Principles of Group Solidarity.* Berkeley: University of California Press, 1987a.

———. "Nationalism as group solidarity." *Ethnic and Racial Studies* 10:415–426, 1987b.

———. "The dynamics of secession." *Acta Sociologica* 35: 267–283, 1992.

Hechter, Michael, and Debra Friedman. "Does rational choice theory suffice? Response to Adam." *International Migration Review* 18:381–388, 1984.

Hechter, Michael, Debra Friedman, and Malka Appelbaum. "A theory of ethnic collective action." *International Migration Review* 16:412–434, 1982.

Hein, Jeremy. "Do 'new immigrants' become 'new minorities?:' The meaning of ethnic minority for Indochinese refugees in the United States." *Sociological Perspectives* 31:61–77, 1991.

———. "From migrant to minority." *Sociological Inquiry* 64, 1994.

Hertzberg, Hazel. *The Search for an American Identity: Modern Pan-Indian Movements.* Syracuse: Syracuse University Press, 1971.

Hobsbawm, Eric. "Introduction: Inventing traditions." In *The Invention of Tradition*, eds. E. Hobsbawm and T. Ranger, 1–14. Cambridge: Cambridge University Press, 1983.

———. *Nations and Nationalism Since 1780.* London: Cambridge University Press, 1990.

Hodson, Randy, Dusko Sekulic, and Garth Massey. "National tolerance in Yugoslavia." *American Journal of Sociology* 99, forthcoming.

———. Holstein, James A., and Gale Miller, eds. *Perspectives on Social Problems: Reconsidering Social Constructionism (Volume 5).* New York: Aldine, 1993.

Horowitz, Donald. *Ethnic Groups in Conflict.* Berkeley: University of California Press, 1985.

Iliffe, John. *A Modern History of Tanganyika.* Cambridge: Cambridge University Press, 1979.

Jaimes, M. Annette. "Federal Indian identification policy: A usurpation of indigenous sovereignty in North America." In *The State of Native America: Genocide, Colonization, and Resistance*, ed. M.A. Jaimes, 123–128. Boston: South End Press, 1992.

James, David R. "City limits on racial equality: The effects of city-suburb boundaries on public-school desegregation, 1968–1976." *American Sociological Review* 54:963–985, 1989.

Johnston, Hank. *Tales of Nationalism: Catalonia: 1939–1979.* New Brunswick: Rutgers University Press, 1991.

Kansas City Star. "Indian art protection law may end up hurting the artists." August 4:J–5, 1991.

Karner, TracyX. "Ideology and nationalism: The Finnish move to independence, 1809–1918." *Racial and Ethnic Studies,* 1991.

Katz, Elaine N. *A Trade Union Aristocracy.* African Studies Institute Communication, No. 3. Johannesburg: University of the Witwatersrand, 1976.

Keith, Verna M., and Cedric Herring. "Skin tone and stratification in the black community." *American Journal of Sociology* 97:760–778, 1991.

Kelly, Mary. "Lithuanian-Americans in the United States and Lithuania." *Sociologija Lietuvoje: Praeitis ir Dabartis* (Kaunas Technological University, Lithuania) 3:158–159, 1993.

———. "Ethnic pilgrimages: People of Lithuanian descent in Lithuania." Paper presented at the annual meeting of the Midwest Sociological Society, St. Louis, 1994.

Kivisto, Peter, ed. *The Ethnic Enigma: The Salience of Ethnicity for European-Origin Groups*. Philadelphia: The Balch Institute Press, 1989.

Kuhlmann, Annette. "Steelheads and walleyes: Changes in political culture in and around Indian country and the fishing rights struggle in the Pacific Northwest and the Great Lakes." In *Research in Human Capital and Development*, eds. C. Ward and C.M. Snipp. Greenwich, Conn.: JAI Press, Forthcoming.

Laitin, David D. "Hegemony and religious conflict: British imperial control and political cleavages in Yorubaland." In *Bringing the State Back In*, eds. P.B. Evans, D. Rueschemeyer, and T. Skocpol, 285–312. Cambridge: Cambridge University Press, 1985.

Larimore, Jim, and Rick Waters. "American Indians speak out against ethnic fraud in college admissions." Paper presented at a conference sponsored by the American Council on Education: "Educating One-Third of a Nation IV: Making our Reality Match our Rhetoric," Houston, 1993.

Lauwagie, Beverly. "Ethnic boundaries in modern states: Romano Lavo-Lil revisited." *American Journal of Sociology* 87:23–47, 1979.

Layne, Linda L. "The dialogics of tribal self-representation in Jordan." *American Ethnologist* 16:24–39, 1989.

Lee, Sharon M. "Racial classification in the U.S. census: 1890–1990." *Racial and Ethnic Studies* 17:75–94, 1993.

Lelyveld, Joseph. *Move Your Shadow: South Africa, Black and White*. New York: Penguin, 1985.

Lemann, Nicholas. *The Promised Land: The Great Black Migration and How it Changed America*. New York: A.A. Knopf, 1991.

Lichtenstein, Grace. "Custer's defeat commemorated by entreaties of peace." New York Times, June 1976 25II–1.

Lieberson, Stanley. "Unhyphenated whites in the United Sates." *Ethnic and Racial Studies* 8:159–180, 1985.

Light, Ivan, and Edna Bonacich. *Immigrant Entrepreneurs: Koreans in Los Angeles, 1965–1982*. Berkeley: University of California Press, 1988.

Lister, Julius. *Look Out Whitey! Black Power's Gon' Get Your Mama*. New York: The Dial Press, Inc., 1968.

Lupul, M.R. "Multiculturalism and Canada's white ethnics." *Multiculturalism* 6:14–18, 1983.

Maarseveen, Henc T., and Ger van der Tang. *Written Constitutions: A computerized Comparative Study*. Dobbs Ferry, NY: Oceana Publications, 1978.

Martin, Ben L. "From Negro to black to African-American: The power of names and naming." *Political Science Quarterly* 106:83–105, 1991.

Massey, Douglas S. "Ethnic residential segregation: A theoretical syntheses and empirical review." *Sociology and Social Research* 69:315–350, 1985.

Massey, Douglas S., and Nancy Denton. *American Apartheid*. Chicago: University of Chicago Press, 1993.

McBeth, Sally. "Layered identity systems in western Oklahoma Indian communities." Paper presented at the annual meeting of the American Anthropological Association, 1989.

Means, Gordon P. *Malaysian Politics*. London: Hodder and Stoughton, 1976.

Melson, Robert, and Howard Wolpe, eds. *Nigeria: Modernization and the Politics of Communalism*. East Lansing: Michigan State University Press, 1971.

Mercer, John. *Scotland: the Devolution of Power*. London: Calder, 1978.

Moerman, Michael. "Ethnic identification in a complex civilization: Who are the Lue?" *American Anthropologist* 76:1215–1230, 1965.

———. "Accomplishing ethnicity." In *Ethnomethodology,* ed. R. Turner, 54–68. New York: Penguin Education, 1974.

Morris, Aldon. *The Origins of the Civil Rights Movement*. New York: The Free Press, 1984.

Morris, Aldon D., and Carol M. Mueller, eds. *Frontiers in Social Movement Theory*. New Haven: Yale University Press, 1992.

Murray, Janice. *Canadian Cultural Nationalism*. New York: New York University Press, 1977.

Nagel, Beverly. "Gypsies in the United States and Great Britain: Ethnic boundaries and political mobilization." In *Competitive Ethnic Relations*, eds. S. Olzak and J. Nagel, 69–90. New York: Academic Press, 1986.

Nagel, Joane. "The political construction of ethnicity." In *Competitive Ethnic Relations*, eds. S. Olzak and J. Nagel, 93–112. New York: Academic Press, 1986.

———. *American Indian Ethnic Renewal: Red Power and the Resurgence of Identity and Culture*. New York: Oxford University Press, 1994.

Nagel, Joane, and Susan Olzak. "Ethnic mobilization in new and old states: An extension of the competition model." *Social Problems* 30:127–143, 1982.

Nayar, Baldev Raj. *Politics in the Punjab*. New Haven: Yale University Press, 1966.

Olzak, Susan. "Labor unrest, immigration, and ethnic conflict in urban America, 1880–1914." *American Journal of Sociology* 94:1303–1333, 1989.

———. *The Dynamics of Ethnic Competition and Conflict*. Stanford: Stanford University Press, 1992.

Padilla, Felix. *Latino Ethnic Consciousness: The Case of Mexican Americans and Puerto Ricans in Chicago*. Notre Dame: University of Notre Dame Press, 1985.

———. "Latino ethnicity in the city of Chicago." In *Competitive Ethnic Relations*, eds. S. Olzak and J. Nagel, 153–171. New York: Academic Press, 1986.

Pedraza, Silvia. "Ethnic identity: Developing a Hispanic-American identity." Paper presented at the 5th Congreso Internacional sobre las Culturas Hispanas de los Estados Unidos, Madrid, Spain, 1992.

Pedraza-Bailey, Silvia. *Political and Economic Migration in America: Cubans and Mexicans*. Austin: University of Texas Press, 1985.

Petonito, Gina. "Constructing 'Americans:' 'Becoming American,' 'loyalty' and Japanese internment during World War II." In *Perspectives on Social Problems*., eds. G. Miller and J. Holstein. Greenwich, Conn.: JAI Press, 1991a.

———. "Racial discourse, claims making and Japanese internment during World War II." Paper presented at the annual meeting of the American Sociological Association, Cincinnati, 1991b.

Plascov, Avi. *The Palestinian Refugees in Jordon*, 1948–1957. London: Frank Cass, 1981.

Portes, Alejandro, and Reuben Rumbaut. *Immigrant America: A Portrait*. Berkeley: University of California Press, 1990.

Prebble, John. *The Highland Clearances*. London: Secker and Warburg, 1963.

Prucha, Francis P. *The Great Father. The United States Government and the American Indians*. Lincoln: University of Nebraska Press, 1984.

Quinn, William W., Jr. "The southeast syndrome: Notes on Indian descendant recruitment organizations and their perceptions of Native American culture." *American Indian Quarterly* 14:147–154, 1990.

Rhoodie, Eschel. *Discrimination in the Constitutions of the World*. Atlanta: Orbis, 1983.

Roediger, David R. *The Wages of Whiteness: Race and the Making of the American Working Class*. London: Verso, 1991.

Roosens, Eugeen E. *Creating Ethnicity: The Process of Ethnogenesis*. Newbury Park: Sage Publications, 1989.

Rubin, Lillian B. *Busing and Backlash: White Against White in a California School District*. Berkeley: University of California Press, 1972.

Rudolph, Lloyd, and Susanne Rudolph. *The Modernity of Tradition: Political Development in India*. Chicago: University of Chicago Press, 1967.

Salamone, Frank A., ed. *Missionaries and Anthropologists, Part II*. Athens, Ga.: University of Georgia, Department of Anthropology, 1985.

Sanneh, Lamin. *Translating the Message: The Missionary Impact on Culture*. New York: Orbis Books, 1989.

Sassen, Saskia. *The Mobility of Labor and Capital*. New York: Cambridge University Press, 1988.

———. *The Global City*. NJ: Princeton University Press, 1991.

Schermerhorn, R.A. *Ethnic Plurality in India*. Tucson: University of Arizona Press, 1978.

Scott, James C. *Domination and the Arts of Resistance: Hidden Transcripts*. New Haven: Yale University Press, 1990.

Simmons, Ron. *Affirmative Action: Conflict and Change in Higher Education After Bakke*. Cambridge, Mass.: Schenkman, 1982.

Smith, Anthony D. *The Ethnic Origins of Nations*. New York: B. Blackwell, 1986.

———. *Ethnicity and Nationalism*. Leiden: E.J. Brill, 1992.

Smith, Tom W. "Changing racial labels: From colored to Negro to black to African American." Chicago, University of Chicago, *General Social Survey Topical Report No. 22, 1992*.

Snipp, C. Matthew. "Some observations about racial boundaries and the experiences of American Indians." Paper presented at the University of Washington, Seattle, April, 1993.

Snow, D.A., E.B. Rochford, Jr., S.K. Worden, and R.D. Benford. "Frame alignment processes, micromobilization, and movement participation." *American Sociological Review* 51:464–481, 1986.

Snow, D.A. and Robert D. Benford. "Ideology, frame resonance, and participant mobilization." In *International Social Movements* Research., eds. B. Klandermans, B. Kriesi, and S. Tarrow, 197–217. Greenwich, Conn.: JAI Press, 1988.

———. "Master frames and cycles of protest." In *Frontiers in Social Movement Theory*, eds. A.D. Morris and C.M. Mueller, 133–155. New Haven: Yale University Press, 1992.

Spector, Malcolm, and John I. Kitsuse. *Constructing Social Problems*. New York: Aldine, 1977.

Steele, C. Hoy. "Urban Indian identity in Kansas: Some implications for research." In *The New Ethnicity: Perspectives from Ethnology*, ed. J.W. Bennett, 167–178. St. Paul: West Publishing Company, 1975.

Stein, Judith. "Defining the race, 1890–1930." In *The Invention of Ethnicity*, ed. W. Sollors, 77–104. New York: Oxford University Press, 1989.

Sullivan, John. *ETA and Basque Nationalism: The Fight for Euskadi, 1890–1986*. Rutledge: New York, 1988.

Swidler, Ann. "Culture as action: Symbols and strategies." *American Sociological Review* 51:273–286, 1986.

Taber, Charles R. *The World is Too Much with Us: "Culture" in Modern Protestant Missions*. Macon, Ga.: Mercer University Press, 1991.

Tilly, Charles. *The Contentious French*. Cambridge: Harvard University Press, 1986.

Tonkin, Elizabeth, Maryon McDonald, and Malcolm Chapman, eds. *History and Ethnicity*. New York: Routledge, 1989.

Trevor-Roper, Hugh. "The invention of tradition: The highland tradition of Scotland." In *The Invention of Tradition*, eds. E. Hobsbawm and T. Ranger, 15–42. Cambridge: Cambridge University Press, 1983.

U.S. Bureau of the Census. *U.S. Census of Population and Housing Public Use Microdata Sample* (PUMS) file (1% sample), 1980.

———. *Census of Population, Subject Reports, Characteristics of American Indians by Tribes and Selected Areas, 1980, Vol 2, Sections 1 and 2*. Washington, D.C.: Government Printing Office, 1989.

———. *1990 March Current Population Survey* (CPS) file, 1990.

———. "Census Bureau completes distribution of 1990 redistricting tabulations to states." *Census Bureau Press Release* CB91–100, Monday, March 11, 1991.

United States Congress. *United States Statutes at Large*, 101st Congress, 2nd Session. Volume 104, Part 6:4662–4665. Washington, D.C.: U.S. Government Printing Office, 1990.

Wagner, Roy. *The Invention of Culture*. Chicago: University of Chicago Press, 1975.

Wallerstein, Immanuel. "Ethnicity and national integration." *Cahiers d'Etudes Africaines* 3:129–138, 1960.

Waters, Mary. *Ethnic Options: Choosing Identities in America*. Berkeley: University of
     California Press, 1990.
————. "The Intersection of race and ethnicity: Generational changes among Caribbean
     immigrants to the United States." Paper presented at the annual meeting of the American
     Sociological Association, Cincinnati, 1991.
Weibel-Orlando, Joan. *Indian Country, L.A.* Champaign: University of Illinois Press, 1991.
Whitaker, Mark. "White and black lies." *Newsweek* (November 15):52–63, 1993.
Whitehorse, David. *Pow-wow: The Contemporary Pan-Indian Celebration*. San Diego: San
     Diego State University, Publications in American Indian Studies, No. 5., 1988.
Whiteman, Darrell L., ed. *Missionaries and Anthropologists, Park I*. Athens, GA.:
     University of Georgia, Department of Anthropology, 1985.
Whorton, Brad. "The transformation of American refugee policy in the 1970s and 1960s."
     Paper presented at the annual meeting of the Midwest Sociological Society, St. Louis,
     1994.
Willhelm, Sidney. *Who Needs the Negro?* Cambridge, Mass.: Schenkman, 1970.
Wilson, William J. *The Truly Disadvantaged: The Inner City, the Underclass, and Public
     Policy*. Chicago: University of Chicago Press, 1987.
Wright, Carole. "What people have formed backlash groups?" *Yakima Nation Review*, July
     18:10, 1977.
Yancey, William L., Eugene P. Ericksen, and R. Juliani. "Emergent ethnicity: A review and
     reformulation." *American Sociological Review* 41:391–402, 1976.
Yetman, Norman R. "The 'new immigrant wave': Migration pressures and the American
     presence." Paper presented at the annual meeting of the American Studies Association,
     Philadelphia, 1983.
————. "Race and ethnicity in 1980s America." In *Majority and Minority: The Dynamics of
     Race and Ethnicity in American Life*, ed. N. Yetman, 379–401. Boston: Allyn and Bacon,
     1991.
Young, Crawford, *The Politics of Cultural Pluralism*. Madison: University of Wisconsin
     Press, 1976.
Zulaika, Joseba. *Basque Violence: Metaphor and Sacrament*. Reno: University of Nevada
     Press, 1988.

"Soulmaning": Using Race for Political and Economic Gain

Luther Wright, Jr.

Philip and Paul Malone, twin brothers from Boston, applied to be firefighters in 1975, but were not hired because of low civil service test scores. The brothers reapplied in 1977, changing their racial classifications from "white" to "black."[1] Due to a court mandate requiring Boston to hire more minority firefighters and police,[2] the Malones were hired in 1978, even though their test scores remained the same. Had the Malones listed their race as white in 1977, they most likely would have been denied employment a second time. In 1988, ten years after being hired, the Malone brothers' racial classifications were questioned by a Boston Fire Commissioner when the twins applied for promotions. The commissioner, who knew the twins personally, was puzzled that they listed their race as black. After a state hearing, Philip and Paul Malone were fired for committing "Racial fraud."[3]

Hispanic and black organizations in Boston criticized the city government for allowing the Malones to work for ten years before questioning their racial identity. These organizations called for a full investigation of the Malones' case and for prompt investigation of other allegations of racial fraud. One Boston official claimed that as many as sixty other firefighters had engaged in racial fraud, but other officials estimated that the actual number was closer to ten. Shortly after the Malones' hearing, eleven Boston firefighters classifying themselves as Hispanic were investigated; two resigned. [4]

In the mid-1980s, allegations of racial fraud also surfaced in the political arena. In 1984, Stockton, California, City Councilman Mark Stebbins survived a recall election organized by a black councilman he had defeated.[5] Stebbins, described as a man with a "broad nose, light complexions, blue eyes and curly brown hair...worn in a short Afro style," had run as a black candidate in the city council election. While the birth certificates of Stebbins's parents and grandparents listed their race as white, and Stebbins acknowledged that his siblings were white, he contended that he was black. At the time of the elections, Stebbins's council district was forty-six percent Latino and thirty-seven percent black. Accused of lying about his race to get votes, Stebbins argued that he first believed he was black when he was growing up and other children referred to him as "niggerhead." Stebbins also hinted he believed he had a black ancestor who had passed as white. Despite this somewhat tenuous assertion, many of the black leaders in the community accepted him as black, apparently to gain more minority influence on the council.[6]

American society has long differentiated among individuals on the basis of race. Paul Finkelman recently noted, "the word 'race' defines precise definition in American Law."[7] No physical attribute or collection of physical attributes adequately defines "race." This lack of a precise definition led to accusations of racial fraud in the Malones and Stebbins cases. The make-shift definition of race used during the Malones' hearing encompassed appearance, self-identification of the family in the community, and ancestry. In the Stebbins election, California voters and leaders created a definition of race premised on physical features and personal self-identification, but paid absolutely no attention to Stebbins's obviously white ancestry. Finkelman argues, and the Malones and Stebbins cases support the assertion, that the American definition of race is much like Justice Potter Stewart's definition of obscenity—"I know it when I see it."[8] The problem with race, as with pornography, is that people "see it" differently.

From slavery to the present, some blacks have passed for white. In recent years, incidents of whites claiming to be black have become more and more frequent. I use the term "soulmaning"[9] to describe whites passing for black to gain employment, education, and political opportunities. The Malones and Stebbins incidents illustrate soulmaning.

While the case of Mark Stebbins may seem unbelievable, his case is probably more common. The "Black Pride" movement of the 1960s encouraged people to take pride in and embrace their fractional black heritage. Mark Stebbins may have been one of these individuals, but that seems highly unlikely. The political benefit that he received by identifying himself as black in a district composed of thirty-seven percent blacks and eighty-three percent minorities is a classic example of soulmaning. Running as a white candidate against a black incumbent would have resulted in defeat if the voters voted along racial lines. It is not unreasonable to argue that Stebbins declared himself black in order to win.

Regardless of his motivations, blacks in the district were willing to embrace Stebbins because of the much needed black political power he could generate as a black council member. In a society so heavily reliant on race, it is advantageous for all minority groups to accept those who self-identify with the group. Consequently, minority groups may welcome those who are soulmaning when it is beneficial to the group. However, when the benefit is only incurred by the individual, the attitude is usually more hostile.

The case of the Malone twins demonstrates soulmaning in employment. The Malones were found guilty of committing racial fraud to obtain work. The Malones apparently believed that there was some benefit to be gained by classifying themselves as blacks. Soulmaning in obtaining work did not elicit the open-armed response that Stebbins received in the political arena. As Massachusetts Department of Personnel administrator David Hayley pointed out at the time of the Malone incident, the reaction of minorities in that instance was much different. Hayley argued that because the Malones denied two minorities the opportunity to serve as Boston firefighters, no one would ever know what those two minority firefighters might have accomplished. The Malones took advantage of a hiring policy designed to remedy past and present discrimination. In this remedial context, a standardless definition of race allows racial fraud to continue with no remedy for past discrimination. The reality of affirmative action, calls for diversity, and even political campaigns may make soulmaning a recurring phenomenon. Failure to develop intelligent rules in this arena could lead to strained racial tensions and the blatant abuse of policies designed to bring about social justice.

Notes

1. Peggy Hernandez, *Firemen Who Claimed to be Black Lose Appeal,* Boston Globe 13
    (July 26, 1989).

2. For a history of the court mandate to hire minorities in the Boston firefighting and police
    departments, see *Boston Chapter NAACP v. Beecher,* 679 F.2d 965 (5th Cir. 1982).

3. Peggy Hernandez and John Ellement, *Two Fight Firing Over Disputed Claim That They
    are Black,* Boston Globe 29 (Sept. 29, 1988). Id. Affirming the decision of the State
    Department of Personnel Administration, Justice Wilkins of the State Supreme Judicial
    Court asserted that the Malones "had a powerful incentive to seize on any means to en-
    hance their chances of appointment as firefighters." Id. The term "racial fraud" is used to
    characterize situations in which individuals racially misclassify themselves in order to ob-
    tain some tangible benefit. In the black community, "racial fraud" has been called "pass-
    ing" (i.e., blacks misclassifying themselves as white). See Gunnar Myrdal, *An American
    Dilemma: The Negro Problem and Modern Democracy* 683–86 (Harper, 1944).

4. Hernandez and Ellement, *supra* at 29, 32; Hernandez, *supra* at 14.

5. *City Council Member Survives Recall Vote,* Wash. Post A6 (May 15, 1984).

6. United Press Int'l, *Black or White? Race Becomes Political Issue* (April 19, 1984).
    Stebbins claimed that the fact that Latinos outnumbered blacks in the district meant
    that lying about his race would not have been very beneficial. Id. Interestingly enough,
    Stebbins won 39% of the vote in a district that was only 17% white. Id. If groups in
    the district had voted along strict racial lines, a white candidate would have had no
    chance to be elected.

7. Paul Finkelman, *The Color of Law,* 87 Nw. U.L. Rev. 937, 937 n.3 (1993) (book review).

8. See *Jacobellis v. Ohio,* 378 U.S. 184, 197 (1964) (Stewart, J., concurring); Finkelman,
    87 Nw. U. L. REV. at 937 N.3 (cited in note 24). This standardless conception of race
    is particularly troubling since race, unlike hard-core pornography, has broad signifi-
    cance in American society.

9. *Soul Man* was a 1986 movie starring C. Thomas Howe, Rae Dawn Chong, and James
    Earl Jones. In the movie, Howe plays Mark Watson, a wealthy California student who
    is admitted to Harvard Law School, but whose father refuses to pay the tuition. Unable
    to qualify for student aid and loans because of his father's wealthy status, Watson
    takes tanning pills and puts on make-up to make himself appear black, so that he can
    win a minority scholarship for which no minority has applied.

Article 2.4

"I'm Just Who I am: Race Is No Longer Black or White. So, What Does This Mean for America?"

Jack E. White

His nickname notwithstanding, professional golfer Frank ("Fuzzy") Zoeller saw Tiger Woods quite clearly. He gazed upon the new king of professional golf, through whose veins runs the blood of four continents, and beheld neither a one-man melting pot nor even a golfing prodigy but a fried-chicken-and-collard-greens-eating Sambo. Zoeller saw Woods, in short, as just another stereotype, condemned by his blackness to the perpetual status of "little boy."

Zoeller soon paid a price for saying openly what many others were thinking secretly. K Mart, the discount chain with a big African-American clientele, unceremoniously dumped him as the sponsor of a line of golf clothing and equipment, and he abjectly withdrew from the Greater Greensboro Open tournament. "People who know me know I'm a jokester. I just didn't deliver the line well," Zoeller tearfully explained. But his real crime was not, as he and his defenders seem to think, merely a distasteful breach of racial etiquette or an inept attempt at humor. The real crime was falling behind the times. The old black-white stereotypes are out of date, and Zoeller is just the latest casualty of America's failure to come to grips with the perplexing and rapidly evolving significance of racial identity in what is fast becoming the most polyglot society in history.

If current demographic trends persist; midway through the 21st century whites will no longer make up a majority of the U.S. population. Blacks will have been overtaken as the largest minority group by Hispanics. Asians and Pacific Islanders will more than double their number of 9.3 million in 1995 to 19.6 million by 2020. An explosion of interracial, interethnic and interreligious marriages will swell the ranks of children whose mere existence makes a mockery of age-old racial categories and attitudes. Since 1970, the number of multiracial children has quadrupled to more than 2 million, according to the Bureau of the Census. The color line once drawn between blacks and white—or more precisely between whites and nonwhites—is breaking into a polygon of dueling ethnicities, each fighting for its place in the sun.

For many citizens the "browning of America" means a disorienting plunge into an un-

From *Time*, May 5, 1997. Reprinted by permission.

MELDING POT

Children of interracial marriages in millions

Interracial marriages in millions

1970   1980   1990

Percentage of African Americans marrying whites   8.9

Women   3.9
Men
1.9
0.7
1970   1993

charted sea of identity. Zoeller is far from alone in being confused about the complex tangle of genotypes and phenotypes and cultures that now undercut centuries-old verities about race and race relations in the U.S. Like many others, he hasn't got a clue about what to call the growing ranks of people like Woods who inconveniently refuse to be pigeonholed into one of the neat, oversimplified racial classifications used by government agencies—and, let's face it, most people. Are they people of color? Mixed race? Biracial? Whatever they like?

And if we don't know what to call them, how are we supposed to cope with them? Are they a new and distinct category of "real" Americans, due the same respectful recognition—and governmental protections—as more familiar groups? Or should they be lumped into the demeaning catchall category of "minorities" or "other"? How we eventually answer these questions will affect everything from the first Census forms of the 21st century, which will be issued a mere three years from now, to university admissions policies to the way civil rights laws are enforced. Even more important, it may ultimately transform the way Americans identify themselves and the tribe or tribes they belong to. In one grandiose vision, shared by conservative analyst Douglas Besharov of the American Enterprise Institute and communitarian sociologist Amitai Etzioni of American University, the ambiguous racial identity of mixed-race children may be "the best hope for the future of American race relations," as Besharov puts it. Letting people define themselves as multiracial, Etzioni argues, "has the potential to soften the racial lines that now divide America by rendering them more like economic differences and less like harsh, almost immutable, caste lines." Those who blend many streams of ethnicity within their own bodies, the argument goes, will render race a meaningless concept, providing a biological solution to the problem of racial justice. This idea reflects a deeply pessimistic view of human nature. It suggests that people can get along with each other only if they are all the same, instead of learning to accept and respect differences.

In any event, the way Americans think and talk about race will have to catch up with the new reality. Just how anachronistic our racial vocabulary has become was made clear by Woods in an appearance last week on *The Oprah Winfrey Show*. When asked if it bothered him, the only child of a black American father and a Thai mother, to be called an African American, he replied, "It does. Growing up, I came up with this name: I'm a 'Cablinasian,'" which he explained is a self-crafted acronym that reflects his one-eighth Caucasian, one-fourth black, one-eighth American Indian, one-fourth Thai and one-fourth Chinese roots with a precision that a racial-classifications expert under South African apartheid would admire. He said that when he was asked to check a box for racial background, he couldn't settle on just one. "I checked off 'African American' and 'Asian.' Those are the two I was raised under, and the only two I know."

Kerboom! A mini-racial fire storm erupted. Woods' remarks infuriated many African Americans who hailed his record-setting triumph at the Masters as a symbol of racial progress but see him as a traitor. To them Woods appeared to be running away from being an African American—a condition, they were quick to point out, that he himself had emphasized when he paid tribute to black golf pioneers Teddy Rhodes, Charlie Sifford and Lee Elder in his graceful victory speech. In a mirror image of Zoeller's constricted views, some blacks saw Woods' assertion of a multiracial identity as a sellout that could touch off an epidemic of "passing." Arthur Fletcher, a black member of the U.S. Commission on Civil Rights, testified at a 1993 congressional hearing devoted to whether a new, "multiracial' category should be added to U.S. Census forms that "I can see a whole host of light-skinned black Americans running for the door the minute they have another choice. All of a sudden they have a way of saying, 'In this discriminatory culture of ours, I am something other than black.'"

In their rush to judgment, the fearful apparently never stopped to consider that Woods was not turning his back on any part of his identity but instead was embracing every aspect of it. As he put it, "I'm just who I am, whoever you see in front of you"—and that includes his Asian side. "The influence of Tiger's mother Kultida in his life is very important," declares a family friend. "He goes to the temple with her occasionally. She's a devout Buddhist. He wears a family heirloom Buddha around his neck. He's a hybrid of a lot of things, and that's how he sees himself. He honestly sees himself as a somewhat separate person from the norm—not in terms of talent but in terms of his makeup."

Woods grew up in a suburb of Los Angeles with mostly white friends. But over the years he has made four visits to Thailand, where locals like to say he's "Asian from the eyes up," and he has also embraced the role model of his father Earl, who was the first black to play baseball in the Big Eight (for Kansas State). Now Tiger seems to be saying that if acknowledging the totality of his genetic and cultural makeup is difficult for many Americans, they will just have to try harder.

If history is any guide, a lot of them don't try at all. "It's very hard for other folks to embrace our philosophy without thinking we are being racist or trying to create a new race," says Nancy G. Brown, a Jewish woman who is married to a black man and is a past president of the 10-year-old advocacy group Multiracial Americans of Southern California. "It's hard for people to believe we are just looking for equality and that we are able to live with the concept of duality. Constantly calling Tiger Woods black is a good example of what we are talking about."

Groups like Brown's have lobbied for a multiracial category on government forms, but they also point out that recognizing multiracialism is more than just a matter of "psychic comfort." There are important health issues, for example, such as bone-marrow matching and how such race-specific syndromes as Tay-Sachs manifest themselves and get treated in biracial individuals. And most multiracial Americans have had the experience of being arbitrarily assigned an ethnic identity by a school principal, a caseworker or an employer that may differ from other family members'—or from one form to the next.

The noxious practice of pigeonholing people in narrow racial classifications is a deeply ingrained American habit that predates independence. It began with a desire to enforce firm distinctions between free citizens and slaves. In 1661, for example, Virginia decreed that the legal status of the mother would determine whether a black child was a slave or free. Three years later, Maryland went a step further, declaring that if either of a child's parents was a slave, the child would also be. The purpose of this law, its authors said, was to deter "divers freeborn English women" from marrying black slaves. But it did nothing to deter white male slave owners from trying to expand their human holdings by impregnating black female slaves.

Eventually, these pioneering efforts at codifying racial distinctions hardened into so-called miscegenation laws, which aimed to preserve the "purity" of the white race by making interracial sex a crime. Though upholding such laws required ever more tortured legal definitions of who was black and who wasn't, 16 states continued to ban interracial marriages until 1967, when the U.S. Supreme Court struck down such laws. In what was perhaps the most ridiculous example of racial pigeonholing, Louisiana ordained that anyone with a "trace" of black ancestry would be classified as black. Then, in an ostensibly "humane" 1970 reform, it enacted the "one thirty-second rule," by which anyone with a single black great-great-great-great-grandparent and 31 white great-great-great-great-grandparents was legally black. That regulation went unchallenged until Susie Guillory Phipps, the wife of a wealthy seafood importer who had always considered herself white, got a look at her birth certificate when applying for a passport and discovered that according to the state, she was black. In 1982 she sued the state, which hired a genealogist to delve into Phipps' ancestry. He dug up, among other ancestors, Phipps' great-great-great-great-grandmother—the black mistress of an Alabama plantation owner back in 1760—and concluded that Phipps was precisely three thirty-seconds black. The preposterous law stayed on the books until 1983.

For many decades, people on all sides of the color line chafed at these legal restraints on their ability to love and procreate. Even where black-white marriages were legal, these couples had to seek refuge in more tolerant black neighborhoods and raise their children as African Americans. But in the past 20 years, as the number of mixed-race marriages has increased dramatically, to more than 3 million by some estimates, attitudes among all racial groups have evolved. Tracey Mandell, 26, is an English instructor at Loyola Marymount University. Her partner Michael Bartley is a black man from Jamaica, and their son Noah is coming up on his first birthday. Mandell remembers last March, when she and members of her family were taking a get-acquainted tour of the maternity ward at Santa Monica Hospital. "There were about 50 couples on the tour," she says. "At least half of them were multiracial. My cousin, who lives in Minnesota, pointed it out to me. I hadn't even noticed. I think in L.A. there are so many multiracial people you don't even pay attention. But it's different when you leave Los Angeles."

It is precisely because they feel under attack and in need of solidarity that many American minorities fear the blurring of racial lines. Congressional black leaders argue that adding a multiracial category to Census forms, which the Office of Management and Budget will be considering through June of this year, would make it much harder to detect and combat racial discrimination. For example, according to a recent article in *Emerge,* the black newsmagazine, in 1991 some 35,000 people chose "other" on Home Mortgage Disclosure Act papers meant to track bias in lending. Allowing people to opt out of traditional race categories, says Congressional Black Caucus chairwoman Maxine Waters, a California Democrat, "just blurs everything. [People pushing for a multiracial category] want to be seen for all they are, but I don't think they're making the connection about how it could affect how they're represented, or who's being an advocate for them when they get mistreated." Among the many programs administered on the basis of racial tallies: minority employment on government contracts, court ordered school desegregation plans and protection of minority voting rights. All would have to be retooled, at great cost, if the categories change.

In the end, however, the impact of multiracialism will be decided not by the content of a Census form but in the hearts of Americans. Tiger Woods can proclaim his personal diversity, but if most people, like Zoeller, just see a "boy," it won't make much difference. Multiracial Americans will not get the right to define themselves as they choose without a fight.

Article 2.5

A Black Spy in White America

Danzy Senna

When I was 10 years old, I hung out with a group of white girls from my neighborhood. After school, we'd watch reruns of Welcome Back, Kotter and gossip about our classmates: who was cool, who wasn't. Occasionally, some of the girls would refer to "jungle bunnies," the black students who were bused to our school from the other side of town. When I heard such remarks, I'd pretend to be too absorbed by the television to hear what they were saying.

One day, one of the girls noticed my silence and whispered to another, "Yo, Chrissy, isn't Danzy's father colored?"

Christine, the leader of the pack, laughed and said, "Yeah, but *she* isn't. Just look at her." The rest of the group smiled at me warmly, and I forced a smile in return.

I am mixed, the daughter of a white mother and an African American father. Although I was raised by my parents to strongly identify as black, my straight hair and pale complexion suggest otherwise. As a result, I've often been privy to racist remarks like the ones that my fifth-grade companions made.

I can't count the number of times that people, unaware of my ethnicity, have whispered to me about the trouble with "them," meaning black people. At a retail job during college, my employer told me I should keep a closer eye on the "niggers" for fear they might steal. When I worked at a magazine, a colleague, a self-proclaimed liberal, warned me never to let black bike messengers past the front desk. "Maybe I'm racist," she confided, "but I don't feel safe with those homeboys around."

Even when I *told* white people I was black, they eventually slipped up. In one of my most painful experiences, a white guy I was dating drunkenly imitated black slang for his friend's amusement. In the middle of his routine, he looked at me, still laughing, and asked what was wrong. When I told him to guess, he turned four shades of pink.

Over the years, I've developed a sixth sense about white people. Like a horse that can predict a storm before it actually hits, my body can sense a racist remark before it is actually spoken. A friend once told me I'm like a spy, a 007 for the black race. She considered me lucky: At least I knew what white people said among their own.

But I didn't feel fortunate. In fact, white people's bigotry seemed to implicate me, bond me to their racism. I felt ashamed of my physical resemblance to them, contaminated by their confidences. It was like being let in on a dirty little secret you never asked to know. Afterward, you can't wash it off of you.

Nonetheless, I've grown adept at dealing with racist attitudes. Rather than sitting quietly as I did back in fifth grade, I've worked up some responses that are much more sarcastic and aggressive. Once, at a dinner party where the guests began telling racist jokes, I announced that I was black and said I was doing an anthropological study on what white people say when they think they're alone. I thanked them for the material and left abruptly, ignoring everyone's embarrassed apologies.

Another time, when I was looking for an apartment, my real estate agent assured me I would like a certain neighborhood. "Most of the blacks and Mexicans have moved out," she whispered with a conspiratorial smile, "You'll feel safe there." I nodded and said, "But have all the racist white people moved out too? Because I'm black, and that's really more of a concern for me." Her jaw dropped and she fumbled for words until I told her I would find another agent.

Despite my sharp comebacks and feigned coolness, incidents like this always leave me angry, disappointed and—most of all—exhausted by the feeling that I'm bearing a lonely burden. Recently, a white friend told me how his coworker often made bigoted comments to him. He said he wished I was there to "go off" on the guy. I asked him why I needed to be there; why didn't he speak up against what he knew was wrong? My friend was silent.

In a society as politely racist as ours, it is rare for anyone to speak up for those who are spared the blatant comments but who feel their effects. My black friends never hear the word *nigger* spoken at cocktail parties, but instead they must face racism's more subtle consequences: condescension at school, a glass ceiling at the office and a sense that they are forever being judged as a group rather than as individuals.

As a young girl, I thought I had no choice but to accept the invisibility my appearance afforded me. I believed I needed to look black in order to defend black people. I often wished for darker skin, curlier hair, some sign to the world of who I was. I thought that race was simply about color, a trait you inherited at birth.

Over time, though, I've learned that my black identity is not at all diminished simply because it is hidden. In fact, the identities we choose are the ones that define us, far more than the identities that we're given. I've chosen to let my thoughts and my words, not my skin and my hair, tell the world who I am.

Article 2.6

What Am I?

Laura Hymson

I was born out of love
Fostered in confusion
Came to stumble on pride and inner strength
Found power within myself
I never knew what I was but I knew what I was not
I knew then I did not fit into one of your small boxes of identity
I know now I am too big, too strong to curl up into one of your conventional
convenient categories of existence
I knew then I was different, special, unique
I know now just how special I am
I am the small minded man's fear
The fear of the unknown
The nameless
The outsider
The fear of a perfect union of the oppressor and the oppressed
But they still don't know what to call me
Could it be true, is it right, could the two co-exist in one bodily vessel
After all the looks and questions I looked around for some answers
What I saw was the zebra; such an animal to my delight
Nobody questions the zebra with his stripes worn proudly across his back
So with the grace of the zebra I stand and stride throughout my day
But still I pressed on looking for more within myself
I looked down one morning at the coffee in my cup
What a beautiful rich shade of mahogany I saw there
As I lifted the cream I peered inside to see its colors crisp as snow
I looked on with joy as I poured the cream in
I watched as the ribbons of color swam around in my cup with the wondrous
shades of ivory, mocha and mahogany and all that lies in between
I saw my answer becoming clear before me as the colors began to blend in
With each cup a new flavor, a new color
Each cup more spectacular in perfect harmony

Although my strength I found in the untamed zebra
And my confidence in a steaming cup of coffee
Each one of our answers lies out there somewhere before us
Our identities waiting to be claimed
Claimed not by a checked off box nor society nor anyone else other than you,
the individual, the perfect combination, the union of two beautiful cultures, backgrounds,
and colors

Article 2.7

What Are You?

Ryan Trammel

The questions that seems to plague me the most is, "What are you?"
I've been asked this question countless times
throughout my life. I understand how it might be difficult for people to figure out what I am,
especially when I wasn't sure myself.
I am multiracial.
My last name can be traced back to Europe,
    but I definitely wouldn't be mistaken for being white. Trammell,
my last name, comes from my paternal grandmother's side. To add to my diversity,
my mother is Korean and my father is Mexican

Needless to say,
I had a hard time figuring out who or what I was. All I wanted was to fit in.
The last thing I wanted was to stick
out like a piece of corn on top a mountain of mashed potatoes.
    I sometimes wondered what went through people's minds
when they looked at me.
I wondered what their reactions were when the teacher called my
Caucasian-sounding name,
only to be answered by an unusual looking Asian guy.

Being of mixed race was uncomfortable
for me.
I was either ashamed that I wasn't Korean enough or Mexican enough or white enough.
    When I was with my Korean
friends, my dark skin would stick out.
When I was with my Mexican friends, my Asian features would stick out.
I did not realize the beauty of my uniqueness. Instead,
I was ashamed of it.

I still find myself dealing with the same problems I dealt with as a child.
    However, from the knowledge I have

Reprinted by permission of Ryan Trammel.

gained from years of struggling
to figure out my identity,
I now have a new perspective on how to deal with my unique background.

As my life, and especially my education progressed, I learned to deal with being multiracial.
    I opened up myself to
learn about the ancient kingdoms of Korea.
I learned about the ancient Mexica (Aztec) people of Mexico,
who had established one of the most impressive kingdoms of all time.
    And I learned about the rich culture
of my European ancestors.

I began to appreciate and celebrate my diverse cultural background.
    As I learned more about each of my cultures and
their contributions to mankind,
I started to realize that I had something special. My journey is, and has been, very enlightening.

I'll always gain new knowledge about my cultures
because one never obtains full knowledge. We are always learning.
    I am always learning new and exciting things
about my Korean, Mexican and European heritage.
I'm absolutely proud to be from such a diverse ethnic background.
I used to believe that being multiracial
was a burden, but now I realize that I've been truly blessed
and am fortunate for it. The part of being multiracial
that I really feel fortunate for is the fact that I can celebrate and live more cultures than most.

I can eat my abuelita's (grandmother's) tamales one day,
my mom's kim-chee the next and eat a hamburger and fries another.
    I can celebrate Cinco de Mayo, the
Korean New Year and Octoberfest.
I appreciate the variety I have,
but I try not to emphasize one culture over another. Each culture that
    I belong to is beautiful in its own unique
way, and they affect me tremendously everyday.

Because of my diverse background,
I feel I can see with a variety of perspectives,
and hence,
be more open-minded and objective when I look at people.

I have dreams of one day
returning to Korea to my relatives again. I want to go to Mexico and find out who
exactly the Guerra's were.
I want to go to Germany and Alsace-Lorraine in France to find out where the Trammells
originated.

I will forever be Ryan,
a Korean, Mexican, and European American. There is no way that will ever change and
I would never want it to change.
I wouldn't be the Ryan Trammell I am today,
and I would never have reaped all the benefits of being part of such a diverse group
of people if it hadn't been for my culturally diverse upbringing.

No longer will I see my multiracial face as a burden.
It's like the saying goes, "When life gives you lemons, make lemonade." I'd have to say
that I've definitely made some lemonade,
but with a little added kick to it. I will always celebrate all my cultures.
   I will always look at Korea,
Mexico and Europe as my spiritual homelands.
However, I will always consider myself a person first
and a person of color second. I embrace my uniqueness and stand proudly.
One thing I know for sure,
I wouldn't change a thing.

CHAPTER 3

Ethnic Stratification

Of fundamental concern of ethnic studies is ethnic stratification, or institutionalized inequality among ethnic groups. To achieve ethnic equality, one must understand how ethnic stratification emerges in human societies in the first place. The two selections in this chapter mainly address the origins of ethnic stratification. Donald Noel proposes a theory that explains the origins of ethnic stratification by a combination of three conditions: ethnocentrism; competition of different ethnic groups for scarce resources; and unequal power among different ethnic groups. While Noel's theory is probably the most comprehensive among existing frameworks, it does not take class into account. In explaining the origins of the black slavery system—one of the best examples of ethnic stratification, Ronald Takaki vividly shows how class conflict between white planters and white indentured servants in the colony of Virginia played a pivotal role in the emergence of the black slavery system.

1.   A Theory of the Origin of Ethnic Stratification
     Donald Noel

2.   The "Giddy Multitude": The Hidden Origins of Slavery
     Ronald Takaki

A Theory of the Origin of Ethnic Stratification

Donald Noel

While a great deal has been written about the nature and consequences of ethnic stratification, there have been few theoretical or empirical contributions regarding the causes of ethnic stratification.[1] It is the purpose of this paper to state a theory of the origin of ethnic stratification and then test it by applying the theory to an analysis of the origin of slavery in the United States. A number of recent contributions have clarified our knowledge of early Negro-white stratification[2] but there has been no attempt to analyze slavery's origin from the standpoint of a general theoretical framework. The present attempt focuses upon ethnocentrism, competition, and differential power as the key variables which together constitute the necessary and sufficient basis for the emergence and initial stabilization of ethnic stratification.

Ethnic stratification is, of course, only one type of stratification. Social stratification as a generic form of social organization is a structure of social inequality manifested via differences in prestige, power, and/or economic rewards. Ethnic stratification is a system of stratification wherein some relatively fixed group membership (e.g., race, religion, or nationality) is utilized as a major criterion for assigning social positions with their attendant differential rewards.

Prior to the emergence of ethnic stratification there must be a period of recurrent or continuous contact between the members of two or more distinct ethnic groups. This contact is an obvious requisite of ethnic stratification, but it is equally a requisite of equalitarian intergroup relations. Hence, intergroup contact is assumed as given and not treated as a theoretical element because in itself it does not provide a basis for predicting whether ethnic relations will be equalitarian or inequalitarian (i.e., stratified). Distinct ethnic groups can interact without super-subordination.[3] Factors such as the nature of the groups prior to contact, the agents of contact, and the objectives of the contacting parties affect the likelihood of an equalitarian or inequalitarian outcome but only as they are expressed through the necessary and sufficient variables.[4]

The Theory and Its Elements

In contrast to intergroup contact per se, the presence of ethnocentrism, competition, and differential power provides a firm basis for predicting the emergence of ethnic stratification. Conversely, the absence of any one or more of these three elements means that ethnic stratification will not emerge. This is the essence of our theory. Each of the three elements is a variable but for present purposes they will be treated as attributes because our knowledge is not sufficiently precise to allow us to say what degrees of ethnocentrism, competition, and differential power are necessary to generate ethnic stratification. Recognition of the crucial importance of the three may stimulate greater efforts to precisely measure each of them. We shall examine each in turn.

Ethnocentrism is a universal characteristic of autonomous societies or ethnic groups. As introduced by Sumner, the concept refers to that "...view of things in which one's own group is the center of everything, and all others are scaled and rated with reference to it."[5] From this perspective the values of the in-group are equated with abstract, universal standards of morality and the practices of the in-group are exalted as better or more "natural" than those of any out-group. Such an orientation is essentially a matter of in-group glorification and not of hostility toward any specific out-group. Nevertheless, an inevitable consequence of ethnocentrism is the rejection or downgrading of all out-groups to a greater or lesser degree as a function of the extent to which they differ from the in-group. The greater the difference the lower will be the relative rank of any given out-group, but any difference at all is grounds for negative evaluation.[6] Hence, English and Canadian immigrants rank very high relative to other out-groups in American society, *but* they still rank below old American WASPs.[7]

Ethnocentrism is expressed in a variety of ways including mythology, condescension, and a double standard of morality in social relations. Becker has labeled this double standard a "dual ethic" in which in-group standards apply only to transactions with members of the in-group.[8] The outsider is viewed as fair game. Hence, intergroup economic relations are characterized by exploitation. Similarly, sexual relations between members of different groups are commonplace even when intermarriage is rare or prohibited entirely. The practice of endogamy is itself a manifestation of and, simultaneously, a means of reinforcing ethnocentrism. Endogamy is, indeed, an indication that ethnocentrism is present in sufficient degree for ethnic stratification to emerge.[9]

Insofar as district ethnic groups maintain their autonomy, mutual ethnocentrism will be preserved. Thus Indians in the Americas did not automatically surrender their ethnocentrism in the face of European technological and scientific superiority. Indeed, if the cultural strengths (including technology) of the out-group are not relevant to the values and goals of the in-group they will, by the very nature of ethnocentrism, be negatively defined. This is well illustrated in the reply (allegedly) addressed to the Virginia Commission in 1744 when it offered to educate six Indian youths at William and Mary:

> Several of our young people were formerly brought up at Colleges of the Northern
> Provinces; they were instructed in all your sciences; but when they came back to us,

they were bad runners, ignorant of every means of living in the woods, unable to
bear either cold or hunger, knew neither how to build a cabin, take a deer or kill an
enemy, spoke our language imperfectly, were therefore neither fit for hunters, war-
riors, or counsellors; they were totally good for nothing. We are, however, not the
less obliged by your kind offer, though we decline accepting it; and to show our
grateful Sense of it, if the Gentlemen of Virginia will send us a Dozen of their Sons
we will take great care of their education, instruct them in all we know, and make
Men of them.[10]

Ethnocentrism in itself need not lead to either interethnic conflict or ethnic stratification,
however. The Tungus and Cossacks have lived in peace as politically indepentdent but economically interdependent societies for several centuries. The groups remain racially and culturally dissimilar and each is characterized by a general ethnocentric preference for the
in-group. This conflict potential is neutralized by mutual respect and admission by each that
the other is superior in certain specific respects, by the existence of some shared values and
interests, and by the absence of competition due to economic complementarity and low population density.[11]
    The presence of competition, structured along ethnic lines, is an additional prerequisite
for the emergence of ethnic stratification. Antonovsky has suggested that a discriminatory
system of social relations requires both shared goals and scarcity of rewards,[12] and competition here refers to the interaction between two or more social units striving to achieve *the
same scarce goal* (e.g., land or prestige). In the absence of shared goals members of the various ethnic groups involved in the contact situation would have, in the extreme case, mutually exclusive or nonoverlapping value hierarchies. If one group is not striving for a given
goal, this reduces the likelihood of discrimination partly because members of the group are
unlikely to be perceived as competitors for the goal. In addition, the indifference of one
group toward the goal in effect reduces scarcity—i.e., fewer seekers enhance the probability
of goal attainment by any one seeker. However, if the goal is still defined as scarce by members of one group they may seek to establish ethnic stratification in order to effectively exploit the labor of the indifferent group and thereby maximize goal attainment. In such a
situation the labor (or other utility) of the indifferent group may be said to be the real object
of competition. In any event the perceived scarcity of a socially valued goal is crucial and
will stimulate the emergence of ethnic stratification unless each group perceives the other
as: (1) disinterested in the relevant goal, *and* (2) nonutilitarian with respect to its own attainment of the goal.
    In actuality the various goals of two groups involved in stable, complex interaction will
invariably overlap to some degree and hence the likelihood of ethnic stratification is a function of the arena of competition. The arena includes the shared object(s) sought, the terms of
the competition, and the relative adaptability of the groups involved.[13] Regarding the objects
(or goals) of competition, the greater the number of objects subject to competition, the more
intense the competition. Moreover, as Wagley and Harris observe, "It is important to know
the objects of competition, for it would seem that the more vital or valuable the resource

over which there is competition, the more intense is the conflict between the groups."[14] Barring total annihilation of one of the groups, these points can be extended to state that the more intense the competition or conflict the greater the likelihood—other things being equal—that it will culminate in a system of ethnic stratification. In other words, the number and significance of the scarce, common goals sought determine the degree of competition, which in turn significantly affects the probability that ethnic stratification will emerge.

The terms of the competition may greatly alter the probability of ethnic stratification, however, regardless of the intensity of the competition. The retention of a set of values or rules which effectively regulates—or moderates—ethnic interrelations is of particularly crucial significance. If a framework of regulative values fails to emerge, or breaks down, each group may seek to deny the other(s) the right to compete with the result that overt conflict emerges and culminates in annihilation, expulsion, or total subjugation of the less powerful group. If, in contrast, regulative values develop and are retained, competition even for vital goals need not result in ethnic stratification—or at least the span of stratification may be considerably constricted.[15]

Even where the groups involved are quite dissimilar culturally, the sharing of certain crucial values (e.g., religion or freedom, individualism, and equality) may be significant in preventing ethnic stratification. This appears to have been one factor in the enduring harmonious relations between the Cossacks and the Tungus. The influence of the regulative values upon the span of ethnic stratification is well illustrated by Tannenbaum's thesis regarding the differences between North American and Latin American slavery.[16] In the absence of a tradition of slavery the English had no established code prescribing the rights and duties of slaves and the racist ideology which evolved achieved its ultimate expression in the Dred Scott decision of 1857. This decision was highly consistent with the then widely held belief that the Negro "had no rights which the white man was bound to respect...." By contrast the Iberian code accorded certain rights to the Latin American slave (including the right to own property and to purchase his freedom), which greatly restricted the extent of inequality between free man and slave.[17]

In addition to the regulative values, the structural opportunities for or barriers to upward mobility which are present in the society may affect the emergence and span of ethnic stratification. Social structural barriers such as a static, nonexpanding economy are a significant part of the terms of competition and they may be more decisive than the regulative values as regards the duration of the system. Finally, along with the goals and the terms of competition, the relative adaptive capacity of the groups involved is an aspect of competition which significantly affects the emergence of ethnic stratification.

Wagley and Harris assume that ethnic stratification is given and focus their analysis on the adaptive capacity of *the minority group* in terms of its effect upon the span and the duration of ethnic stratification. Thus they view adaptive capacity as:

> those elements of a minority's cultural heritage which provide it with a basis for competing more or less effectively with the dominant group, which afford protection against exploitation, which stimulate or retard its adaptation to the total social

environment, and which facilitate or hinder its upward advance through the socio-economic hierarchy.[18]

We shall apply the concept to an earlier point in the intergroup process—i.e., prior to the emergence of ethnic stratification—by broadening it to refer to those aspects of any ethnic group's sociocultural heritage which affect its adjustment to a given social and physical environment. The group with the greater adaptive capacity is apt to emerge as the dominant group[19] while the other groups are subordinated to a greater or lesser degree—i.e., the span of the stratification system will be great or slight—dependent upon the extent of their adaptive capacity relative to that of the emergent dominant group.

The duration, as well as the origin and span, of ethnic stratification will be markedly influenced by adaptive capacity. Once a people have become a minority, flexibility on their part is essential if they are to efficiently adjust and effectively compete within the established system of ethnic stratification and thereby facilitate achievement of equality. Sociocultural patterns are invariably altered by changing life conditions. However, groups vary in the alacrity with which they respond to changing conditions. A flexible minority group may facilitate the achievement of equality or even dominance by readily accepting modifications of their heritage which will promote efficient adaptation to their subordination and to subsequent changes in life conditions.

Competition and ethnocentrism do not provide a sufficient explanation for the emergence of ethnic stratification. Highly ethnocentric groups involved in competition for vital objects will not generate ethnic stratification unless they are of such unequal power that one is able to impose its will upon the other.[20] Inequality of power is the defining characteristic of dominant and minority groups, and Lenski maintains that differential power is the foundation element in the genesis of any stratification system.[21] In any event differential power is absolutely essential to the emergence of ethnic stratification and the greater the differential the greater the span and durability of the system, other things being equal.

Technically, power is a component of adaptive capacity, as Wagley and Harris imply in their definition by referring to "protection against exploitation." Nevertheless, differential power exerts an effect independent of adaptive capacity in general and is of such crucial relevance for ethnic stratification as to warrant its being singled out as a third major causal variable. The necessity of treating it as a distinct variable is simply demonstrated by consideration of those historical cases where one group has the greater adaptive capacity in general but is subordinated because another group has greater (military) power. The Dravidians overrun by the Ayrans in ancient India and the Manchu conquest of China are illustrative cases.[22]

Unless the ethnic groups involved are unequal in power, intergroup relations will be characterized by conflict, symbiosis, or a pluralist equilibrium. Given intergroup competition, however, symbiosis is unlikely and conflict and pluralism are inevitably unstable. Any slight change in the existing balance of power may be sufficient to establish the temporary dominance of one group and this can be utilized to allow the emerging dominant group to perpetuate and enhance its position.[23]

Once dominance is established the group in power takes all necessary steps to restrict the now subordinated groups, thereby hampering their effectiveness as competitors,[24] and to institutionalize the emerging distribution of rewards and opportunities. Hence, since power tends to beget power, a slight initial alteration in the distribution of power can become the basis of a stable inequalitarian system.

We have now elaborated the central concepts and propositions of a theory of the emergence and initial stabilization of ethnic stratification. The theory can be summarized as follows. When distinct ethnic groups are brought into sustained contact (via migration, the emergence and expansion of the state, or internal differentiation of a previously homogeneous group), ethnic stratification will invariably follow if—and only if—the groups are characterized by a significant degree of ethnocentrism, competition, *and* differential power. Without ethnocentrism the groups would quickly merge and competition would not be structured along ethnic lines. Without competition there would be no motivation or rationale for instituting stratification along ethnic lines. Without differential power it would simply be impossible for one group to achieve dominance and impose subordination to its will and ideals upon the other(s).

The necessity of differential power is incontestable, but it could be argued that neither competition or ethnocentrism is dispensable. For example, perhaps extreme ethnocentrism independent of competition is sufficient motive for seeking to impose ethnic stratification. Certainly ethnocentrism could encourage efforts to promote continued sharp differentiation, but it would not by itself motivate stratification unless we assume the existence of a *need* for dominance or aggression. Conversely, given sociocultural differences, one group may be better prepared for and therefore able to more effectively exploit a given environment. Hence, this group would become economically dominant and might then perceive and pursue the advantages (especially economic) of ethnic stratification quite independent of ethnocentrism. On the other hand, while differential power and competition alone are clearly sufficient to generate stratification, a low degree of ethnocentrism could readily forestall *ethnic* stratification by permitting assimilation and thereby eliminating differential adaptive capacity. Ethnocentrism undeniably heightens awareness of ethnicity and thereby promotes the formation and retention of ethnic competition, but the crucial question is whether or not some specified degree of ethnocentrism is *essential* to the emergence of ethnic stratification. Since autonomous ethnic groups are invariably ethnocentric, the answer awaits more precise measures of ethnocentrism which will allow us to test hypotheses specifying the necessary degree of ethnocentrism.[25]

Given the present state of knowledge it seems advisable to retain both competition and ethnocentrism, as well as differential power, as integral elements of the theory. Our next objective, then, is to provide an initial test of the theory by applying it to an analysis of the genesis of slavery in the seventeenth century mainland North American colonies.

The Origin of American Slavery

There is a growing consensus among historians of slavery in the United States that Negroes were not initially slaves but that they were gradually reduced to a position of chattel slavery over several decades.[26] The historical record regarding their initial status is so vague and incomplete, however, that it is impossible to assert with finality that their status was initially no different from that of non-Negro indentured servants.[27] Moreover, while there is agreement that the statutory establishment of slavery was not widespread until the 1660s, there is disagreement regarding slavery's emergence in actual practice. The Handlins maintain that "The status of Negroes was that of servants; and so they were identified and treated down to the 1660s."[28] Degler and Jordan argue that this conclusion is not adequately documented and cite evidence indicating that some Negroes were slaves as early as 1640.[29]

Our central concern is to relate existing historical research to the theory elaborated above, *not* to attempt original historical research intended to resolve the controversy regarding the nature and extent of the initial status differences (if any) between white and Negro bondsmen. However, two findings emerging from the controversy are basic to our concern: (1) although the terms servant and slave were frequently used interchangeably, whites were never slaves in the sense of serving for life and conveying a like obligation to their offspring; and (2) many Negroes were not slaves in this sense at least as late as the 1660s. Concomitantly with the Negroes' descent to slavery, white servants gained increasingly liberal terms of indenture and, ultimately, freedom. The origin of slavery for the one group and the growth of freedom for the other are explicable in terms of our theory as a function of differences in ethnocentrism, the arena of competition, and power vis-à-vis the dominant group or class.[30]

Degler argues that the status of the Negro evolved in a framework of discrimination and therefore, "The important point is not the evolution of the legal status of the slave, but the fact that discriminatory legislation regarding the Negro long preceded any legal definition of slavery."[31] The first question then becomes one of explaining this differential treatment which foreshadowed the descent to slavery. A major element in the answer is implied by the Handlins' observation that "The rudeness of the Negroes' manners, the strangeness of their languages, the difficulty of communicating to them English notions of morality and proper behavior occasioned sporadic laws to regulate their conduct."[32] By itself this implies a contradiction of their basic thesis that Negro and white indentured servants were treated similarly prior to 1660. They maintain, however, that there was nothing unique nor decisive in this differential treatment of Negroes, for such was also accorded various Caucasian outgroups in this period.[33] While Jordan dismisses the Handlins' evidence as largely irrelevant to the point and Degler feels that it is insufficient, Degler acknowledges that "Even Irishmen, who were white, Christian, and European, were held to be literally 'beyond the Pale,' and some were even referred to as 'slaves'."[34] Nevertheless, Degler contends that the overall evidence justifies his conclusion that Negroes were generally accorded a lower position than any white, bound or free.

That the English made status distinctions between various out-groups is precisely what one would expect, however, given the nature of ethnocentrism. The degree of ethnocentric rejection is primarily a function of the degree of difference, and Negroes were markedly different from the dominant English in color, nationality, language, religion, and other aspects of culture.[35] The differential treatment of Negroes was by no means entirely due to a specifically anti-Negro *color* prejudice. Indeed color was not initially the most important factor in determining the relative status of Negroes; rather, the fact that they were non-Christian was of major significance.[36] Although beginning to lose its preeminence, religion was still the central institution of society in the seventeenth century and religious prejudice toward non-Christians or heathens was widespread. The priority of religious over color prejudice is amply demonstrated by analysis of the early laws and court decisions pertaining to Negro-white sexual relations. These sources explicitly reveal greater concern with Christian-non-Christian than with white-Negro unions.[37] During and after the 1660s laws regulating racial intermarriage arose but for some time their emphasis was generally, if not invariably, upon religion, nationality, or some basis of differentiation other than race per se. For example, a Maryland law of 1681 described marriages of white women with Negroes as lascivious and "to the disgrace not only of the English but also [sic] of many *other Christian* Nations,"[38] Moreover, the laws against Negro-white marriage seem to have been rooted much more in economic considerations than they were in any concern for white racial purity.[39] In short, it was not a simple color prejudice but a marked degree of ethnocentrism, rooted in a multitude of salient differences, which combined with competition and differential power to reduce Negroes to the status of slaves.[40]

Degler has noted that Negroes initially lacked a status in North America and thus almost any kind of status could have been worked out.[41] Given a different competitive arena, a more favorable status blurring the sharp ethnic distinctions could have evolved. However, as the demand for labor in an expanding economy began to exceed the supply, interest in lengthening the term of indenture arose.[42] This narrow economic explanation of the origin of slavery has been challenged on the grounds that slavery appeared equally early in the northern colonies although there were too few Negroes there to be of economic significance.[43] This seemingly decisive point is largely mitigated by two considerations.

First, in the other colonies it was precisely *the few* who did own slaves who were not only motivated by vested interests but were also the men of means and local power most able to secure a firm legal basis for slavery.[44] The distribution of power and motivation was undoubtedly similar and led to the same consequences in New England. For the individual retainer of Negro servants the factual and legal redefinition of Negroes as chattel constitutes a vital economic interest whether or not the number of slaves is sufficient to vitally affect the economy of the colony. Our knowledge of the role of the elite in the establishment of community mores suggests that this constitutes at least a partial explanation of the northern laws.[45] In addition, the markedly smaller number of Negroes in the North might account for the fact that "although enactments in the northern colonies recognized the legality of lifetime servitude, no effort was made to require all Negroes to be placed in that condition."[46] We surmise that the laws were passed at the behest of a few powerful individuals who had relatively many Negro servants and were indifferent to the status of Negroes in general so long as their own vested interests were protected.

The explanation for the more all-encompassing laws of the southern colonies is rooted in the greater homogeneity of interests of the southern elite. In contrast to the northern situation, the men of power in the southern colonies were predominantly planters who were unified in their need for large numbers of slaves. The margin of profit in agricultural production for the commercial market was such that the small landholder could not compete and the costs of training and the limitations on control (by the planter) which were associated with indentured labor made profitable exploitation of such labor increasingly difficult.[47] Hence, it was not the need for labor per se which was critical for the establishment of the comprehensive southern slave system but rather the requirements of the emerging economic system for a particular kind of labor. In short, the southern power elite uniformly needed slave labor while only certain men of power shared this need in the North, and hence the latter advocated slave laws but lacked the power (or did not feel the need) to secure the all-encompassing laws characteristic of the southern colonies.

There is a second major consideration in explaining the existence of northern slavery. Men do not compete only for economic ends. They also compete for prestige and many lesser objects, and there is ample basis for suggesting that prestige competition was a significant factor in the institutionalization of slavery, North and South. Degler calls attention to the prestige motive when he discusses the efforts to establish a feudal aristocracy in seventeenth-century New York, Maryland, and the Carolinas. He concludes that these efforts failed because the manor was "dependent upon the scarcity of land."[48] The failure of feudal aristocracy in no way denies the fundamental human desire for success or prestige. Indeed, this failure opened the society. It emphasized success and mobility for "it meant that wealth, rather than family or tradition, would be the primary determinant of social stratification."[49] Although the stress was on economic success, there were other gains associated with slavery to console those who did not achieve wealth. The desire for social prestige derivable from "membership in a superior caste" undoubtedly provided motivation and support for slavery among both northern and southern whites, slaveholders and nonslaveholders.[50]

The prestige advantage of slavery would have been partially undercut, especially for non-slaveholders, by enslavement of white bondsmen, but it is doubtful that this was a significant factor in their successfully eluding hereditary bondage. Rather the differential treatment of white and Negro bondsmen, ultimately indisputable and probably present from the very beginning, is largely attributable to differences in ethnocentrism and relative power. There was little or no ethnocentric rejection of the majority of white bondsmen during the seventeenth century because most of them were English.[51] Moreover, even the detested Irish and other non-English white servants were culturally and physically much more similar to the English planters than were the Africans. Hence, the planters clearly preferred white bondsmen until the advantages of slavery became increasingly apparent in the latter half of the seventeenth century.[52]

The increasing demand for labor after the mid-seventeenth century had divergent consequences for whites and blacks. The colonists became increasingly concerned to encourage immigration by counteracting "the widespread reports in England and Scotland that servants were harshly treated and bound in perpetual slavery" and by enacting "legislation designed to improve servants' conditions and to enlarge the prospect of a meaningful release, a release that was not the start of a new period of servitude, but of life as a free-man and landowner."[53] These improvements curtailed the exploitation of white servants without directly affecting the status of the Africans.

Farthest removed from the English, least desired, [the Negro] communicated with no friends who might be deterred from following. Since his coming was involuntary, nothing that happened to him would increase or decrease his numbers. To raise the status of Europeans by shortening their terms would ultimately increase the available hands by inducing their compatriots to emigrate; to reduce the Negro's term would produce an immediate loss and no ultimate gain. By mid-century the servitude of Negroes seems generally lengthier than that of whites; and thereafter, the consciousness dawns that the blacks will toil for the whole of their lives...[54]

The planters and emerging agrarian capitalism were unconstrained in a planter-dominated society with no traditional institutions to exert limits. In this context even the common law tradition helped promote slavery.[55]

Ethnocentrism set the Negroes apart but their almost total lack of power and effective spokesmen, in contrast to white indentured servants, was decisive in their enslavement. Harris speaks directly to the issue and underscores the significance of (organized) power for the emergence of slavery:

The facts of life in the New World were such...that Negroes, being the most defenseless of all the immigrant groups, were discriminated against and exploited more than any others....Judging from the very nasty treatment suffered by the white indentured servants, it was obviously not sentiment which prevented the Virginia planters from enslaving their fellow Englishmen. They undoubtedly would have done so had they been able to get away with it. but such a policy was out of the question as long as there was a King and a Parliament in England.[56]

The Negroes, in short, did not have any organized external government capable of influencing the situation in their favor.[57] Moreover, "there was no one in England or in the colonies to pressure for the curtailment of the Negro's servitude or to fight for his future."[58]

The Negroes' capacity to adapt to the situation and effectively protest in their own behalf was greatly hampered by their cultural diversity and lack of unification. They did not think of themselves as "a kind." They did not subjectively share a common identity and thus they lacked the group solidarity necessary to effectively "act as a unit in competition with other groups."[59] Consciousness of shared fate is essential to effective unified action but it generally develops only gradually as the members of a particular social category realize that they are being treated alike despite their differences. "People who find themselves set apart eventually come to recognize their common interests," but for those who share a subordinate position common identification usually emerges "only after repeated experiences of denial and humiliation."[60] The absence of a shared identification among seventeenth-century Negroes reflected the absence of a shared heritage from which to construct identity, draw strength, and organize protest. Hence, Negroes were easily enslaved and reduced to the status of chattel. This point merits elaboration.

We have defined adaptive capacity in terms of a group's sociocultural heritage as it affects adjustment to the environment. Efficient adaptation may require the members of a group to modify or discard a great deal of their heritage. A number of factors, including ethnocentrism and the centrality of the values and social structures requiring modification, affect willingness to alter an established way of life.[61] Even given a high degree of willingness, however, many groups simply have not possessed the cultural complexity or social structural similarity to the dominant group necessary to efficient adaptation. Many Brazilian and United States Indian tribes, for example, simply have not had the knowledge (e.g., of writing, money, markets, etc.) or the structural similarity to their conquerors (e.g., as regards the division of labor) necessary to protect themselves from exploitation and to achieve a viable status in an emerging multiethnic society.[62]

By comparison with most New World Indians the sociocultural heritage of the Africans was remarkably favorable to efficient adaptation.[63] However, the discriminatory framework within which white-Negro relations developed in the seventeenth century ultimately far outweighed the cultural advantages of the Negroes vis-à-vis the Indians in the race for status.[64] The Negroes from any given culture were widely dispersed and their capacity to adapt *as a group* was thereby shattered. Like the Negroes, the Indians were diverse culturally but they retained their cultural heritage and social solidarity, and they were more likely to resist slavery because of the much greater probability of reunion with their people following escape. Hence, Negroes were preferred over Indians as slaves both because their cultural background had better prepared them for the slave's role in the plantation system (thus enhancing the profits of the planters) and because they lacked the continuing cultural and group support which enabled the Indians to effectively resist slavery.[65] By the time the Africans acquired the dominant English culture and social patterns *and* a sense of shared fate, their inability to work out a more favorable adaptation was assured by the now established distribution of power and by the socialization processes facilitating acceptance of the role of slave.[66]

Conclusion

We conclude that ethnocentrism, competition, and differential power provide a comprehensive explanation of the origin of slavery in the seventeenth-century English colonies. The Negroes were clearly more different from the English colonists than any other group (*except* the Indians) by almost any criterion, physical or cultural, that might be selected as a basis of social differentiation. Hence, the Negroes were the object of a relatively intense ethnocentric rejection from the beginning. The opportunity for great mobility characteristic of a frontier society created an arena of competition which dovetailed with this ethnocentrism. Labor, utilized to achieve wealth, and prestige were the primary objects of this competition. These goals were particularly manifest in the southern colonies, but our analysis provides a rationale for the operation of the same goals as sources of motivation to institutionalize slavery in the northern colonies also.

The terms of the competition for the Negro's labor are implicit in the evolving pattern of differential treatment of white and Negro bondsmen prior to slavery and in the precarious position of free Negroes. As slavery became institutionalized the moral, religious, and legal values of the society were increasingly integrated to form a highly consistent complex which acknowledged no evil in the "peculiar institution."[67] Simultaneously, Negroes were denied any opportunity to escape their position of lifetime, inheritable servitude. Only by the grace of a generous master, not by any act of his own, could a slave achieve freedom and, moreover, there were "various legal structures aimed at impeding or discouraging the process of private manumission."[68] The rigidity of the "peculiar institution" was fixed before the Negroes acquired sufficient common culture, sense of shared fate, and identity to be able to effectively challenge the system. This lack of unity was a major determinant of the Africans' poor adaptive capacity as a group. They lacked the social solidarity and common cultural resources essential to organized resistance and thus in the absence of intervention by a powerful external ally they were highly vulnerable to exploitation.

The operation of three key factors is well summarized by Stampp:

> Neither the provisions of their charters nor the policy of the English government limited the power of colonial legislatures to control Negro labor as they saw fit....Their unprotected condition encouraged the trend toward special treatment, and their physical and cultural differences provided handy excuses to justify it....[T]he landholders' growing appreciation of the advantages of slavery over the older forms of servitude gave a powerful impetus to the growth of the new labor system.[69]

In short, the present theory stresses that *given* ethnocentrism, the Negroes' lack of power, and the dynamic arena of competition in which they were located, their ultimate enslavement was inevitable. The next task is to test the theory further, incorporating modifications as necessary, by analyzing subsequent accommodations in the pattern of race relations in the United States and by analyzing the emergence of various patterns of ethnic stratification in other places and eras.

Notes

1. The same observation regarding social stratification in general has recently been made by Gerhard Lenski, *Power and Privilege*, New York: McGraw-Hill, 1966, p. ix.

2. See Joseph Boskin, "Race Relations in Seventeenth Century America: The Problem of the Origins of Negro Slavery," *Sociology and Social Research*, 49 (July, 1965), pp. 446–455, including references cited therein; and David B. Davis, *The Problem of Slavery in Western Culture*, Ithaca: Cornell U., 1966.

3. A classic example is provided by Ethel John Lindgren, "An Example of Culture Contact Without Conflict: Reindeer Tungus and Cossacks of Northwest Manchuria," *American Anthropologist*, 40 (October–December, 1938), pp. 605–621.

4. The relevance of precontact and of the nature and objectives of the contacting agents for the course of intergroup relations has been discussed by various scholars, including Edward B. Reuter in his editor's "Introduction" to *Race and Culture Contacts*, New York: McGraw-Hill, 1934, pp. 1–18; and Clarence E. Glick, "Social Roles and Types in Race Relations" in Andrew W. Lind, editor, *Race Relations in World Perspective*, Honolulu: U. of Hawaii, 1955, pp. 239–262.

5. William G. Summer, *Folkways*, Boston: Ginn, 1940, p. 13. The essence of ethnocentrism is well conveyed by Catton's observation that "Ethnocentrism makes us see out-group behavior as deviation from in-group mores rather than as adherence to out-group mores." William R. Catton, Jr., "The Development of Sociological Thought" in Robert E.L. Faris, editor, *Handbook of Modern Sociology*, Chicago: Rand McNally, 1964, p. 930.

6. Williams observes that "in various *particular* ways an out-group may be seen as superior" insofar as its members excel in performance vis-à-vis certain norms that the two groups hold in common (e.g., sobriety or craftsmanship in the production of a particular commodity). Robin M. Williams, Jr., *Stranger Next Door*, Englewood Cliffs, N.J.: Prentice-Hall, 1964, p. 22 (emphasis added. A similar point is made by Marc J. Swartz, "Negative Ethnocentrism," *Journal of Conflict Resolution*, 5 (March, 1961), pp. 75–81. It is highly unlikely, however, that the out-group will be so consistently objectively superior in the realm of shared values as to be seen as generally superior to the in-group unless the in-group is subordinate to or highly dependent upon the out-group.

7. Emory S. Bogardus, *Social Distance*, Yellow Springs: Antioch, 1959.

8. Howard P. Becker, *Man in Reciprocity*, New York: Praeger, 1956, Ch. 15.

9.   Endogamy is an overly stringent index of the degree of ethnocentrism essential to eth-
     nic stratification and is not itself a prerequisite of the emergence of ethnic stratifica-
     tion. However, where endogamy does not precede ethnic stratification, it is a
     seemingly invariable consequence. Compare this position with that of Charles Wagley
     and Marvin Harris, who treat ethnocentrism and endogamy as independent structural
     requisites of intergroup hostility and conflict. See *Minorities in the New World*, New
     York: Columbia, 1958, pp. 256–263.

10. Quoted in T. Walker Wallbank and Alastair M. Taylor, *Civilization: Past and Present*,
     Chicago: Scott, Foresman, 1949, rev. ed., Vol. 1, pp. 559–560. The offer and counter-
     offer also provide an excellent illustration of mutual ethnocentrism.

11. Lindgren, *op. cit.*

12. Aaron Antonovsky, "The Social Meaning of Discrimination," *Phylon*, 21 (Spring,
     1960), pp. 81–95.

13. This analysis of the arena of competition is a modification of the analysis by Wagley
     and Harris, *op. cit.*, esp. pp. 263–264. These authors limit the concept "arena" to the
     objects sought *and* the regulative values which determine opportunity to compete and
     then partly confound their components by including the regulative values, along with
     adaptive capacity and the instruments necessary to compete, as part of the "terms" of
     competition.

14. *Ibid.*, p. 263. They suggest that competition for scarce subsistence goals will produce
     more intense conflict than competition for prestige symbols or other culturally defined
     goals.

15. Discussing the ideological aspect of intergroup relations, Wagley and Harris note that
     equalitarian creeds have generally not been effective in preventing ethnic stratifica-
     tion. *Ibid.*, pp. 280ff. The operation of ethnocentrism makes it very easy for the bound-
     aries of the in-group to become the boundaries of adherence to group values.

16. Frank Tannenbaum, *Slave and Citizen: The Negro in the Americas*, New York:
     Random House, 1963.

17. *Ibid.*, esp. pp. 49ff. Marvin Harris has criticized Tannenbaum's thesis, arguing that the
     rights prescribed by the Iberian code were largely illusory and that there is no certainty
     that *slaves* were treated better in Latin America. Harris in turn provides a functional
     (economic necessity) explanation for the historical difference in treatment of *free*
     Negroes in the two continents. See Marvin Harris, *Patterns of Race in the Americas*,
     New York: Walker, 1964, esp. Chs. 6 and 7.

18. Wagley and Harris, *op. cit.*, p. 264.

19. This point is explicitly made by Tamotsu Shibutani and Kian M. Kwan, Ethnic Stratification: A Comparative Approach, New York: Macmillan, 1965, p. 147; see also Ch. 9.

20. This point is made by Antonovsky, *op. cit.*, esp. p. 82, and implied by Wagley and Harris in their discussion of the role of the state in the formation of minority groups, *op. cit.*, esp. pp. 240–244. Stanley Lieberson's recent modification of Park's cycle theory of race relations also emphasizes the importance of differential power as a determinant of the outcome of intergroup contacts. See "A Societal Theory of Race and Ethnic Relations," *American Sociological Review*, 26 (December, 1961), pp. 902–910.

21. Lenski, *op. cit.*, esp. Ch. 3.

22. See Wallbank and Taylor, *op. cit.*, p. 95; and Shibutani and Kwan, *op. cit.*, pp. 129–130.

23. See *ibid.*, esp. Chs. 6, 9, and 12; and Richard A. Schermerhorn, *Society and Power*, New York: Random House, 1961, pp. 18–26.

24. Shibutani and Kwan observe that dominance rests upon victory in the competitive process and that competition between groups is eliminated or greatly reduced once a system of ethnic stratification is stabilized, *op. cit.*, pp. 146 and 235, and Ch. 12. The extent to which competition is actually stifled is highly variable, however, as Wagley and Harris note in their discussion of minority adaptive capacity and the terms of competition. *op. cit.*, pp. 263ff.

25. The issue is further complicated by the fact that the necessary degree of any one of the three elements may vary as a function of the other two.

26. The main relevant references in the recent literature include Carl N. Degler, *Out of Our Past*, New York: Harper and Row, 1959 and "Slavery and the Genesis of American Race Prejudice," *Comparative Studies in Society and History*, 2 (October, 1959), pp. 49–66; Stanley M. Elkins, *Slavery: A Problem in American Institutional and Intellectual Life*, Chicago: U. of Chicago, 1959; Oscar and Mary F. Handlin, "Origins of the Southern Labor System," *William and Mary Quarterly*, 3rd Series, 7 (April, 1950), pp. 199–222; and Winthrop D. Jordan, "Modern Tensions and the Origins of American Slavery," *The Journal of Southern History*, 28 (February, 1962), pp. 18–30, and *White over Black*, Chapel-Hill: U. of North Carolina, 1968. See also Boskin, *op. cit.*, and "Comment" and "Reply" by the Handlins and Degler in the cited volume of *Comparative Studies…*, pp. 488–495,

27. Jordan, *The Journal…*, p. 22.

28. Handlin and Handlin, *op. cit.*, p. 203.

29. Degler, *Comparative Studies...*, pp. 52–56 and Jordan, *The Journal...*, pp. 23–27 and *White over Black*, pp. 73–74. Also see Elkins, *op. cit.*, pp. 38–42 (esp. fns. 16 and 19).

30. Our primary concern is with the emergence of Negro slavery but the theory also explains how white bondsmen avoided slavery. Their position vis-à-vis the dominant English was characterized by a different "value" of at least two of the key variables.

31. Degler, *Out of Our Past*, p. 35. Bear in mind, however, that slavery was not initially institutionalized in law or in the mores.

32. Handlin and Handlin, *op. cit.*, pp. 208–209.

33. *Ibid.* They note that "It is not necessary to resort to racist assumptions to account for such measures;...[for immigrants in a strange environment] longed...for the company of familiar men and singled out to be welcomed those who were most like themselves." See pp. 207–211 and 214.

34. Jordan, *The Journal...*, esp. pp. 27 (fn. 29) and 29 (fn. 34); and Degler, *Out of Our Past*, p. 30.

35. Only the aboriginal Indians were different from the English colonists to a comparable degree and they were likewise severely dealt with via a policy of exclusion and annihilation after attempts at enslavement failed. See Boskin, *op. cit.*, p. 453; and Jordan, *White over Black*, pp. 85–92.

36. The priority of religious over racial prejudice and discrimination in the early seventeenth century is noted in *ibid.*, pp. 97–98 and by Edgar J. McManus, *A History of Negro Slavery in New York*, Syracuse: Syracuse U., 1966, esp. pp. 11–12.

37. Jordan, *The Journal...*, p. 28 and *White over Black*, pp. 78–80.

38. Quoted in *ibid.*, pp. 79–80 (emphasis added). Also see pp. 93–97, however, where Jordan stresses the necessity of carefully interpreting the label "Christian."

39. See Handlin and Handlin, *op. cit.*, pp. 213–216; and W.D. Zabel, "Interracial Marriage and the Law," *The Atlantic* (October, 1965), pp. 75–79.

40. The distinction between ethnocentrism (the rejection of out-groups *in general* as a function of in-group glorification) and prejudice (hostility toward the members of a *specific* group because they are members of that group) is crucial to the controversy regarding the direction of causality between discrimination, slavery, and prejudice. Undoubtedly these variables are mutually causal to some extent but Harris, *op. cit.*, esp. pp. 67–70, presents evidence that prejudice is primarily a consequence and is of minor importance as a cause of slavery.

Chapter 3

41. Degler, *Comparative Studies...*, p. 51. See also Boskin, *op. cit.*, pp. 449 and 454 (esp. fn. 14); Elkins, *op. cit.*, pp. 39–42 (esp. fn. 16); and Kenneth M. Stampp, *The Peculiar Institution*, New York: Knopf, 1956, p. 21. The original indeterminacy of the Negroes' status is reminiscent of Blumer's "sense of group position" theory of prejudice and, in light of Blumer's theory, is consistent with the belief that there was no widespread prejudice toward Negroes prior to the institutionalization of slavery. See Herbert Blumer, "Race Prejudice as a Sense of Group Position," *Pacific Sociological Review,* 1 (Spring, 1958), pp. 3–7.

42. Handlin and Handlin, *op. cit.*, p. 210. Differential power made this tactic as suitable to the situation of Negro bondsmen as it was unsuitable in regard to white bondsmen.

43. Degler acknowledges that the importance of perpetuating a labor force indispensable to the economy later became a crucial support of slavery but he denies that the need for labor explains the origin of slavery. His explanation stresses prior discrimination which, in the terms of the present theory, was rooted in ethnocentrism and differential power. See *Comparative Studies...*, including the "Reply" to the Handlins, "Comment"; and *Out of Our Past*, pp. 35–38 and 162–168.

44. Elkins, *op. cit.*, pp. 45 (esp. fn. 26) and 48.

45. Historical precedent is provided by the finding that "The vagrancy laws emerged in order to provide the powerful landowners with a ready supply of cheap labor." See William J. Chambliss, "A Sociological Analysis of the Law of Vagrancy," *Social Problems* 12 (Summer, 1964), pp. 67–77. Jordan, *White over Black*, pp. 67 and 69, provides evidence that the economic advantages of slavery were clearly perceived in the northern colonies.

46. Elkins, *op. cit.*, p. 41 (fn. 19).

47. By the 1680s, "The point had clearly passed when white servants could realistically, on any long-term appraisal, be considered preferable to Negro slaves." *Ibid.*, p. 48.

48. Degler, *Out of Our Past*, p. 3. Also see Hubert M. Blalock, Jr., *Toward a Theory of Minority Group Relations*, New York: Wiley, 1967, pp. 44–48.

49. Degler, *Out of Our Past*, p. 5; see also pp. 45–50. Elkins, *op. cit.*, esp. pp. 43–44, also notes the early emphasis on personal success and mobility.

50. Stampp, *op. cit.*, pp. 29–33, esp. 32–33. Also see J.D.B. DeBow, "The Interest in Slavery of the Southern Non-Slaveholder," reprinted in Eric L. McKitrick, editor, *Slavery Defended: The Views of the Old South*, Englewood Cliffs, N.J.: Prentice-Hall, 1963, pp. 169–177.

51. Stampp, *op. cit.*, p. 16; and Degler, *Out of Our Past*, pp. 50–51. Consistent with the nature of ethnocentrism, "The Irish and other aliens, less desirable, at first received longer terms. But the realization that such discrimination retarded 'the people of the country' led to an extension of the identical privilege to all Christians." Handlin and Handlin, *op. cit.*, pp. 210–211.

52. Elkins, *op. cit.*, pp. 40 and 48; and Handlin and Handlin, *op. cit.*, pp. 207–208.

53. *Ibid.*, p. 210.

54. *Ibid.*, p. 211 (emphasis added). That the need for labor led to improvements in the status of white servants seems very likely but Degler in *Comparative Studies…*effectively challenges some of the variety of evidence presented by the Handlins, *op. cit.*, pp. 210 and 213–214 and "Comment."

55. Elkins, *op. cit.*, pp. 38 (fn. 14), 42 (fn. 22), 43, and 49–52; and Jordan, *White over Black*, pp. 49–51.

56. Harris, *op. cit.*, pp. 69–70.

57. The effectiveness of intervention by an external government is illustrated by the halting of Indian emigration to South Africa in the 1860s as a means of protesting "the indignities to which indentured 'coolies' were subjected in Natal,…" See Pierre L. van den Berghe, *South Africa, A Study in Conflict*, Middletown: Wesleyan U., 1965, p. 250.

58. Boskin, *op. cit.*, p. 448. Also see Stampp. *op. cit.*, p. 22; and Elkins, *op. cit.*, pp. 49–52.

59. Shibutani and Kwan, *op. cit.*, p. 42. See also William O. Brown, "Race Consciousness among South African Natives," *American Journal of Sociology*, 40 (March, 1935), pp. 569–581.

60. Shibutani and Kwan, *op. cit.*, Ch. 8, esp. pp. 202 and 212.

61. See the discussion in Brewton Berry, *Race and Ethnic Relations*, Boston: Houghton-Mifflin, 1965, 3rd ed. esp. pp. 147–149; Shibutani and Kwan, op. cit., esp. pp. 217f.; and Wagley and Harris, op. cit., pp. 40–44.

62. *Ibid.*, pp. 15–86 and 265–268.

63. *Ibid.*, p. 269; Harris, *op. cit.*, p. 14; and Stampp, *op. cit.*, pp. 13 and 23.

64. The Indians were also discriminated against but to a much lesser extent. The reasons for this differential are discussed by Jordan, *White over Black*, pp. 89–90; and Stampp, *op. cit.*, pp. 23–24.

65. Harris, *op. cit.*, pp. 14–16, an otherwise excellent summary of the factors favoring the
     enslavement of Negroes rather than Indians, overlooks the role of sociocultural sup-
     port. The importance of this support is clearly illustrated by the South African policy
     of importing Asians in preference to the native Africans who strenuously resisted en-
     slavement and forced labor. Shibutani and Kwan, *op. cit.*, p. 126. Sociocultural unity
     was also a significant factor in the greater threat of revolt posed by the Helots in
     Sparta as compared to the heterogeneous slaves in Athens. Alvin W. Gouldner, *Enter
     Plato*, New York: Basic Books, 1965, p. 32.

66. Shibutani and Kwan, *op. cit.*, esp. Chs. 10–12. Stampp observes that the plantation
     trained Negroes to be slaves, not free men, *op. cit.*, p. 12. Similarly, Wagley and Harris
     note that the Negroes were poorly prepared for survival in a free-market economic
     system even when they were emancipated, *op. cit.*, p. 269.

67. Davis asserts that while slavery has always been a source of tension, "in Western cul-
     ture it was associated with certain religious and philosophical doctrines that gave it the
     highest sanction." *Op. cit.*, p. ix.

68. Wagley and Harris, *op. cit.*, p. 124.

69. Stampp, *op. cit.*, p. 22.

The "Giddy Multitude":
The Hidden Origins of Slavery

Ronald Takaki

That "something" occurred within white society in Virginia. To understand race relations by focusing on race sometimes obscures; indeed, the "hidden" origins of slavery
were rooted in class. Here again, *The Tempest* might be illuminating. The theatergoers
were given a scenario that was uncanny in its anticipation of what would happen in
Virginia. What they say on the stage was an interracial class revolt to overthrow Prospero.
When the jester Trinculo and the butler Stephano first encountered Caliban, they found
him repulsive—a fishlike monster and a devil. They gave him wine, and the inebriated
Caliban offered to show Trinculo every "fertile inch o' of the island" and worship him as a
god. Defying Prospero, Caliban chanted:

> 'Ban, 'Ban, Ca-Caliban
> Has a new master. Get a new man.

A fierce desire drove the subversive stance: "Freedom, highday! highday, freedom! freedom, highday, freedom!" Complaining about how Prospero had colonized his island,
Caliban concocted a plot for rebellion. If Stephano would kill Prospero ("knock a nail into
his head"), Caliban declared, the butler would become the lord of the island and husband of
Miranda. Caliban promised Stephano: "She will become thy bed." Stirred by these promis-
es, the butler exclaimed: "Lead, monster; we'll follow." Warned in advance about the "foul
conspiracy of the beast Caliban and his confederates," Prospero unleashed his hunting dogs
against the rebels: "Fury, Fury! There, Tyrant, there! Go, charge my goblins that they grind
their joints...." A victim, Caliban was also an actor, a participant in the making of events.
What attracted Stephano and Trinculo to his revolutionary leadership was their shared "oth-
erness" rooted in class.[1]

Like Prospero, the English settlers had brought to America not only racial prejudice but
also a hierarchical class structure. While a few were from the aristocracy and many were
from what could be called the middle class, most English colonists migrated to Virginia as
indentured servants. They planned to complete their period of indenture and become

landowners. According to Governor William Berkeley, white servants came with a "hope of bettering their condition in a Growing Country." They thought the American expanse offered the possibility of starting over, creating new selves and new lives. Land in Virginia, taken from the Indians, was available and cheap, and each freeman could claim title to fifty acres. Perhaps they could even become wealthy, for a new cash crop, tobacco, offered farmers the opportunity to enter the market. Like the butler Stephano and the jester Trinculo, they wanted to become "lords" of land in America.[2]

The very abundance of land and the profitability of tobacco production, however, unleashed a land boom and speculation. Colonists with financial advantage quickly scrambled to possess the best lands along the navigable rivers. Representing a landed elite, they dominated the Virginia Assembly and began to enact legislation to advance and protect their class interests. They passed laws that extended the time of indentured servitude for whites and increased the length of service for white runaways. In this way, they minimized competition for lands and at the same time maximized the supply of white laborers by keeping them in servitude for as long as possible.[3]

Consequently, white freemen increasingly found it difficult to become landowners. In 1663, the House of Burgesses turned down a proposal to levy taxes on land instead of polls. Such a basis for taxation, it was argued, would limit the suffrage to landholders, and such a restriction would be resented by "the other freemen" who were "the more in number." The majority of freemen, the burgesses were acknowledging, did not own land. Thirteen years later, two members of the Virginia council, Thomas Ludwell and Robert Smith, estimated that at least one-fourth of the population consisted of "merchants and single freemen and such others as have no land." A growing group of tenant farmers existed.[4]

Hopes of landownership became dreams deferred for many English colonists. Frustrated and angry, many white workers felt they had been duped into coming to America. In 1649, pamphleteer William Bullock warned planters about the men and women who, "not finding what was promised," had become "dejected" and recalcitrant workers. In England, they had been viewed as the "Surcharge of necessitous people, the matter or fuel of dangerous insurrections." In Virginia, they became an even greater threat to social order, forming what the planter elite fearfully called a "giddy multitude"—a discontented class of indentured servants, slaves, and landless freemen, both white and black, the Stephanos and Trinculos as well as the Calibans of Virginia. They constituted a volatile element. In the early 1660s, for example, indentured servant Isaac Friend led a conspiracy to band together forty servants and "get Arms." He issued the rebellious cry: "who would be for Liberty, and free from bondage." Others would join the revolt, Friend promised, and together they would "go through the Country and kill those that made any opposition," and would "either be free or die for it." The authorities were informed about Friend's plan and quickly suppressed the plot. Again, in 1663, a Gloucester court accused nine "Laborers" of conspiring to overthrow the Virginia government and sentenced several of them to be executed. This incident gave planters a frightening example of "the horror" in Virginia—the presence of "villains" engaged in a "barbarous design" to subvert "rights and privileges" in the colony.[5]

But unruliness and discontent continued to grow. Fearing this landless class, the Virginia legislature restricted the suffrage to landowners in 1670. Governor William Berkeley was worried about the explosive class conditions in his colony where "six parts of seven" of the people were "Poor Indebted Discontented and Armed." The ownership of guns was widespread among whites, for every white man had a right to bear arms and was required by law to have a gun in order to help defend the colony. The landed elite distrusted this armed lower class of whites so much that they were even afraid to organize them for military service. On one occasion, in 1673, Governor Berkeley raised troops to defend Virginia against Dutch warships, but he did so very reluctantly. Of the men he enlisted in his army, Berkeley apprehensively noted, at least one-third were freemen or debtors. They could not be trusted, he cautioned, for in battle, they might revolt and join the enemy "in hopes of bettering their Condition by Sharing the Plunder of the Country with them."[6]

Three years later, the very revolt Berkeley feared took place. One of the landholders in the upcountry was Nathaniel Bacon, a friend of Berkeley's and a member of the Virginia council. Seeking to protect settlers against the Indians, he helped raise a militia. Bacon recognized the danger of organizing armed men who came from the ranks of the "giddy multitude." But Bacon calculated that an expedition against the Indians would serve a dual purpose—eliminate a foe and redirect the white lower class's anger away from the white elite to the Indians. The unruly and armed poor would focus on the external red enemy, rather than on the legislature's high taxes and the governor's failure to provide for defense against the Indians. "Since my being with the volunteers," he wrote to Berkeley, "the Exclaiming concerning forts and Leavys has been suppressed and the discourse and earnestness of the people is against the Indians...."[7]

Bacon's actions shocked Berkeley and his council, who were more worried about armed white freemen than hostile Indians. In their view, Bacon's followers were a "Rabble Crew, only the Rascallity and meanest of the people...there being hardly two amongst them that we have heard of who have Estates or are persons of Reputation and indeed very few who can either write or read." Ignoring their concerns, Bacon led a march against the Indians, killing Susquehannahs as well as friendly Occaneechees. He justified his expedition as a "Glorious" defense of the country. But the governor angrily declared Bacon a rebel and charged him with treason, an act punishable by death. Bacon retaliated by marching five hundred armed men to Jamestown.[8]

Blacks joined Bacon's army: they realized that they had a greater stake in the rebellion than their white brothers in arms, for many of them were bound servants for life. White and black, Bacon's soldiers formed what contemporaries described as "an incredible Number of the meanest People," "every where Armed." They were the "tag, rag, and bobtayle," the "Rabble" against "the better sort of people." A colonial official reported that Bacon had raised hundreds of soldiers "whose fortunes & Inclinations" were "desperate," and that almost all of them were either "Idle" and would not work, or in debt because of "Debaucherie or Ill Husbandry." Bacon had unleashed a radical class boundlessness that threatened the very foundations of order in Virginia.[9]

The rebels forced Berkeley to escape by ship and burned Jamestown to the ground. Shortly afterward, Bacon died, probably from dysentery; Berkeley then returned with armed ships. Like Prospero with his hunting dogs, the governor violently suppressed the rebellion. At one of the rebel fortifications, Captain Thomas Grantham encountered some four hundred "English and Negroes in Armes." Lying to them, Grantham said they had been "pardoned and freed from their Slavery." Most of them accepted his offer, but eighty black and twenty white rebels refused to surrender. Promised safe passage across the York River, the holdouts were captured when Grantham threatened to blow them out of the water. All of the captured "Negroes & Servants," Grantham reported, were returned "to their Masters."[10]

By force and deceit, the rebels of the "giddy multitude" had been defeated, but they had fought in what historian Edmund Morgan called "the largest rebellion known in any American colony before the [American] Revolution." Bacon's Rebellion had exposed the volatility of class tensions within white society in Virginia. During the conflict, the specter of class revolution had become a reality, and the scare shook the elite landholders: they were no longer confident they could control the "giddy multitude." Five years after the rebellion, planters continued to harbor fears of class disorder and urged the king to keep royal soldiers in Virginia to "prevent or suppress any Insurrection that may otherwise happen during the necessitous unsettled condition of the Colony." Large landowners could see that the social order would always be in danger so long as they had to depend on white labor. They had come to a crossing. They could open economic opportunities to white workers and extend political privileges to them. But this would erode their own economic advantage and potentially undermine their political hegemony. Or they could try to reorganize society on the basis of class *and* race. By importing and buying more slaves, they would decrease the proportion of white indentured servants. They would then be able to exploit a group of workers who had been enslaved and denied the right to bear arms because of their race. To increase the black population would mean to create a biracial society. However, such a development could help the planters control an armed white labor force and possibly solve the class problem within white society.[11]

While such a scenario of the "hidden" origins of slavery might not have been a deliberate strategy, what was so striking about the transition from white to black labor was its timing. The planter elite were becoming increasingly concerned about the growing discontent and rebelliousness among white servants during the 1660s—the very moment when the legislature made slavery *de jure*. During this time, the black population began to increase, an indication that planters had started shifting to this source of labor. But it was still not clear whether Africans would become the major work force and slavery would become the primary system of labor. After Bacon's Rebellion, however, the turn to slavery became sharp and significant. Even though the supply of white indentured servants seemed to have declined at this time, planters did not try to expand their recruitment efforts. Instead, they did something they had resisted until then—prefer black slaves over white indentured servants. In a letter to Ralph Wormely in 1681, William Fitzhugh noted that there were "some Negro Ships expected into York now every day." "If you intend to buy any for yours self, and it be not too much trouble," Fitzhugh added, "...secure me five or six." The growing dependency on slave laborers rather than white indentured servants can be measured decade by decade from the tax lists of Surry County. Slaves constituted 20 percent of households in 1674, 33 percent in 1686, and 48 percent in 1694. In other words, by the end of the century, nearly half the work force in Surry County was black and enslaved.[12]

Moreover, what the landed gentry systematically developed after the rebellion was a racially subordinated labor force. After 1680, they enacted laws that denied slaves freedom of assembly and movement. The "frequent meeting of considerable number of negroe slaves under pretense of feasts and burials" was "judged of dangerous consequence." Masters and overseers were prohibited from allowing "any Negro or Slave not properly belonging to him or them, to Remain or be upon his or their Plantation above the space of four hours." Militia patrollers were authorized to visit "negro quarters and other places suspected of entertaining unlawful assemblies," and to "take up" those assembling "or any other, strolling about from one plantation to another, without a pass from his or her master, mistress, or overseer." The gentry also disarmed blacks: in an act entitled "Preventing Negroes Insurrections," the legislature ordered that "it shall not be lawful for any negro or other slave to carry or arm himself with any club, staff, gun, sword, or any other weapon." The planter class saw that black slaves could be more effectively controlled by state power than white servants, for they could be denied certain rights based on the color of their skin.[13]

Although the number of white indentured servants entering Virginia declined sharply after 1700, the white lower class did not disappear. In 1720, in Christ Church, Virginia, out of 146 householders, only 86 were landowners. The landed elite continued to view the white lower class as a bothersome problem. The planters offered a carrot: in 1705, the assembly provided that upon completion of their term, white servants would not only be entitled to fifty acres of land but would also be given ten bushels of Indian corn, thirty shillings, and a musket. The planters also wielded a stick: they petitioned the legislature in 1699 to pass a law punishing "Vagrant Vagabond and Idle Persons and to assess the Wages of Common Labourers." In 1723, the assembly enacted a poor law that empowered county courts to punish "vagrants" by giving them thirty-nine lashes or by binding them out as servants. The law complained that "diverse Idle and disorderly persons," who had "no visible Estates or Employments," frequently "strolled from One County to another" and would not labor or pay their taxes.[14]

By then, landless white Stephanos and Trinculos were less likely to join with enslaved black Calibans on a class basis. The cultural gap between white and black workers had widened in the late seventeenth century. Where the early black arrivals had been "seasoned" in the Barbados and were often able to speak some English, new blacks were transported directly from Africa. These Africans must have seemed especially strange to whites, even to those who occupied a common exploited class position.[15]

This cultural chasm between the whites and blacks of the "giddy multitude" was transformed into a political separation as the landed gentry instituted new borders between white and black laborers. Four years after Bacon's Rebellion, the Virginia Assembly repealed all penalties imposed on white servants for plundering during the revolt, but did not extend this pardon to black freemen and black indentured servants. Moreover, the gentry reinforced the separate labor status for each group: blacks were forced to occupy a racially subordinate and stigmatized status, one below all whites regardless of their class. Black was made to signify slave. In 1691, the assembly prohibited the manumission of slaves unless the master paid for transporting them out of the colony. New laws sharpened the lines of a caste system: who was "black" was given expanded definition. Earlier, in 1662, the legislature had declared that children born in Virginia should be slave or free according to the condition of the mother. In 1691, the Virginia Assembly passed a law that prohibited the "abominable mixture and spurious issue" of interracial unions and that provided for the banishment of white violators. The assembly took special aim at white women: the law specified that a free white mother of a racially mixed illegitimate child would be fined fifteen pounds and that that child would be required to be in servitude for thirty years. The effect of these laws was not only to make mulattoes slaves but also to stigmatize them as black. Moreover, the legislature also denied free blacks the right to vote, hold office, and testify in court.[16]

Meanwhile, the Virginia elite deliberately pitted white laborers and black slaves against each other. The legislature permitted whites to abuse blacks physically with impunity: in 1680, it prescribed thirty lashes on the bare back "if any negro or other slave shall presume to lift up his hand in opposition against any christian." Planters used landless whites to help put down slave revolts. In the early eighteenth century, Hugh Jones reported that each county had "a great number of disciplined and armed militia, ready in case of any sudden eruption of Indians or insurrection of Negroes." In 1705, Virginia legislated that "all horses, cattle, and hogs, now belonging, or that hereafter shall belong to any slave, or of any slaves mark...shall be seized and sold by the churchwardens of the parish...and the profit thereof applied to the use of the poor." "Here was a policy to transfer farm animals and food from slaves to poor whites. Later, during the American Revolution, the Virginia Assembly went even farther: to recruit white men for the struggle for liberty, the legislature rewarded each soldier with a bounty of three hundred acres of land and a slave— "a healthy, sound Negro between ten and thirty years of age."[17]

Notes

1. Shakespeare, *Tempest*, Act II, sc. ii, 180–190; Act II, sc. ii, 60–70; Act III, sc. ii, 110–140; Act IV, sc. i, 250–260.

2. Breen, "Changing Labor Force," p. 4.

3. Morgan, *American Slavery—American Freedom*, pp. 215–220.

4. Morgan, *American Slavery—American Freedom*, p. 221.

5. Breen, "Changing Labor Force," pp. 3, 8, 9; Breen and Innes, *"Myne Owne Grounde,"* p. 60; Smith, *Colonists in Bondage*, p. 138.

6. Breen, "Changing Labor Force," pp. 3–4; Morgan, *American Slavery—American Freedom*, pp. 241–242.

7. Morgan, *American Slavery—American Freedom*, p. 257. The House of Burgesses used the term "giddy multitude" to describe the followers of Nathaniel Bacon. H. R. McIlwaine (ed.), *Journals of the House of Burgesses of Virginia, 1659/60–1693* (Richmond, 1914). See Breen, "Changing Labor Force," p. 18.

8. Morgan, *American Slavery—American Freedom*, pp. 258, 260.

9. Breen, "Changing Labor Force," p. 10.

10. Breen, "Changing Labor Force," p. 11.

11. Morgan, *American Slavery—American Freedom, p. 308; Breen, "Changing Labor Force," p. 12. Morgan is reluctant to press his analysis as far as I do. "The substitution of slaves for servants gradually eased and eventually ended the threat that the freedmen posed,"* he wrote. *"As the annual number of imported servants dropped, so did the number of men turning free.....*Planters who bought slaves instead of servants did not do so with any apparent consciousness of the social stability to be gained thereby." Perhaps not, but perhaps they did, though not apparently. See Theodore Allen, "'...They Would Have Destroyed Me': Slavery and the Origins of Racism," *Radical America*, vol. 9, no. 3 (May–June 1975), pp. 41–63, which I read after completing my analysis of Bacon's Rebellion, for an argument that the planters acted deliberately and consciously.

12. Darrett B. and Anita H. Rutman, *A Place in Time: Middlesex County, Virginia, 1650–1750* (New York, 1984), p. 165; Morgan, *American Slavery—American Freedom*, p. 306.

13. Hening, *Statutes*, vol. 2, pp. 481, 493.

14. Morgan, *American Slavery—American Freedom*, pp. 222, 339; Hening, *Statutes*, vol. 3, p. 451.

15. Breen and Innes, *"Mine Owne Grounde,"* p. 108.

16. Allen, "'They Would Have Destroyed Me,'" p. 55; Hening, *Statutes*, vol. 3, pp. 86–87; Morgan, *American Slavery—American Freedom*, pp. 333, 335–337.

17. Hening, *Statutes*, vol. 2, p. 481; vol. 3, pp. 459–460; vol. 10, p. 331; Breen, "Changing Labor Force," p. 17; Benjamin Quarles, *The Negro in the American Revolution* (Chapel Hill, N.C., 1961), p. 108.

CHAPTER 4

Ethnic Adaptation

The core of the readings in this chapter is the process and outcome of interaction or adaptation among different ethnic groups in America. Milton Gordon summarizes three approaches to this issue: (1) the Anglo-conformity perspective, also called assimilation theory; (2) the melting-pot perspective; and (3) the cultural pluralism perspective. The ethnogenesis perspective proposed by Andrew Greeley is an attempt to integrate the useful elements of the foregoing three theories by highlighting partial assimilation, partial retention of ethnic culture, and especially the modification and creation of ethnic cultural elements in response to the host environment. In his selection, Robert Blauner emphasizes the internal colonization of minority groups by the dominant group as the most salient process and outcome of ethnic interaction for ethnic minorities.

To be sure, interracial marriage is one of the salient adaptation processes in America. It has gained momentum in recent decades as shown in Jack White's article in Chapter 2. Some even view it as a biological solution to the problem of racial injustice. While interracial marriage is still unfavored and often prejudiced, Terry Hong's personal narrative sheds some positive light on it by showing the changing attitudes of her grandmother toward her interracial union.

1. Assimilation in America: Theory and Reality
    Milton Gordon

2. An Alternative Perspective for Studying American Ethnicity
    Andrew Greeley

3. Colonized and Immigrant Minorities
    Robert Blauner

4. The Prodigal Daughter
    Terry Hong

Article 4.1

Assimilation in America
Theory and Reality

Milton M. Gordon

Three ideologies or conceptual models have competed for attention on the American scene as explanations of the way in which a nation, in the beginning largely white, Anglo-Saxon, and Protestant, has absorbed over 41 million immigrants and their descendants from variegated sources and welded them into the contemporary American people. These ideologies are Anglo-conformity, the melting pot, and cultural pluralism. They have served at various times, and often simultaneously, as explanations of what has happened—descriptive models—and of what should happen—goal models. Not infrequently they have been used in such a fashion that it is difficult to tell which of these two usages the writer has had in mind. In fact, one of the more remarkable omissions in the history of American intellectual thought is the relative lack of close analytical attention given to the theory of immigrant adjustment in the United States by its social scientists.

The result has been that this field of discussion—an overridingly important one since it has significant implications for the more familiar problems of prejudice, discrimination, and majority-minority group relations generally—has been largely preempted by laymen, representatives of belles lettres, philosophers, and apologists of various persuasions. Even from these sources the amount of attention devoted to ideologies of assimilation is hardly extensive. Consequently, the work of improving intergroup relations in America is carried out by dedicated professional agencies and individuals who deal as best they can with day-to-day problems of discriminatory behavior, but who for the most part are unable to relate their efforts to an adequate conceptual apparatus. Such an apparatus would, at one and the same time, accurately describe the present structure of American society with respect to its ethnic groups (I shall use the term "ethnic group" to refer to any racial, religious, or national-origins collectivity), and allow for a considered formulation of its assimilation or integration goals for the foreseeable future. One is reminded of Alice's distraught question in her travels in Wonderland. "Would you tell me, please, which way I ought to go from here?" "That depends a good deal," replied the Cat with irrefutable logic, "on where you want to get to."

The story of America's immigration can be quickly told for our present purposes. The white American population at the time of the Revolution was largely English and Protestant

Reprinted by permission from *Daedalus*, Journal of the American Academy of Arts and Sciences, Boston, Massachusetts, Volume 90, Number 2 (Spring 1961), pp. 263–285.

in origin, but had already absorbed substantial groups of Germans and Scotch-Irish and smaller contingents of Frenchmen, Dutchmen, Swedes, Swiss, South Irish, Poles, and a handful of migrants from other European nations. Catholics were represented in modest numbers, particularly in the middle colonies, and a small number of Jews were residents of the incipient nation. With the exception of the Quakers and a few missionaries, the colonists had generally treated the Indians and their cultures with contempt and hostility, driving them from the coastal plains and making the western frontier a bloody battleground where eternal vigilance was the price of survival.

Although the Negro at the time made up nearly one-fifth of the total population, his predominantly slave status, together with racial and cultural prejudice, barred him from serious consideration as an assimilable element of the society. And while many groups of European origin started out as determined ethnic enclaves, eventually, most historians believe, considerable ethnic intermixture within the white population took place. "People of different blood" [sic]—write two American historians about the colonial period, "English, Irish, German, Huguenot, Dutch, Swedish—mingled and intermarried with little thought of any difference."[1] In such a society, its people predominantly English, its white immigrants of other ethnic origins either English-speaking or derived largely from countries of northern and western Europe whose cultural divergences from the English were not great, and its dominant white population excluding by fiat the claims and considerations of welfare of the non-Caucasian minorities, the problem of assimilation understandably did not loom unduly large or complex.

The unfolding events of the next century and a half with increasing momentum dispelled the complacency which rested upon the relative simplicity of colonial and immediate post-Revolutionary conditions. The large-scale immigration to America of the famine-fleeing Irish, the Germans, and later the Scandinavians (along with additional Englishmen and other peoples of northern and western Europe) in the middle of the nineteenth century (the so-called "old immigration"), the emancipation of the Negro slaves and the problems created by post-Civil War reconstruction, the placing of the conquered Indian with his broken culture on government reservations, the arrival of the Oriental, first attracted by the discovery of gold and other opportunities in the West, and finally, beginning in the last quarter of the nineteenth century and continuing to the early 1920s, the swelling to proportions hitherto unimagined of the tide of immigration from the peasantries and "pales" of southern and eastern Europe—the Italians, Jews, and Slavs of the so-called "new immigration," fleeing the persecutions and industrial dislocations of the day—all these events constitute the background against which we may consider the rise of the theories of assimilation mentioned above. After a necessarily foreshortened description of each of these theories and their historical emergence, we shall suggest analytical distinctions designed to aid in clarifying the nature of the assimilation process, and then conclude by focusing on the American scene.

Anglo-Conformity

"Anglo-conformity"[2] is a broad term used to cover a variety of viewpoints about assimilation and immigration; they all assume the desirability of maintaining English institutions (as modified by the American Revolution), the English language, and English-oriented cultural patterns as dominant and standard in American life. However, bound up with this assumption are related attitudes. These may range from discredited notions about race and "Nordic" and "Aryan" racial superiority, together with the nativist political programs and exclusionist immigration policies which such notions entail, through an intermediate position of favoring immigration from northern and western Europe on amorphous, unreflective grounds ("They are more like us"), to a lack of opposition to any source of immigration, as long as these immigrants and their descendants duly adopt the standard Anglo-Saxon cultural patterns. There is by no means any necessary equation between Anglo-conformity and racist attitudes.

It is quite likely that "Anglo-conformity" in its more moderate aspects, however explicit its formulation, has been the most prevalent ideology of assimilation goals in America throughout the nation's history. As far back as colonial times, Benjamin Franklin recorded concern about the clannishness of the Germans in Pennsylvania, their slowness in learning English, and the establishment of their own native-language press.[3] Others of the founding fathers had similar reservations about large-scale immigration from Europe. In the context of their times they were unable to foresee the role such immigration was to play in creating the later greatness of the nation. They were not all men of unthinking prejudices. The disestablishment of religion and the separation of church and state (so that no religious group— whether New England Congregationalists, Virginian Anglicans, or even all Protestants combined—could call upon the federal government for special favors or support, and so that man's religious conscience should be free) were cardinal points of the new national policy they fostered. "The Government of the United States," George Washington had written to the Jewish congregation of Newport during his first term as president, "gives to bigotry no sanction, to persecution no assistance."

Political differences with ancestral England had just been written in blood; but there is no reason to suppose that these men looked upon their fledgling country as an impartial melting pot for the merging of the various cultures of Europe, or as a new "nation of nations," or as anything but a society in which, with important political modifications, Anglo-Saxon speech and institutional forms would be standard. Indeed, their newly won victory for democracy and republicanism made them especially anxious that these still precarious fruits of revolution should not be threatened by a large influx of European peoples whose life experiences had accustomed them to the bonds of despotic monarchy. Thus, although they explicitly conceived of the new United States of America as a haven for those unfortunates of Europe who were persecuted and oppressed, they had characteristic reservations about the effects of too free a policy. "My opinion, with respect to immigration," Washington wrote to John Adams in 1794, "is that except of useful mechanics and some particular descriptions of men or professions, there is no need of encouragement, while the policy or advantage of its taking place in a body (I mean the settling of them in a body) may be much questioned; for, by so doing, they retain the language, habits and principles (good or bad) which they bring with them."[4] Thomas Jefferson, whose views on race and attitudes towards slavery were notably liberal and advanced for his time, had similar doubts concerning the effects of mass immigration on American institutions, while conceding that immigrants, "if they come of them-selves…are entitled to all the rights of citizenship."[5]

The attitudes of Americans toward foreign immigration in the first three-quarters of the nineteenth century may correctly be described as ambiguous. On the one hand, immigrants were much desired, so as to swell the population and importance of states and territories, to man the farms of expanding prairie settlement, to work the mines, build the railroads and canals, and take their place in expanding industry. This was a period in which no federal leg-islation of any consequence prevented the entry of aliens, and such state legislation as exist-ed attempted to bar on an individual basis only those who were likely to become a burden on the community, such as convicts and paupers. On the other hand, the arrival in an over-whelmingly Protestant society of large numbers of poverty-stricken Irish Catholics, who set-tled in groups in the slums of Eastern cities, roused dormant fears of "Popery" and Rome. Another source of anxiety was the substantial influx of Germans, who made their way to the cities and farms of the mid-West and whose different language, separate communal life, and freer ideas on temperance and sabbath observance brought them into conflict with the Anglo-Saxon bearers of the Puritan and Evangelical traditions. Fear of foreign "radicals" and suspicion of the economic demands of the occasionally aroused workingmen added fuel to the nativist fires. In their extreme form these fears resulted in the Native-American move-ment of the 1830s and 1840s and the "American" or "Know-Nothing" party of the 1850s, with their anti-Catholic campaigns and their demands for restrictive laws on naturalization procedures and for keeping the foreign-born out of political office. While these movements scored local political successes and their turbulences so rent the national social fabric that the patches are not yet entirely invisible, they failed to influence national legislative policy on immigration and immigrants; and their fulminations inevitably provoked the expected re-actions from thoughtful observers.

The flood of newcomers to the westward expanding nation grew larger, reaching over one and two-thirds million between 1841 and 1850 and over two and one-half million in the decade before the Civil War. Throughout the entire period, quite apart from the excesses of the Know-Nothings, the predominant (though not exclusive) conception of what the ideal immigrant adjustment should be was probably summed up in a letter written in 1818 by John Quincy Adams, then Secretary of State, in answer to the inquiries of the Baron von Fürstenwaerther. If not the earliest, it is certainly the most elegant version of the sentiment, "If they don't like it here, they can go back where they came from." Adams declared:[6]

> They (immigrants to America) come to life of independence, but to a life of labor—
> and, if they cannot accommodate themselves to the character, moral, political and
> physical, of this country with all its compensating balances of good and evil, the
> Atlantic is always open to them to return to the land of their nativity and their fa-
> thers. To one thing they must make up their minds, or they will be disappointed in
> every expectation of happiness as Americans. They must cast off the European skin,
> never to resume it. They must look forward to their posterity rather than backward
> to their ancestors; they must be sure that whatever their own feelings may be, those
> of their children will cling to the prejudice of this country.

The events that followed the Civil War created their own ambiguities in attitude toward the immigrant. A nation undergoing wholesale industrial expansion and not yet finished with the march of westward settlement could make good use of the never faltering waves of newcomers. But sporadic bursts of labor unrest, attributed to foreign radicals, the growth of Catholic institutions and the rise of Catholics to municipal political power, and the continuing association of immigrant settlement with urban slums revived familiar fears. The first federal selective law restricting immigration was passed in 1882, and Chinese immigration was cut off in the same year. The most significant development of all, barely recognized at first, was the change in the source of European migrants. Beginning in the 1880s, the countries of southern and eastern Europe began to be represented in substantial numbers for the first time, and in the next decade immigrants from these sources became numerically dominant. Now the notes of a new, or at least hitherto unemphasized, chord from the nativist lyre began to sound—the ugly chord, or discord, of racism. Previously vague and romantic notions of Anglo-Saxon peoplehood, combined with general ethnocentrism, rudimentary wisps of genetics, selected tidbits of evolutionary theory, and naive assumptions from an early and crude imported anthropology produced the doctrine that the English, Germans, and others of the "old immigration" constituted a superior race of tall, blonde, blue-eyed "Nordics" or "Aryans," whereas the peoples of eastern and southern Europe made up the darker Alpines or Mediterraneans—both "inferior" breeds whose presence in America threatened, either by intermixture or supplementation, the traditional American stock and culture. The obvious corollary to this doctrine was to exclude the allegedly inferior breeds; but if the new type of immigrant could not be excluded, then everything must be done to instill Anglo-Saxon virtues in these benighted creatures. Thus, one educator writing in 1909 could state:[7]

> These southern and eastern Europeans are of a very different type from the north Europeans who preceeded them. Illiterate, docile, lacking in self-reliance and initiative, and not possessing the Anglo-Teutonic conceptions of law, order, and government, their coming has served to dilute tremendously our national stock, and to corrupt our civic life....Everywhere these people tend to settle in groups or settlements, and to set up here their national manners, customs, and observances. Our task is to break up these groups or settlements, to assimilate and amalgamate these people as a part of our American race, and to implant in their children, so far as can be done, the Anglo-Saxon conception of righteousness, law and order, and popular government, and to awaken in them a reverence for our democratic institutions and for those things in our national life which we as a people hold to be of abiding worth.

Anglo-conformity received its fullest expression in the so-called Americanization which gripped the nation during World War I. While "Americanization" in its various stages had more than one emphasis, it was essentially a consciously articulated movement to strip the immigrant of his native culture and attachments and make him over into an American along Anglo-Saxon lines—all this to be accomplished with great rapidity. To use an image of a later day, it was an attempt at "pressure-cooking assimilation." It had prewar antecedents, but it was during the height of the world conflict that federal agencies, state governments, municipalities, and a host of private organizations joined in the effort to persuade the immigrant to learn English, take out naturalization papers, buy war bonds, forget his former origins and culture, and give himself over to the patriotic hysteria.

After the war and the "Red scare" which followed, the excesses of the Americanization movement subsided. In its place, however, came the restriction of immigration through federal law. Foiled at first by presidential vetoes, and later by the failure of the 1917 literacy test to halt the immigrant tide, the proponents of restriction finally put through in the early 1920s a series of acts culminating in the well-known national-origins formula for immigrant quotas which went into effect in 1929. Whatever the merits of a quantitative limit on the number of immigrants to be admitted to the United States, the provisions of the formula, which discriminated sharply against the countries of southern and eastern Europe, in effect institutionalized the assumptions of the rightful dominance of Anglo-Saxon patterns in the land. Reaffirmed with only slight modification in the McCarran-Walter Act of 1952, these laws, then, stand as a legal monument to the creed of Anglo-conformity and a telling reminder that this ideological system still has numerous and powerful adherents on the American scene.

The Melting Pot

While Anglo-conformity in various guises has probably been the most prevalent ideology of assimilation in the American historical experience, a competing viewpoint with more generous and idealistic overtones has had its adherents and exponents from the eighteenth century onward. Conditions in the virgin continent, it was clear, were modifying the institutions which the English colonists brought with them from the mother country. Arrivals from non-English homelands such as Germany, Sweden, and France were similarly exposed to this fresh environment. Was it not possible, then, to think of the evolving American society not as a slightly modified England but rather as a totally new blend, culturally and biologically, in which the stocks and folkways of Europe, figuratively speaking, were indiscriminately mixed in the political pot of the emerging nation and fused by the fires of American influence and interaction into a distinctly new type?

Such, at any rate, was the conception of the new society which motivated that eighteenth-century French-born writer and agriculturalist, J. Hector St. John de Crèvecoeur, who, after many years of American residence, published his reflections and observations in *Letters from an American Farmer*.[8] Who, he asks, is the American?

> He is either an European, or the descendant of an European, hence that strange mixture of blood, which you will find in no other country. I could point out to you a family whose grandfather was an Englishman, whose wife was Dutch, whose son married a French woman, and whose present four sons have now four wives of different nations. He is an American, who leaving behind him all his ancient prejudices and manners, receives new ones from the new mode of life he has embraced, the new government he obeys, and the new rank he holds. He becomes an American by being received in the broad lap of our great Alma Mater. Here individuals of all

nations are melted into a new race of men, whose labours and posterity will one day cause great changes in the world.

Some observers have interpreted the open-door policy on immigration of the first three-quarters of the nineteenth century as reflecting an underlying faith in the effectiveness of the American melting pot, in the belief "that all could be absorbed and that all could contribute to an emerging national character."[9] No doubt many who observed with dismay the nativist agitation of the times felt as did Ralph Waldo Emerson that such conformity-demanding and immigrant-hating forces represented a perversion of the best American ideals. In 1845, Emerson wrote in his Journal:[10]

> I hate the narrowness of the Native American Party. It is the dog in the manger. It is precisely opposite to all the dictates of love and magnanimity; and therefore, of course, opposite to true wisdom....Man is the most composite of all creatures....Well, as in the old burning of the Temple at Corinth, by the melting and intermixture of silver and gold and other metals a new compound more precious than any, called Corinthian brass, was formed: so in this continent,—asylum of all nations,—the energy of Irish, Germans, Swedes, Poles and Cossacks, and all the European tribes,—of the Africans, and the Polynesians,—will construct a new race, a new religion, a new state, a new literature, which will be as vigorous as the new Europe which came out of the smelting-pot of the Dark Ages, or that which earlier emerged from the Pelasgic and Etruscan barbarism. La Nature aime les croisements.

Eventually, the melting-pot hypothesis found its way into historical scholarship and inter-pretation. While many American historians of the late nineteenth century, some fresh from graduate study at German universities, tended to adopt the view that American institutions derived in essence from Anglo-Saxon (and ultimately Teutonic) sources, others were not so sure.[11] One of these was Frederick Jackson Turner, a young historian from Wisconsin, not long emerged from his graduate training at Johns Hopkins. Turner presented a paper to the American Historical Association meeting in Chicago in 1893. Called "The Significance of the Frontier in American History," this paper proved to be one of the most influential essays in the history of American scholarship, and its point of view, supported by Turner's subse-quent writings and his teaching, pervaded the field of American historical interpretation for at least a generation. Turner's thesis was that the dominant influence in the shaping of American institutions and American democracy was not this nation's European heritage in any of its forms, nor the forces emanating from the eastern seaboard cities, but rather the experiences created by a moving and variegated western frontier. Among the many effects attributed to the frontier environment and the challenges it presented was that it acted as a solvent for the national heritages and the separatist tendencies of the many nationality groups which had joined the trek westward, including the Germans and Scotch-Irish of the eighteenth century and the Scandinavians and Germans of the nineteenth. "The frontier," asserted Turner, "pro-moted the formation of a composite nationality for the American people....In the crucible of the frontier the immigrants were Americanized, liberated, and fused into a mixed race,

English in neither nationality nor characteristics. The process has gone on from the early days to our own." And later, in an essay on the role of the Mississippi Valley, he refers to "the tide of foreign immigration which has risen so steadily that it has made a composite American people whose amalgamation is destined to produce a new national stock."[12]

Thus far, the proponents of the melting pot idea had dealt largely with the diversity produced by the sizeable immigration from the countries of northern and western Europe alone—the "old immigration," consisting of peoples with cultures and physical appearance not greatly different from those of the Anglo-Saxon stock. Emerson, it is true, had impartially included Africans, Polynesians, and Cossacks in his conception of the mixture; but it is was only in the last two decades of the nineteenth century that a large-scale influx of peoples from the countries of southern and eastern Europe imperatively posed the question of whether these uprooted newcomers who were crowding into the large cities of the nation and industrial sector of the economy could also be successfully "melted." Would the "urban melting pot" work as well as the "frontier melting pot" of an essentially rural society was alleged to have done?

It remained for an English-Jewish writer with strong social convictions, moved by his observation of the role of the United States as a haven for the poor and oppressed of Europe, to give utterance to the broader view of the American melting pot in a way which attracted public attention. In 1908, Israel Zangwill's drama, *The Melting Pot*, was produced in this country and became a popular success. It is a play dominated by the dream of its protagonist, a young Russian-Jewish immigrant to America, a composer, whose goal is the completion of a vast "American" symphony which will express his deeply felt conception of his adopted country as a divinely appointed crucible in which all the ethnic division of mankind will divest themselves of their ancient animosities and differences and become fused into one group, signifying the brotherhood of man. In the process he falls in love with a beautiful and cultured Gentile girl. The play ends with the performance of the symphony and, after numerous vicissitudes and traditional family opposition from both sides, with the approaching marriage of David Quixano and his beloved. David, in rhetoric of the time, delivers himself of such sentiments as these:[13]

> America is God's crucible, the great Melting Pot where all the races of Europe are melting and reforming! Here you stand, good folk, think I, when I see them at Ellis Island, here you stand in your fifty groups, with your fifty languages and histories, and your fifty blood hatreds and rivalries. But you won't be long like that, brother, for these are the fires of God you've come to—these are the fires of God. A fig for your feuds and vendettas! Germans and Frenchmen, Irishmen and Englishmen, Jews and Russians—into the Crucible with you all! God is making the American.

Here we have a conception of a melting pot which admits of no exceptions or qualifications with regard to the ethnic stocks which will fuse in the great crucible. Englishmen, Germans, Frenchmen, Slavs, Greeks, Syrians, Jews, Gentiles, even the black and yellow races, were specifically mentioned in Zangwill's rhapsodic enumeration. And this pot patently was to boil in the great cities of America.

Thus around the turn of the century the melting pot idea became embedded in the ideals of the age as one response to the immigrant receiving experience of the nation. Soon to be challenged by a new philosophy of group adjustment (to be discussed below) and always competing with the more pervasive adherence to Anglo-conformity, the melting-pot image, however, continued to draw a portion of the attention consciously directed toward this aspect of the American scene in the first half of the twentieth century. In the mid-1940s a sociologist who had carried out an investigation of intermarriage trends in New Haven, Connecticut, described a revised conception of the melting process in that city and suggested a basic modification of the theory of that process. In New Haven, Ruby Jo Reeves Kennedy[14] reported from a study of intermarriages from 1870 to 1940 that there was a distinct tendency for the British-Americans, Germans, and Scandinavians to marry among themselves—that is, within a Protestant "pool"; for the Irish, Italians, and Poles to marry among themselves—a Catholic "pool"; and for the Jews to marry other Jews. In other words, intermarriage was taking place across lines of nationality background, but there was a strong tendency for it to stay confined within one or the other of the three major religious groups, Protestants, Catholics, and Jews. Thus, declared Mrs. Kennedy, the picture in New Haven resembled a "triple melting pot" based on religious division, rather than a "single melting pot." Her study indicated, she stated, that "while strict endogamy is loosening, religious endogamy is persisting and the future cleavages will be along religious lines rather than along nationality lines as in the past. If this is the case, then the traditional 'single-melting-pot' idea must be abandoned, and a new conception, which we term the 'triple-melting-pot' theory of American assimilation, will take its place as the true expression of what is happening to the various nationality groups in the United States."[15] The triple melting-pot thesis was later taken up by the theologian Will Herberg, and formed an important sociological frame of reference for his analysis of religious trends in American society, *Protestant-Catholic-Jew*.[16] But the triple melting-pot hypothesis patently takes us into the realm of a society pluralistically conceived. We turn now to the rise of an ideology which attempts to justify such a conception.

Cultural Pluralism

Probably all the non-English immigrants who came to American shores in any significant numbers from colonial times onward—settling either in the forbidding wilderness, the lonely prairie, or in some accessible urban slum—created ethnic enclaves and looked forward to the preservation of at least some of their native cultural patterns. Such a development, natural as breathing, was supported by the later accretion of friends, relatives, and countrymen seeking out oases of familiarity in a strange land, by the desire of the settlers to rebuild (necessarily in miniature) a society in which they could communicate in the familiar tongue and maintain familiar institutions, and, finally, by the necessity to band together for mutual aid and mutual protection against the uncertainties of a strange and frequently hostile environment. This was as true of the "old" immigrants as of the "new." In fact, some of the liberal intellectuals who fled to America from an inhospitable political climate in Germany in the 1830s, 1840s, and 1850s looked forward to the creation of an all-German state within the union, or, even more hopefully, to the eventual formation of a separate German nation, as soon as the expected dissolution of the union under the impact of the slavery controversy should have taken place.[17] Oscar Handlin, writing of the sons of Erin in mid-nineteenth-century Boston, recent refugees from famine and economic degradation in their homeland, points out: "Unable to participate in the normal associational affairs of the community, the Irish felt obliged to erect a society within a society, to act together in their own way. In every contact therefore the group, acting apart from other sections of the community, became intensely aware of its peculiar and exclusive identity."[18] Thus cultural pluralism was a fact in American society before it became a theory—a theory with explicit relevance for the nation as a whole, and articulated and discussed in the English-speaking circles of American intellectual life.

Eventually, the cultural enclaves of the Germans (and the later arriving Scandinavians) were to decline in scope and significance as succeeding generations of their native-born attended public schools, left the farms and villages to strike out as individuals for the Americanizing city, and generally became subject to the influences of a standardizing industrial civilization. The German-American community, too, was struck a powerful blow by the accumulated passions generated by World War I—a blow from which it never fully recovered. The Irish were to be the dominant and pervasive element in the gradual emergence of a pan-Catholic group in America, but these developments would reveal themselves only in the twentieth century. In the meantime, in the last two decades of the nineteenth, the influx of immigrants from southern and eastern Europe had begun. These groups were all the more sociologically visible because the closing of the frontier, the occupational demands of an expanding industrial economy, and their own poverty made it inevitable that they would remain in the urban areas of the nation. In the swirling fires of controversy and the steadier flame of experience created by these new events, the ideology of cultural pluralism as a philosophy for the nation was forged.

The first manifestations of an ideological counterattack against draconic Americanization came not from the beleaguered newcomers (who were, after all, more concerned with survival than with theories of adjustment), but from those idealistic members of the middle class who, in the decade or so before the turn of the century, had followed the example of their English predecessors and "settled" in the slums to "learn to sup sorrow with the poor."[19] Immediately, these workers in the "settlement houses" were forced to come to grips with the realities of immigrant life and adjustment. Not all reacted in the same way, but on the whole the settlements developed an approach to the immigrant which was sympathetic to his native cultural heritage and to his newly created ethnic institutions.[20] For one thing, their workers, necessarily in intimate contact with the lives of these often pathetic and bewildered newcomers and their daily problems, could see how unfortunate were the effects of those forces which impelled rapid Americanization in their impact on the immigrants' children, who not infrequently became alienated from their parents and the restraining influence of family authority? Were not their parents ignorant and uneducated "Hunkies," "Sheenies," or "Dagoes," as that limited portion of the American environment in which they moved defined the matter? Ethnic "self-hatred" with its debilitating psychological consequences, family disorganization, and juvenile delinquency, were not unusual results of this state of affairs. Furthermore, the immigrants themselves were adversely affected by the incessant attacks on their cultures, their language, their institutions, their very conception of themselves. How were they to maintain their self-respect when all that they knew, felt, and dreamed, beyond their sheer capacity for manual labor—in other words, all that they *were*—was despised or scoffed at in America? And—unkindest cut of all—their own children had begun to adopt the contemptuous attitude of the "Americans." Jane Addams relates in a moving chapter of her *Twenty Years at Hull House* how, after coming to have some conception of the extent and depth of these problems, she created at the settlement a "Labor Museum," in which the immigrant women of the various nationalities crowded together in the slums of Chicago could illustrate their native methods of spinning and weaving, and in which the relation of these earlier techniques to contemporary factory methods could be graphically shown. For the first time these peasant women were made to feel by some part of their American environment that they possessed valuable and interesting skills—that they too had something to offer—and for the first time, the daughters of these women who, after a long day's work at their dank "needletrade" sweatshops, came to Hull House to observe, began to appreciate the fact that their mothers, too, had a "culture," that this culture possessed its own merit, and that it was related to their own contemporary lives. How aptly Jane Addams concludes her chapter with the hope that "our American citizenship might be built without disturbing these foundations which were laid of old time."[21]

This appreciative view of the immigrant's cultural heritage and of its distinctive usefulness both to himself and his adopted country received additional sustenance from another source: those intellectual currents of the day which, however overborne by their currently more powerful opposites, emphasized liberalism, internationalism, and tolerance. From time to time an occasional educator or publicist protested the demands of the "Americanizers," arguing that the immigrant, too, had an ancient and honorable culture, and that this culture had much to offer an America whose character and destiny were still in the process of formation, an America which must serve as an example of the harmonious cooperation of various heritages to a world inflamed by nationalism and war. In 1916 John Dewey, Norman Hapgood, and the young literary critic Randolph Bourne published articles or addresses elaborating various aspects of this theme.

The classic statement of the cultural pluralist position, however, had been made over a year before. Early in 1915 there appeared in the pages of *The Nation* two articles under the title "Democracy *versus* the Melting-Pot." Their author was Horace Kallen, a Harvard-educated philosopher with a concern for the application of philosophy to societal affairs, and, as an American Jew, himself derivative of an ethnic background which was subject to the contemporary pressures for dissolution implicit in the "Americanization," or Anglo-conformity, and the melting-pot theories. In these articles Kallen vigorously rejected the usefulness of these theories as models of what was actually transpiring in American life or as ideals for the future. Rather he was impressed by the way in which the various ethnic groups in America were coincident with particular areas and regions, and with the tendency for each group to preserve its own language, religion, communal institutions, and ancestral culture. All the while, he pointed out, the immigrant has been learning to speak English as the language of general communication, and has participated in the over-all economic and political life of the nation. These developments in which "the United States are in the process of becoming a federal state not merely as a union of geographical and administrative unities, but also as a cooperation of cultural diversities, as a federation or commonwealth of national cultures,"[22] the author argued, far from constituting a violation of historic American political principles, as the "Americanizers" claimed, actually represented the inevitable consequences of democratic ideals, since individuals are implicated in groups, and since democracy for the individual must by extension also mean democracy for his group.

The processes just described, however, as Kallen develops his argument, are far from having been thoroughly realized. They are menaced by "Americanization" programs, assumptions of Anglo-Saxon superiority, and misguided attempts to promote "racial" amalgamation. Thus America stands at a kind of cultural crossroads. It can attempt to impose by force an artificial, Anglo-Saxon oriented uniformity on its peoples, or it can consciously allow and encourage its ethnic groups to develop democratically, each emphasizing its particular cultural heritage. If the latter course is followed, as Kallen puts it at the close of his essay, then,[23]

> The outlines of a possible great and truly democratic commonwealth become discernible. Its form would be that of the federal republic: its substance a democracy of nationalities, cooperating voluntarily and autonomously through common institutions in the enterprise of self-realization through the perfection of men according to their kind. The common language of the commonwealth, the language of its great tradition, would be English, but each nationality would have for its emotional and involuntary life its own peculiar dialect or speech, its own individual and inevitable esthetic and intellectual forms. The political and economic life of the commonwealth is a single unit and serves as the foundation and background for the realization of the distinctive individuality of each nation that composes it and of the pooling of these in a harmony above them all. Thus "American civilization" may come to mean the perfection of the cooperative harmonies of "European civilization"—the waste, the squalor and the distress of Europe being eliminated—a multiplicity in a unity, an orchestration of mankind.

Within the next decade Kallen published more essays dealing with the theme of American multiple-group life, later collected in a volume.[24] In the introductory note to this book he used for the first time the term "cultural pluralism" to refer to his position. These essays reflect both his increasingly sharp rejection of the onslaughts on the immigrant and his culture which the coming of World War I and its attendant fears, the "Red scare," the projection of themes of racial superiority, the continued exploitation of the newcomers, and the rise of the Ku Klux Klan all served to increase in intensity, and also his emphasis on cultural pluralism as the democratic antidote to these ills. He has since published other essays elaborating or annotating the theme of cultural pluralism. Thus, for at least forty-five years, most of them spent teaching at the New School for Social Research, Kallen has been acknowledged as the originator and leading philosophical exponent of the idea of cultural pluralism.

In the late 1930s and early 1940s the late Louis Adamic, the Yugoslav immigrant who had become an American writer, took up the theme of America's multicultural heritage and the role of these groups in forging the country's national character. Borrowing Walt Whitman's phrase, he described America as "a nation of nations," and while his ultimate goal was closer to the melting-pot idea than to cultural pluralism, he saw the immediate task as that of making America conscious of what it owed to all its ethnic groups, not just to the Anglo-Saxons. The children and grandchildren of immigrants of non-English origins, he was convinced, must be taught to be proud of the cultural heritage of their ancestral ethnic group and of its role in building the American nation; otherwise, they would not lose their sense of ethnic inferiority and the feeling of rootlessness he claimed to find in them.

Thus in the twentieth century, particularly since World War II, "cultural pluralism" has become a concept which has worked its way into the vocabulary and imagery of specialists in intergroup relations and leaders of ethnic communal groups. In view of this new pluralistic emphasis, some writers now prefer to speak of the "integration" of immigrants rather than of their "assimilation."[25] However, with a few exceptions,[26] no close analytical attention has been given either by social scientists or practitioners of intergroup relations to the meaning of cultural pluralism, its nature and relevance for a modern industrialized society, and its implications for problems of prejudice and discrimination—a point to which we referred at the outset of this discussion.

Conclusions

In the remaining pages I can make only a few analytical comments which I shall apply in context to the American scene, historical and current. My view of the American situation will not be documented here, but may be considered as a series of hypotheses in which I shall attempt to outline the American assimilation process.

First of all, it must be realized that "assimilation" is a blanket term which in reality covers a multitude of subprocesses. The most crucial distinction is one often ignored—the distinction between what I have elsewhere called "behavioral assimilation" and "structural assimilation."[27] The first refers to the absorption of the cultural behavior patterns of the "host" society. (At the same time, there is frequently some modification of the cultural patterns of the immigrant-receiving country, as well.) There is a special term for this process of cultural modification or "behavioral assimilation"—namely, "acculturation." "Structural assimilation," on the other hand, refers to the entrance of the immigrants and their descendants into the social cliques, organizations, institutional activities, and general civic life of the receiving society. If this process takes place on a large enough scale, then a high frequency of intermarriage must result. A further distinction must be made between, on the one hand, those activities of the general civic life which involve earning a living, carrying out political responsibilities, and engaging in the instrumental affairs of the larger community, and, on the other hand, activities which create personal friendship patterns, frequent home intervisiting, communal worship, and communal recreation. The first type usually develops so-called "secondary relationships," which tend to be relatively impersonal and segmental; the latter type leads to "primary relationships," which are warm, intimate, and personal.

With these various distinctions in mind, we may then proceed.

Built on the base of the original immigrant "colony" but frequently extending into the life of successive generations, the characteristic ethnic group experience is this: within the ethnic group there develops a network of organizations and informal social relationships which permits and encourages the members of the ethnic group to remain within the confines of the group for all their primary relationships and some of their secondary relationships throughout all the stages of the life cycle. From the cradle in the sectarian hospital to the child's play group, the social clique in high school, the fraternity and religious center in college, the dating group within which he searches for a spouse, the marriage partner, the neighborhood of his residence, the church affiliation and the church clubs, the men's and the women's social and service organizations, the adult clique of "marrieds," the vacation resort, and then, as the age cycle nears completion, the rest home for the elderly and, finally, the sectarian cemetery—in all these activities and relationships which are close to the core of personality and selfhood—the member of the ethnic group may if he wishes follow a path which never takes him across the boundaries of his ethnic structural network.

The picture is made more complex by the existence of social class divisions which cut across ethnic group lines just as they do those of the white Protestant population in America. As each ethnic group which has been here for the requisite time has developed second, third, or in some cases, succeeding generations, it has produced a college-educated group which composes an upper middle class (and sometimes upper class, as well) segment of the larger groups. Such class divisions tend to restrict primary group relations even further, for although the ethnic-group member feels a general sense of identification with all the bearers of his ethnic heritage, he feels comfortable in intimate social relations only with those who also share his own class background or attainment.

In short, my point is that, while *behavioral assimilation* or acculturation has taken place in America to a considerable degree, *structural assimilation*, with some important exceptions has not been extensive.[28] The exceptions are of two types. The first brings us back to the "triple-melting-pot" thesis of Ruby Jo Reeves Kennedy and Will Herberg. The "nationality" ethnic groups have tended to merge within each of the three major religious groups. This has been particularly true of the Protestant and Jewish communities. Those descendants of the "old" immigration of the nineteenth century, who were Protestant (many of the Germans and all the Scandinavians), have in considerable part gradually merged into the white Protestant "sub-society." Jews of Sephardic, German, and Eastern-European origins have similarly tended to come together in their communal life. The process of absorbing the various Catholic nationalities, such as the Italians, Poles and French Canadians, into an American Catholic community hitherto dominated by the Irish has begun, although I do not believe that it is by any means close to completion. Racial and quasi-racial groups such as the Negroes, Indians, Mexican-Americans, and Puerto Ricans still retain their separate sociological structures. The outcome of all this in contemporary American life is thus pluralism—but it is more than "triple" and it is more accurately described as *structural pluralism* than as cultural pluralism, although some of the latter also remains.

My second exception refers to the social structures which implicate intellectuals. There is no space to develop the issue here, but I would argue that there is a social world or subsociety of the intellectuals in America in which true structural intermixture among persons of various ethnic backgrounds, including the religious, has markedly taken place.

My final point deals with the reasons for these developments. If structural assimilation has been retarded in America by religious and racial lines, we must ask why. The answer lies in the attitudes of both the majority and the minority groups and in the way these attitudes have interacted. A saying of the current day is, "It takes two to tango." To apply the analogy, there is no good reason to believe that white Protestant America has ever extended a firm and cordial invitation to its minorities to dance. Furthermore, the attitudes of the minority-group members themselves on the matter have been divided and ambiguous. Particularly for the minority religious groups, there is a certain logic in ethnic communality, since there is a commitment to the perpetuation of the religious ideology and since structural intermixture leads to intermarriage and the possible loss to the group of the intermarried family. Let us, then, examine the situation serially for various types of minorities.

With regard to the immigrant, in his characteristic numbers and socio-economic background, structural assimilation was out of the question. He did not want it, and he had a positive need for the comfort of his own communal institutions. The native American, moreover, whatever the implications of his public pronouncements, had no intention of opening up his primary group life to entrance by these hordes of alien newcomers. The situation was a functionally complementary standoff.

The second generation found a much more complex situation. Many believed they heard the siren call of welcome to the social cliques, clubs, and institutions of white Protestant America. After all, it was simply a matter of learning American ways, was it not? Had they not grown up as Americans, and were they not culturally different from their parents, the "greenhorns"? Or perhaps, an especially eager one reasoned (like the Jewish protagonist of Myron Kaufmann's novel, *Remember Me to God*, aspiring to membership in the prestigious club system of Harvard undergraduate social life) "If only I can go the last few steps in Ivy League manners and behavior, they will surely recognize that I am one of them and take me in." But alas, Brooks Brothers suit notwithstanding, the doors of the fraternity house, the city men's club, and the country club were slammed in the face of the immigrant's offspring. That invitation was not really there in the first place; or, to the extent it was, in Joshua Fishman's phrase, it was a "look me over but don't touch me" invitation to the American minority group child."[29] And so the rebuffed one returned to the homelier but dependable comfort of the communal institutions of his ancestral group. There he found his fellows of the same generation who had never stirred from the home fires. Some of these had been too timid to stray; others were ethnic ideologists committed to the group's survival; still others had never really believed in the authenticity of the siren call or were simply too passive to do more than go along the familiar way. All could not join in the task that was well within the realm of the sociologically possible—the build-up of social institutions and organizations within the ethnic enclave, manned increasingly by members of the second generation and suitably separated by social class.

Those who had for a time ventured out gingerly or confidently, as the case might be, had been lured by the vision of an "American" social structure that was somehow larger than all subgroups and was ethnically neutral. Were they, too, not Americans? But they found to their dismay that at the primary group level a neutral American social structure was a mirage. What at a distance seemed to be a quasi-public edifice flying only the all-inclusive flag of American nationality turned out on closer inspection to be the clubhouse of a particular ethnic group—the white Anglo-Saxon Protestants, its operation shot through with the premises and expectations of its parental ethnicity. In these terms, the desirability of whatever invitation was grudgingly extended to those of other ethnic backgrounds could only become a considerably attenuated one.

With the racial minorities, there was not even the pretense of an invitation. Negroes, to take the most salient example, have for the most part been determinedly barred from the cliques, social clubs, and churches of white America. Consequently, with due allowance for internal class differences, they have constructed their own network of organizations and institutions, their own "social world." There are now many vested interests served by the preservation of this separate communal life, and doubtless many Negroes are psychologically comfortable in it, even though at the same time they keenly desire that discrimination in such areas as employment, education, housing, and public accommodations be eliminated. However, the ideological attachment of Negroes to their communal separation is not conspicuous. Their sense of identification with ancestral African national cultures is virtually nonexistent, although Pan-Africanism engages the interest of some intellectuals and although "black nationalist" and "black racist" fringe groups have recently made an appearance at the other end of the communal spectrum. As for their religion, they are either Protestant or Catholic (overwhelmingly the former). Thus, there are no "logical" ideological reasons for their separate communality; dual social structures are created solely by the dynamics of prejudice and discrimination, rather than being reinforced by the ideological commitments of the minority itself.

Structural assimilation, then, has turned out to be the rock on which the ships of Anglo-conformity and the melting pot have foundered. To understand that behavioral assimilation (or acculturation) without massive structural intermingling in primary relationships has been the dominant motif in the American experience of creating and developing a nation out of diverse peoples is to comprehend the most essential sociological fact of that experience. It is against the background of "structural pluralism" that strategies of strengthening intergroup harmony, reducing ethnic discrimination and prejudice, and maintaining the rights of both those who stay within and those who venture beyond their ethnic boundaries must be thoughtfully devised.

Notes

1. Allen Nevins and Henry Steele Commager, *America: The Story of a Free People* (Boston, Little, Brown, 1942), p. 58.

2. The phrase is the Coles'. See Stewart G. Cole and Mildred Wiese Cole, *Minorities and the American Promise* (New York, Harper & Brothers, 1954), ch. 6.

3. Maurice R. Davie, *World Immigration* (New York, Macmillan, 1936), p. 36, and (cited therein) "Letter of Benjamin Franklin to Peter Collinson, 9th May, 1753, on the condition and character of the Germans in Pennsylvania," in *The World of Benjamin Franklin, with Notes and Life of the Author*, by Jared Sparks (Boston, 1828), vol. 7, pp. 71–73.

4. *The Writings of George Washington*, collected by W.C. Ford (New York, G.P. Putnam's Sons, 1889), vol. 12, p. 489.

5. Thomas Jefferson, "Notes on Virginia, Query 8"; in *The Writings of Thomas Jefferson*, ed. A.E. Bergh (Washington, The Thomas Jefferson Memorial Association, 1907), vol. 2, p. 121.

6. *Niles Weekly Register*, vol. 18, 29 April 1820, pp. 157–158; see also Marcus L. Hansen, *The Atlantic Migration, 1607–1860*, pp. 96–97.

7. Ellwood P. Cubberly, *Changing Conceptions of Education* (Boston, Houghton Mifflin, 1909), pp. 15–16.

8. J. Hector St. John de Crèvecoeur, *Letters from an American Farmer* (New York, Albert and Charles Boni, 1925; reprinted from the 1st edn., London, 1782), pp. 54–55.

9. Oscar Handlin, ed., *Immigration as a Factor in American History* (Englewood, Prentice-Hall, 1959), p. 146.

10. Quoted by Stuart P. Sherman in his Introduction to *Essays and Poems of Emerson* (New York, Harcourt Brace, 1921), p. xxxiv.

11. See Edward N. Saveth, *American Historians and European Immigrants, 1875–1925* (New York, Columbia University Press, 1948).

12. Frederick Jackson Turner, *The Frontier in American History* (New York, Henry Holt, 1920), pp. 22–23, 190.

13. Israel Zangwill, *The Melting Pot* (New York, Macmillan, 1909), p. 37.

14. Ruby Jo Reeves Kennedy, "Single or Triple Melting-Pot? Intermarriage Trends in New Haven, 1870–1940," *American Journal of Sociology*, 1944, 49:331–339. See also her "Single or Triple Melting-Pot? Intermarriage in New Haven, 1870–1950," *ibid.*, 1952, 58:56–59.

15. Kennedy, "Single or Triple Melting-Pot? ...1870–1940," p. 332 (author's italics omitted).

16. Will Herberg, *Protestant-Catholic-Jew* (Garden City, Doubleday, 1955).

17. Nathan Glazer, "Ethnic Groups in America: From National Culture to Ideology," in Morroe Berger, Theodore Abel, and Charles H. Page, eds., *Freedom and Control in Modern Society* (New York, D. Van Nostrand, 1954), p. 161; Marcus Lee Hansen, *The Immigrant in American History* (Cambridge, Harvard University Press, 1940), pp. 129–140; John A. Hawgood, *The Tragedy of German-America* (New York, Putnam's, 1940), *passim*.

18. Oscar Handlin, *Boston's Immigrants* (Cambridge, Harvard University Press, 1959, rev. edn.), p. 176.

19. From a letter (1883) by Sanuel A. Barnett; quoted in Arthur C. Holden, *The Settlement Idea* (New York, Macmillan, 1922), p. 12.

20. Jane Addams, *Twenty Years at Hull House* (New York, Macmillan, 1914), pp. 231–258; Arthur C. Holden, *op. cit.*, pp. 109–131, 182–189; John Higham, *Strangers in the Land* (New Brunswick, Rutgers University Press, 1955), p. 236.

21. Jane Addams, *op. cit.*, p. 258.

22. Horace M. Kallen, "Democracy *versus* the Melting-Pot," *The Nation*, 18 and 25 February 1915; reprinted in his *Culture and Democracy in the United States*, New York, Boni and Liveright, 1924; the quotation is on p. 116.

23. Kallen, *Culture and Democracy...*, p. 124.

24. *Op. cit.*

25. See W.D. Borrie *et al.*, *The Cultural Integration of Immigrants* (a survey based on the papers and proceedings of the UNESCO Conference in Havana, April 1956), Paris, UNESCO, 1959; and William S. Bernard, "The Integration of Immigrants in the United States"(mimeographed), one of the papers for this conference.

26. See particularly Milton M. Gordon, "Social Structure and Goals in Group Relations"; and Nathan Glazer, "Ethnic Groups in America: From National Culture to Ideology," both articles in Berger, Abel, and Page, *op. cit.*; S.N. Eisenstadt, *The Absorption of Immigrants* (London, Routledge and Kegan Paul, 1954) and W.D. Borrie *et al.*, *op. cit.*

27.   Milton M. Gordon, "Social Structures and Goals in Groups Relations," p. 151.

28.   See Erich Rosenthal, "Acculturation without Assimilation?" *American Journal of Sociology*, 1960, 66:275–288.

29.   Joshua A. Fishman, "Childhood Indoctrination for Minority-Group Membership and the Quest for Minority-Group Biculturism in America," in Oscar Handlin, ed., *Group Life in America* (Cambridge, Harvard University Press, forthcoming).

Article 4.2

An Alternative Perspective
for Studying American Ethnicity

It is the intent of this chapter to suggest an alternative perspective for the study of those forms of differentiation in American society that are not attributable to social class (as this concept is normally understood), age, or sex. The most immediate concern of our inquiry will be the study of the descendants of those western European immigrant groups that have become the focus of much social science interest in recent years. However, the perspective (or "model," a word I would prefer to apply only to a perspective that can be stated in mathematical terms) can also be used to study differences based on race, religion, and geography.

"Ethnicity" in the narrow sense refers to the descendants of the European immigrants. "Ethnicity" in the wider sense refers to any differentiation based on nationality, race, religion, or language. Part of the problem in thinking clearly about ethnicity in the American context is that some groups that Americans think of as "ethnic" are constituted by religion (Jews), some by nationality (Poles), some by religion and nationality (Irish Catholics), some by race (blacks), some by language (Spanish-speaking—if indeed such an ethnic group exists), and one by region (Southerners—see Reed 1972). This chapter focuses mainly on ethnicity in the relatively narrow sense as constituted by religion and nationality; such a focus seems to me strategically the best place to begin.

Definitions of ethnicity abound. To a considerable extent the definition one chooses is a function of the "picture" or perspective from which one is making one's analysis or the point one wishes to make. For our present purpose an elaborate but sufficiently general definition of Schermerhorn (1969, p. 123) will be adequate:

> A collectivity within a larger society having real or putative common ancestry, memories of a shared historical past, and a cultural focus on one or more symbolic elements defined as the epitome of their peoplehood. Examples of such symbolic elements are: kinship patterns, physical contiguity (as in localism or sectionalism), religious affiliation, languages or dialect forms, tribal affiliation, nationality, phenotypical features, or any combination of these. A necessary accompaniment is some consciousness of kind among members of the group. This would place it in Bierstedt's category of "societal group."

Any comment on human society, whether it results from common sense analysis or rigorous scholarly research, inevitably utilizes perspectives or pictures or paradigms. Such tools are indispensable for the beginnings of analysis, and though they may be refined in the analytic process, they are rarely discarded. David Matza (1964, pp. 1–2) comments on the functions of such "pictures":

> Pictures are intimately related to the explanation of social systems. Systems of action may usually be typified in ideal fashion. Indeed, this simplification is almost mandatory if the analyst wishes to proceed to the task of explanation. A system, whether it be capitalism or delinquency, has exemplars, basic figures who perpetrate the system. The accurate characterizing of exemplars is a crucial step in the development of explanatory theory. Given the present state of knowledge, pictures are not true or false, but rather plausible or implausible. They more or less remind us of the many discrete individuals who make up a social category.
> Systems of action of exemplars, and a portrayal of them is a crucial step in the elaboration of causal theory. Thus, for example, a plausible picture of the capitalist was implicit in the various theories explaining the rise of capitalism. This hardly means that a system may be reduced to the character of exemplars; rather, an exemplar is a personification or microcosm of the system. A crucial step from a Marxian to a Weberian theory of the origins of capitalism consisted of a basic shift in the portrait of the exemplary capitalist. Somewhere in the dialectic between competing scholars the pirate capitalist of Marx was transformed to the bookkeeper capitalist of Weber. The more authentic ring of Weber's portrait is largely responsible for the more widespread acceptance of his rather than Marx's theory of the emergence of capitalism. Whatever the other virtues of Marx's theory, it suffers from an initial implausibility. It seems conceived on a false note. How, we ask, can we believe in a theory that apparently falsifies the character of the exemplars? Whatever the failings of Weber's theory, it seems more plausible because it is more reminiscent of the early capitalists we have studied or read about.

The assumptions contained in such pictures are both absolutely essential for social research and also dangerous for its goals: "they tend to remain beyond the reach of such intellectual correctives as argument, criticism and scrutiny. ...Left unattended, they return to haunt us by shaping or bending theories that purport to explain major social phenomena" (Matza, 1964, p. 1).

Two "pictures" shape most analyses of the ethnicity phenomenon: the domination (or oppression) picture, and the assimilation (or, in its more popular form, the "melting pot") picture.

The domination image (Mason 1970) is most frequently used in the study of colonialism. It is basically a conflict picture in which one group (white or mixed blood) is perceived as controlling and usually oppressing another (usually nonwhite or native) group. The assimilation image is more accommodationist in its assumptions and focuses on the adjustment of two cultures to each other after encounter and interspersion. Its concerns are "culture contact," in which the culture of the host society is threatened by the culture of a numerically inferior but politically dominant group (Europeans on natives), or "acculturation," in which the culture of the immigrant group is threatened by that of a numerically and politically dominant host society. Both pictures assume a strain toward homogenization—political and structural in the domination picture and social and cultural in the assimilation picture.

Both pictures or images are used to study American society, with the domination perspective applying mostly to relationships between white and nonwhite and the assimilation perspective applying mostly to relationships among the various white groups, particularly between the so-called Anglo-Saxon[1] and later immigrant groups. It is the inadequacy of the latter picture that is the principal concern of this article.[2]

The literature on assimilation in America is immense.[2] Some authors see the process as rapid, others see it as slow. Some think it desirable that ethnic differentiation be eliminated so that a "common culture" may emerge, others think that assimilation ought to be decelerated so that many different cultures may flourish under the American umbrella. Gordon (1964) has distinguished between "structural assimilation," in which ethnicity is no longer pertinent even to primary group formation, and "cultural assimilation" (or acculturation), in which cultural differences diminish but the propensity to choose primary group relationships from within one's own group persists. Gordon argues that the latter process is far along in American society, while the former proceeds much more slowly.

What all the assimilationist literature, popular and serious, sophisticated or simplistic, assumes is that the strain toward homogenization in a modern industrial society is so great as to be virtually irresistible. The influences of the common school, the mass media, common political and social norms, and ethnic and religious intermarriage work toward the elimination of diversity in a society. Basic beliefs, socialization styles, personality characteristics, political participation, social attitudes, expectations of intimate role opposites, all tend toward a similarity that is differentiated only be social class. Social class is generally assumed to be a "rational" basis for differentiation as opposed to differentiation based on religion and national origin, which are "irrational." Race was formerly an irrational focus for differentiation but is now rational.

The picture of American society as stated in the abstract categories of social science or the concrete categories of popular journalism is one of many different cultures merging into one common "American" culture. Only minor differences (such as special foods) persist. It may be debated whether this merging produces either a totally new culture that is a combination of its various inputs, or whether in fact it is rather a matter of the various immigrant cultures adapting themselves to the host culture, which I shall term "Anglo conformity." Whatever theoretical position one may take, in practice, Anglo conformity is what is assumed to occur, even though a few immigrant items, such as Jewish humor and Italian food, may be taken over by the host culture. Once one assumes, as most of the literature does, that the immigrant culture is the dependent variable and the host culture the independent variable, Anglo conformity has entered one's model.

The assimilation picture is pervasive in American society. It is part of our popular folk wisdom as well as an important component of the repertory of pictures available to social science theorists. Politicians, TV commentators, movie critics, social planners, and reform political candidates all take it for granted. The picture has been wedged into our individual and collective unconscious, and has achieved the status not merely of conventional wisdom but of common sense.

There are two things that happen almost inevitably when such a picture becomes common sense. It becomes, as Matza suggested, undiscussed and undiscussable; it begins to become normative. It is now no longer a description of the way things are, it is a description of the way things ought to be. Data that do not fit the picture are ignored or discarded or subjected to the sorts of paralyzing questions against which no data can stand. Instead of being viewed as new and potentially very informative findings, such data are written off as irrelevant or even as potentially dangerous.

It is but a short step from being undiscussably *descriptive* for a picture to become *prescriptive*. The picture becomes not merely an ideal type, it becomes a norm. To untangle the strands of nativism, liberal optimism, vulgar Marxism, secular rationalism, and immigrant self-rejection that underpin the "melting pot" norm is a challenge to which practitioners of the sociology of knowledge might wish to respond. Sociology is supposed to involve questioning assumptions (even criticizing them, if we are to believe the younger members of the profession). That few have asked whether there might be other pictures for looking at the phenomenon of ethnic differentiation in American society beside the "official" assimilationist one, or the moderately revisionist version of it advanced by Gordon, seems to have been a major failure of the profession.

The most basic and fundamental assumption of the assimilationist picture is that in a modern society the forces working for homogenization—at least within broad social class groupings—are so powerful as to be irresistible. With the exception of research by Wilensky (1964), this assumption has been so deeply embedded in the collective unconscious that it is almost never questioned. But one need only look up from one's computer output or one's mathematical model or the latest issue of the *New York Review of Books* to realize that differentiation runs rampant in American society. Processes of homogenization and differentiation are going on simultaneously. We are, to put the matter in popular terms, becoming more like one another and more different from one another. A repertory of pictures of social reality that does not have room for paradoxical models may be neat, clean, and simple. Whether it is helpful for understanding human behavior is another matter.

The assimilationist perspective is indispensable for coping with the social reality of America. The Irish ethnic and the Polish ethnic who live next door to one another have far more in common than their great grandparents did—common language, common citizenship, and a common set of television channels. But in some ways they may be more dissimilar. Their grandparents were in all likelihood peasant farmers, but the two American ethnics may have totally different occupational perspectives. Certain differences rooted in historical heritages may persist between the two Americans with no signs of diminution. For example, more than a member of any other ethnic group, the Irishman is likely to be a political activist; the Pole is less likely. It is at least a researchable question as to whether in some respects the two neighbors are becoming increasingly different from one another. The Irishman may be defecting to the Republican party, while the Pole is much less likely to be doing so, for example. A whole set of pictures, or perhaps one extraordinarily elegant paradoxical picture, is required to do justice to this complex reality. The assimilation picture by itself simply won't do.

Certain limitations of the assimilation picture must be considered. It frequently turns out to be not particularly helpful in generating hypotheses or in ordering data. It is difficult to determine, for example, whether a set of findings we reported in Chapter 3 on the transmission of cultural heritage among the Irish and Italians shows a high rate of "acculturation" or a low rate. The assimilation perspective provided no clue as to why "acculturation" occurred more rapidly for the Italians on some items (attitudes toward the role of women, for example) and on others more rapidly for the Irish (importance of sustaining relationships with one's parents, for example). In other words, when we limit ourselves to the assimilation perspective many research findings on the differentiation among ethnic groups in the United States can neither be predicted nor interpreted.[3]

Glazer has observed that the ethnic groups came into existence in the United States;[11] but no one has seriously investigated the possibilities latent in such an assertion. As Fabian remarked, "It is often overlooked that immigrants when they arrive in a new country do not constitute a group or a community—they *may* become one over time" (Fabian 1972, p. 7).

The acculturation picture offers no insight into why there are presently some self-conscious attempts to create ethnic groups. In the Northeast, for example, there is a deliberate and self-conscious attempt to create a "Spanish-speaking" ethnic group (an attempt that is not supported, incidentally, in the Southwest). An American Indian group is struggling to emerge, with some success; and in Chicago there is even an effort, as yet rather ineffective, to create an Appalachian white ethnic group. Cruse (1971) has also suggested that the black power movement is essentially an attempt to create a black ethnic group, a suggestion that Metzger (1971) has echoed from a very different perspective. The political and social leaderships concerned with the creation of ethnic groups must have insights into how power is exercised in the United States that are quite foreign to the acculturation picture.[4]

Similarly, the acculturation perspective does not take into account the fact noted by many historians that ethnicity was perceived by the immigrants as a way of becoming American. The hypen in the hyphenate American was a symbol of equality, not of inequality. In an urban environment where everyone including the native American was something else besides "American," one had to be an ethnic to find one's place on the map. Furthermore, Brown (1966) notes that the principal argument of the nineteenth and early twentieth-century Irish American nationalists who favored freedom for Ireland was that only when Ireland was a free and independent member of the family of nations would Irish Americans be accepted by the native Americans as being worthy of full-fledged American citizenship. And Greene (1968) has demonstrated that support among Polish Americans and Czech Americans for the nationalist movements in their native countries during World War I came only after the United States entered that war. Such support for free Poland and the new Czech republic was, paradoxically, an exercise in American patriotism more than an expression of Polish or Czech patriotism.

More historical research is obviously required, but there is sufficient reason to state, at least as a tentative hypothesis, that the creation of ethnic groups in the United States was a way for the immigrant population to look at its present and future in America rather than at its past in the Old World. In a complex society of an "unstable pluralism" (Kammen 1972) you had to be "something" if you were going to be "anybody." Such a view of social reality is obviously completely foreign to the acculturation picture.

The acculturationist assumes that "unstable pluralism" is a socially dangerous situation.[5] He expects social harmony to emerge out of the creation and reinforcement of a "common culture." In such a perspective the question becomes, How does a common culture emerge and how does it survive the assaults of periodic regressions to a rational differentiation?

One who operates in the acculturation perspective has no way of addressing himself to the question of how American society manages to keep from tearing itself apart despite its condition of unstable pluralism. During the last quarter of a century, when ethnic, racial, and religious violence has erupted all over the world, the United States has been relatively free from serious violence. The urban riots of the late 1960s were minor in comparison with those of Indonesia, Bangladesh, the Sudan, Burundi, and Ulster. Despite the unstable pluralism, which Kammen tells us worried Americans in 1700, there has been only one civil war, and that was mostly between two British American groups. The pertinent question ought to be not how one protects the "common culture" and propagates it, but rather what there is in the national culture that has legitimated considerable diversity while creating at the same time implicit protocols by which violent social conflict has been avoided in the main. The assimilationist perspective marvels at how homogenous American society is becoming, and hence sees no real need for striving to understand the nation's capacity for observing and coping with our complex racial, religious, nationality, geographic, and social differentiation, a differentiation that came into being in a relatively short period of time as the histories of human societies go.

Another problem with the acculturation picture is that it does not account for the self-conscious manipulation of ethnic symbols in American society, a manipulation which in the acculturation picture ought to be increasingly difficult and infrequent, but which in the social reality around us does not seem to be difficult at all and seems, if anything, to be more frequent in recent years. Polish and Italian self-consciousness, for example, can easily be written off as a response to black militancy. Yet it could also be argued that ethnic consciousness is merely a result of the fact that by accepting black self-consciousness the larger society legitimated the public manipulation of ethnic symbols, which in prior years had been manipulated privately. A particularly interesting example is the appearance of tricolor bumper stickers on the cars of many Italian Americans in the eastern United States. It is safe to assume that most of these self-conscious Italians came from the southern Italy and Sicily where until fairly recently the tricolor represented the "foreign" domination of the Piedmontese. The Sicilians came to the United States and discovered that they were Italian Americans. Now they have discovered that they are Italian, a process exactly the reverse of that suggested by using only the acculturation picture. It is of course a research question as to how widespread the response is to such symbol manipulation. One would presume that sociologists would abstain from dismissing it as an irrelevant and unimportant phenomenon until they have studied it in detail.

As an alternative and complementary perspective, I would suggest the picture of "ethnicization" (Fabian's term) or "ethnogenesis" (a term used by David Greenstone in a NORC seminar) or "the creation of an ethnic group." Ethnic groups come into being in the United States and have a "natural history." The study of their genesis and history, free of the dogmatic assumption that their destiny is obliteration, can be useful in approaching both the history and the sociology of ethnic differentiation in the United States.

• • •

What we are suggesting, then, is a picture of American ethnic differentiation that sees immigrants forming collectivities of limited liability based on presumed common origin, because these collectivities are tolerated and even encouraged by the larger society, provide substantial payoff with marginal risks, and incur only limited costs. In addition to studying the acculturation of immigrants we should also be studying their ethnicization, that is to say, the genesis and natural history of such collectivities. And we should be studying them fully conscious that they are dynamic flexible mechanisms that can grow and change, whose disappearance ought not to be assumed on a priori grounds.

The figure is a development of the four perspectives on ethnicity I presented earlier. It schematizes the "ethnicization" perspective, and is in some measure an extension of the acculturation-assimilation perspective. There are a number of important differences, however.

Figure 1 shows that the host and immigrants may have had something in common to begin with. Some of the Irish, for example, spoke the English language and understood something of the English political style of the eighteenth and nineteenth centuries. The other European groups were part of the broad Western cultural inheritance. Under the influence of education, generation, and the experiences in American society both at the time of immigration and subsequently, the common culture grows larger. Immigrants become more like the host, and the host may become somewhat more like the immigrants. Certain immigrant characteristics persist, but in addition, under the impact of the experience of American life, some traits become more rather than less distinctive. Certain aspects of the immigrant heritage are emphasized and developed in response to the challenge of American society. What appears at the end (the right-hand portion of the figure) is that the ethnic group has a cultural system that is a combination of traits shared with other groups and traits that are distinctive to its own group. For the ethnics, then, the mix of traits and the emphasis within the cultural system are different from those of their immigrant predecessors. They share more with the common culture than they did to begin with, but in some respects they also may be more different from the descendants of the hosts than their ancestors were from their hosts. In principle there is nothing to prevent testing of the various components of my perspective. In practice, however, an immense amount of social and historical research will be required. It is worth noting, incidentally, that while all the lines in Figure 1 are straight, in the reality this chart attempts to schematize the lines might well be jagged. For example, if one considers the variable of ethnic consciousness as part of the original immigrant system of traits, that consciousness may well have waxed and waned through the years, moving away from the common culture, then toward it, and away again in zigzag fashion.

In Figure 1 I have tried to combine the four previous perspectives on American ethnic di-

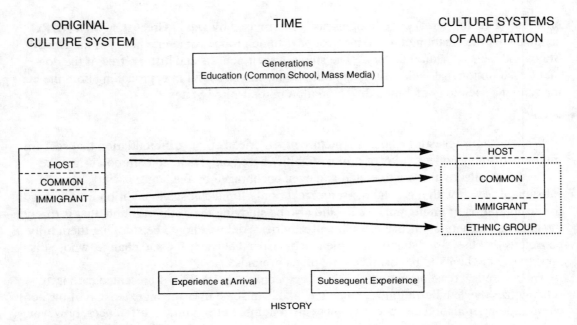

ORIGINAL   TIME   CULTURE SYSTEMS
CULTURE SYSTEM   OF ADAPTATION

Generations
Education (Common School, Mass Media)

HOST
COMMON
IMMIGRANT

HOST
COMMON
IMMIGRANT
ETHNIC GROUP

Experience at Arrival   Subsequent Experience

HISTORY

Figure 1. Ethnogenesis perspective.

versity within a rather more broad and precise framework. I may have only complicated
something already too complex. But the influence of the immigrant groups' experiential history in this country and in the country of origin toward the creation of distinct cultural systems is too important to ignore.

There are two knotty problems to which our picture can at best provide only partial solutions. The first is the question of ethnic origin versus ethnic identification. Approximately
three-quarters of the American public can give an ethnic identification, and approximately
two-thirds have little trouble specifying one such identification. But identification may not
indicate that one's origins are not mixed. Thus one professional colleague, when asked the
nationalities of his four grandparents, claimed French, Dutch, Scots, Irish, and Sioux Indian
ancestry. But when he was asked his ethnic identification he replied "Irish." Such responses
raise two questions. First, How do those of mixed ethnic origins determine which identification they are going to choose? And second, To what extent does such a choice lead to attitudes and behavior that the chooser defines as being pertinent to the identification he has
given himself? Would a "mixed ethnic" with Indian and Irish "blood" in him be more inclined, for example, to political activism because he has defined himself as Irish, and political activism is an "Irish thing"?

The solution to the problem of identification versus origin is in principle relatively easy.
One simply asks both sets of questions and analyzes the interactions between definition and
origin—at least one does so if one has a mammoth sample base that permits the vast variety
of cross-tabulations that would be necessary.

But a far more complex problem is the question of the relationship between ethnic identification and ethnic culture. Three terms must be briefly defined. By "ethnic identification" we mean the place in which one puts oneself in the ethnic chart. By "ethnic heritage" we mean the explicit and conscious recollection of one's past history, either in the Old World or in the United States. By "ethnic culture" we mean attitudes, personality styles, and behaviors that correlate with ethnic identification (or ethnic origin, as the case may be). Thus when an American asserts that he is Polish, he has given his ethnic identification. When he becomes interested in the pro-Jewish legislation of King Casimir the Great and King Stefan Bartori or the Polish involvement in the Little Steel Strike of 1937, he is concerned about his ethnic heritage. When he and his fellow Poles prove more likely on election day to vote than Americans of any other ethnic group and also more likely to vote Democratic, they are manifesting a Polish ethnic culture trait, which probably has far more to do with the experience of the Polish American collectivity than anything in the Polish ancestral past. Ethnic culture, then, is composed of those attitudinal and behavioral traits that correlate with the specific sort of ethnic identification.

Identification, heritage, and culture apparently interrelate in different ways at different times in the natural history of an ethnic group. Thus the American Irish whose ethnic identification may be somewhat weak and whose consciousness of ethnic heritage is weak indeed nonetheless display cultural traits that make them considerably different from other Americans, whether the others be Protestants or their fellow Catholics.

The sorting out of the interrelations of heritage, culture, and identification is a task not even begun. But if one sees the interaction of these three variables as being a part of the natural history of the ethnic group—indeed perhaps the most important part of that natural history—one at least has perspectives from which to begin. Furthermore, one will be fully prepared for the increase in explicit concern about ethnic heritage and the increasingly explicit use of the ethnic identification chart that seems to be occurring among some American ethnic groups at the present time.

Notes

1. I prefer the term "British-American," which was used in pre-Revolutionary days and resurrected before World War I as a response to Irish pressure on the American government.

2. See, for example, Gordon (1964), Lieberson (1963), Zangwill (1917), Kallen (1956), Berkson (1920), and Drachsler (1920).

3. It is true, of course, that a given well-to-do Irishman and the well-to-do Pole may have far more in common with each other than they do with less affluent members of their own ethnic group. I do not want to give the impression here that because I think ethnic differences are important I do not believe that social class differences are important too. Obviously they are.

4. It might be a mistake to conclude that the self-conscious formation of an ethnic group is a new development in American society. One wonders what reason there is to think that the leaders of previous efforts at ethnic group construction were acting unself-consciously.

5. See, for example, the recent writings of Robert Alter, Norman Podhoretz, and Harold Isaacs in *Commentary*.

References

Berkson, Isaac B. *Theories of Americanization: Critical Study*. American Education: Its Men, Institutions and Ideas Series, New York: Arno Press, 1920. Reprinted in 1969.

Brown, Thomas N. *Irish-American Nationalism: Eighteen Seventy to Eighteen Ninety*. Philadelphia: J. B. Lippincott Company, 1966.

Cruse, Harold. *Crisis of the Negro Intellectual*, New York: William Morrow and Company, Inc., 1971.

Drachsler, Julius, *Democracy and Assimilation: The Blending of Immigrant Heritages in America*. Westport, Conn.: Negro University Press, 1920. Reprinted in 1971.

Fabian, Ilona. "The Transformation of Culture Knowledge and the Emergence of Ethnicity Among Czech Immigrants in Chicago." Unpublished research proposal, Department of Anthropology, University of Chicago, 1972.

Gordon, Milton. *Assimilation in American Life*. New York: Oxford University Press, 1964.

Greene, Victor R. *The Slavic Community on Strike*. Notre Dame, Ind.: Notre Dame Press, 1968.

Kallen, Horace M. *Cultural Pluralism and the American Idea*. Philadelphia: University of Pennsylvania Press, 1956.

Kammen, Michael. *People of Paradox*. New York: Alfred A. Knopf, 1972.

Lieberson, Stanley, *Ethnic Patterns in American Cities*. New York: The Free Press, 1963.

Mason, Philip. *Patterns of Dominance*. New York: Oxford University Press, 1970.

Matza, David. *Delinquency and Drift*. New York: John Wiley and Sons, Inc., 1964.

Metzger, L. Paul. "American Sociology and Black Assimilation: Conflicting Perspectives." *American Journal of Sociology*, **76**, 4 (January 1971), pp. 644–647.

Reed, John Shelton. "The Cardinal Test of a Southerner: White Southerners as an Ethnic Group." Unpublished paper, University of North Carolina, 1972.

Schermerhorn, Richard A. *Comparative Ethnic Relations: A Framework for Theory and Research*. New York: Random House, 1969.

Wilensky, Harold L. "Mass Society and Mass Culture." *American Sociological Review*, **29**, 2 (April 1964), pp. 173–197.

Zangwill, Israel. *The Melting Pot*, 2nd revised ed. New York: Macmillan, 1917.

Article 4.3

Colonized and Immigrant Minorities

Robert Blauner

Let us return to the basic assumptions of the third world perspective and examine the idea that a common oppression has created the conditions for effective unity among the constituent racial groups. The third world ideology attempts to promote the consciousness of such common circumstances by emphasizing that the similarities in situation among America's people of color are the essential matter, the differences less relevant. I would like to suggest some problems in this position.

Each third world people has undergone distinctive, indeed cataclysmic, experiences on the American continent that separate its history from the others, as well as from whites. Only Native Americans waged a 300-year war against white encroachment; only they were subject to genocide and removal. Only Chicanos were severed from an ongoing modern nation; only they remain concentrated in the area of their original land base, close to Mexico. Only blacks went through a 250-year period of slavery. The Chinese were the first people whose presence was interdicted by exclusion acts. The Japanese were the one group declared an internal enemy and rounded up in concentration camps. Though the notion of colonized minorities points to a similarity of situation, it should not imply that black, red, yellow, and brown Americans are all in the same bag. Colonization has taken different forms in the histories of the individual groups. Each people is strikingly heterogeneous, and the variables of time, place, and manner have affected the forms of colonialism, the character of racial domination, and the responses of the group.

Because the colonized groups have been concentrated in different regions, geographical isolation has heretofore limited the possibilities of cooperation.* When they have inhabited the same area, competition for jobs has fed ethnic antagonisms. Today, as relatively powerless groups, the racial minorities often find themselves fighting one another for the modicum of political power and material resources involved in antipoverty, model-cities, and educational reform projects. Differences in culture and political style exacerbate these conflicts.

The third world movement will have to deal with the situational differences that are obstacles to coalition and coordinated politics. One of these is the great variation in size between the populous black and Chicano groups and the much smaller Indian and Asian

* The historical accounts also indicate a number of instances of solidarity. A serious study of the history of unity and disunity among third world groups in America is badly needed.

minorities. Numbers affect potential political power as well as an ethnic group's visibility and the possibilities of an assimilative strategy. Economic differentiation may be accelerating both between and within third world groups. The racial minorities are not all poor. The Japanese and, to a lesser extent, the Chinese have moved toward middle-class status. The black middle class also is growing. The ultimate barrier to effective third world alliance is the pervasive racism of the society, which affects people of color as well as whites, furthering division between all groups in America. Colonialism brings into its orbit a variety of groups, which it oppresses and exploits in differing degrees and fashions; the result is a complex structure of racial and ethnic division.

The final assumption of the third world idea remains to be considered. The new perspective represents more than a negation of the immigrant analogy. By its very language the concept assumes an essential connection between the colonized people within the United States and the peoples of Africa, Asia, and Latin America, with respect to whom the idea of *le tiers monde* originated. The communities of color in America share essential conditions with third world nations abroad: economic underdevelopment, a heritage of colonialism and neo-colonialism, and a lack of real political autonomy and power.

This insistence on viewing American race relations from an international perspective is an important corrective to the parochial and ahistorical outlook of our national consciousness. The economic, social, and political subordination of third world groups in America is a microcosm of the position of all peoples of color in the world order of stratification. This is neither an accident nor the result of some essential racial genius. Racial domination in the United States is part of a world historical drama in which the culture, economic system, and political power of the white West has spread throughout virtually the entire globe. The expansion of the West, particularly Europe's domination over non-Western people of color, was the major theme in the almost five hundred years that followed the onset of "The Age of Discovery." The European conquest of Native American peoples, leading to the white settlement of the Western hemisphere, and the African slave trade, were the two leading historical events that ushered in the age of colonialism.* Colonial subjugation and racial domination began much earlier and have lasted much longer in North America than in Asia and Africa, the continents usually thought of as colonial prototypes. The oppression of racial colonies within our national borders cannot be understood without considering worldwide patterns of white European hegemony.

The present movement goes further than simply drawing historical and contemporary parallels between the third world within and third world external to the United States. The new ideology implies that the fate of colonized Americans is tied up with that of the colonial and former colonial peoples of the world. There is at least impressionistic evidence to support this idea. If one looks at the place of the various racial minorities in America's stratified economic and social order, one finds a rough correlation between relative internal status and the international position of the original fatherland. According to most indicators of income, education, and occupation, Native Americans are at the bottom. The Indians alone lack an

---

* The other major event was instituting trade with India.

independent nation, a center of power in the world community to which they might look for political aid and psychic identification. At the other pole, Japanese-Americans are the most successful nonwhite group by conventional criteria, and Japan has been the most economically developed and politically potent non-Western nation during most of the twentieth century. The transformation of African societies from colonial dependency to independent statehood, with new authority and prestige in the international arena, has had an undoubted impact on Afro-Americans in the United States; it has contributed both to civil rights movements and to a developing black consciousness.*

What is not clear is whether an international strategy can in itself be the principle of third world liberation within this country. Since the oppression, the struggle, and the survival of the colonized groups have taken place within our society, it is to be expected that their people will orient their daily lives and their political aspirations to the domestic scene. The racial minorities have been able to wrest some material advantages from American capitalism and empire at the same time that they have been denied real citizenship in the society. Average levels of income, education, and health for the third world in the United States are far above their counterparts overseas; this gap will affect the possibility of internationalism. Besides which, group alliances that transcend national borders have been difficult to sustain in the modern era because of the power of nationalism.

Thus, the situation of the colonized minorities in the United States is by no means identical with that of Algerians, Kenyans, Indonesians, and other nations who suffered under white European rule. Though there are many parallels in cultural and political developments, the differences in land, economy, population composition, and power relations make it impossible to transport wholesale sociopolitical analyses or strategies of liberation from one context to another. The colonial analogy has gained great vogue recently among militant nationalists—partly because it is largely valid, partly because its rhetoric so aggressively condemns white America, past and present. Yet it may be that the comparison with English, French, and Dutch overseas rule lets our nation off too easily! In many ways the special versions of colonialism practices against Americans of color have been more pernicious in quality and more profound in consequences than the European overseas varieties.

In traditional colonialism, the colonized "natives" have usually been the majority of the population, and their culture, while less prestigious than that of the white Europeans, still pervaded the landscape. Members of the third world within the United States are individually and collectively outnumbered by whites, and Anglo-American culture imperatives dominate the society—although this has been less true historically in the Southwest where the

---

* In the early 1970s Pan-Africanism seems to be gaining ground among black American militants and intellectuals. The most celebrated spokesman has been Stokely Carmichael who has virtually eschewed the struggle in the United States. The *Black Scholar* devoted its February and March (1971) issues to Pan-Africanism. Afro-American organizations have been challenging the South African involvements of U.S. business and government, as, for example, in the action of black employees against the Polaroid Corporation. Chicano groups have been taking an active political interest in Mexico and Latin America. On some university campuses Asian militants have taken the lead in protesting American imperialism and genocide in Southeast Asia. Whereas only recently black and brown nationalists tended to see antiwar protest as a white middle-class "trip," the third world perspective has led to an aggressive condemnation of the war in Indochina and a sense of solidarity with the Vietnamese people.

Mexican-American population has never been a true cultural minority. The oppressed masses of Asia and Africa had the relative "advantage" of being colonized in their own land.* In the United States, the more total cultural domination, the alienation of most third world people from a land base, and the numerical minority factor have weakened the group integrity of the colonized and their possibilities for cultural and political self-determination.

Many critics of the third world perspective seize on these differences to question the value of viewing America's racial dynamics within the colonial framework. But all the differences demonstrate is that colonialisms vary greatly in structure and that political power and group liberation are more problematic in our society than in the overseas situation. The fact that we have no historical models for decolonization in the American context does not alter the objective realities. Decolonization is an insistent and irreversible project of the third world groups, although its contents and forms are at present unclear and will be worked out only in the course of an extended period of political and social conflict.

* Within the United States, Native Americans and Chicanos, in general, retain more original culture than blacks and Asians, because they faced European power in their homelands, rather than being transported to the nation of the colonized. Of course the ecological advantage of colonization at home tends to be undermined to the extent to which large European settlements overwhelm numerically the original people, as happened in much of Indo-America. And in much of the Americas a relative cultural integrity among Indian peoples exists at the expense of economic impoverishment and backwardness.

The Prodigal Daughter

Terry Hong

When I was about 11 years old, my grandmother used a Trinitron television to extract a solemn promise: that when the time came, I would agree to marry only a Korean. We sealed the bargain with entwined pinkies and a very expensive, oversized cardboard box marked SONY. As the matriarch of my mother's side of the family (lore has it that we are one of the last direct branches of Korea's final royal dynasty, the Yi* Dynasty), it was a most binding agreement, about equivalent to signing in blood.

The TV lasted much longer than my promise. Because exactly 11 years later, I did the unthinkable—and married someone not of my race.

As recently as four years before my marriage, during a visit to Korea, I remember my grandmother pointing out an interracial couple on the street, and remarking that clearly the Korean girl was either a well-dressed prostitute flaunting her latest client or a wealthy student with her English tutor. So when I married at 22, although my grandmother sent delegates from Korea, she herself did not attend my wedding. Instead she chose to go on a South Seas cruise. It was difficult to leave Korea more than once a year, she explained in a message via my mother, and this year, she needed warmer weather.

Although the relatives who did come managed to enjoy themselves immensely (my mother made sure there was plenty of Korean delicacies in addition to the usual catered wedding fare) and even sent back praise-filled reports of my husband, my grandmother's absence did not go unnoticed.

As I settled into my peripatetic married life (13 moves over the last decade), my grandmother's annual worldly travels waned. Over the past decade, one by one, my at-first resistant relatives met and welcomed my husband. My parents glowed with all the praise heaped on my near-perfect better half. As one aunt raved about his gentleness and generosity, an uncle rejoiced at his sense of humor and adventurousness, a cousin jealously compared him to her spoiled spouse, and so on, until it seemed my husband could do no wrong. All encounters were reported back to my grandmother, every detail intact.

It took eight years and my 30th birthday for my grandmother to actually meet my husband in person; I had decided to face this major milestone in the land of my birth. My parents, who kept an apartment in Seoul, would also be there—to serve as buffers. So we nervously headed for my grandmother's domain. Literally. First stop for us and the en-

* *Different Romanization of same last name: Lee, Yi, Yee, etc.*

tourage of relatives who met us at the airport was my grandmother's apartment, to pay our respects. My husband entered her home and was greeted formally. But he immediately broke all barriers by just stepping up to my grandmother with open arms. The bear hug took my grandmother by complete surprise, but she accepted graciously.

And that set the tone of the 10-day visit. My grandmother chose to accompany us on most of our tourist jaunts to countless palaces, memorials, and historic landmarks. And when she became tired, my husband was right there at her side offering a steady arm. By the end of the trip, the two were actually clowning around. Once he even even carried her on his back for a few paces before my grandmother laughed so hard that they both had to sit down. We left Korea with priceless memories, and my husband with a newly devoted in-law.

Two years later, I was pregnant with our daughter. From throughout the family, scattered whispers still came back to me about how my poor mother worked and sacrificed for her daughter, only to see her betray the family lineage with a biracial daughter. But my mother, more than anyone, was ecstatic. After almost 10 grandchildless years, she had been convinced that she would never have any. When my daughter was born, my mother still claimed that she was far too young to have anyone refer to her as "Halmoni" (Korean for grandmother). But she smiles gleefully every time our daughter calls her so.

But the true test was yet to come. So back it was to Korea, this time for my grandmother's 80th birthday, for which all the relatives were summoned last November. Upon arrival, the greeting entourage again whisked us straight to my grandmother's house. In the car, we primped and preened—not over ourselves, but our one-and-a-half-year-old daughter, for her first true command performance.

This time, it was my grandmother who offered my husband the first hug. Then almost immediately, my grandmother went to our daughter and pointed out the pictures she kept on her mantel—a series of baby pictures, which she announced she rotated regularly, and were the only pictures she kept in her living room, so she could see her great-grandchild every day. Within minutes, our daughter was dancing for her great audience, and squealing with my grandmother in utter, innocent happiness.

In spite of the dread over time changes, not to mention the relatives, the birthday celebration week proved to be a joyful experience. And our daughter, like her father, charmed the entire family, one by one. She was a delightful addition to the Lee family, who took center stage even during my grandmother's actual birthday banquet. As solemn as it was, everyone was smiling at our daughter's antics. Four generations of Lee women, all gathered around to celebrate the rich, long life of the family matriarch. Just imagine the photo opportunities. They did not go unexploited.

We returned from Korea with another child in the making—rather fitting to conceive on home soil. So far, we've only heard congratulations from the Lee relatives. I'm sure some people are still talking about my "poor mother" and her daughter's disloyalty. The child, after all, would be yet another reminder of my 20-year-old broken promise.

In the end, I remain (in)famous as the one—and, still the only—family member to mix the pure blue blood of the Yi dynastic line. But then again, I'm a mere female. Which means that in our Korean family records, neither my name, nor my husband's, nor my daughter's, nor our son-to-be's names will ever be mentioned anywhere. After much meandering, both my brothers have finally found themselves Korean-born spouses, ensuring that even this American-transplanted branch of the Hong family will continue with purity.

In spite of her efforts to preserve the sanctity of Yi blood, the family records will not preserve my grandmother's name either. That absence from the family tree is something my grandmother and I will always have in common, no matter how much my life decisions have diverged from her expectations of me. In the end, I will have cast a mere shadow on the Yi name, as fleeting as the Trinitron that ended up at Goodwill. When we're gone, there will be no records of our existence, on either the Lee or Hong sides, or of my broken promise. But while we're here, we have joy beyond measure in our daughter, in a son about to be born, and in a family bond that has been bent by time and distance, but not broken.

CHAPTER 5

Ethnic Differences in Socioeconomic Achievement

The variation of different ethnic groups in socioeconomic achievement is closely tied to ethnic stratification and ethnic adaptation and is an issue of long-standing concern among scholars, policymakers, and the general public. The four selections in this chapter focus on the causes of ethnic differences in socioeconomic achievement. An excerpt from Richard Herrstein and Charles Murray's 1994 controversial book The Bell Curve *reveals a modern version of the biological argument that stresses genetic differences in intelligence as the key determinant of ethnic inequalities. Thomas Sowell advances a cultural argument that underscores the role of cultural differences in explaining group variation in achievement. While Steven Steinberg does not negate the role of culture, he emphasizes the class position of a group at the time of arrival as an antecedent and more important factor than culture. Alejandro Portes and Rubén Rumbaut take a contextual perspective that accentuates the contexts of receptions encountered by immigrant groups in America and the interaction between individual attributes and contextual factors.*

1. Ethnic Differences in IQ and Ethnic Inequalities
    Richard Herrstein and Charles Murray

2. Culture
    Thomas Sowell

3. Education and Ethnic Mobility
    Stephen Steinberg

4. Making It in America
    Alejandro Portes and Rubén G. Rumbaut

Article 5.1

Ethnic Differences in IQ and Ethnic Inequalities

Richard Herrstein and Charles Murray

Despite the forbidding air that envelops the topic, ethnic differences in cognitive ability are neither surprising nor in doubt. Large human populations differ in many ways, both cultural and biological. It is not surprising that they might differ at least slightly in their cognitive characteristics. That they do is confirmed by the data on ethnic differences in cognitive ability from around the world. One message of this chapter is that such differences are real and have consequences. Another is that the facts are not as alarming as many people seem to fear.

East Asians (e.g., Chinese, Japanese), whether in America or in Asia, typically earn higher scores on intelligence and achievement tests than white Americans. The precise size of their advantage is unclear; estimates range from just a few to ten points. A more certain difference between the races is that East Asians have higher nonverbal intelligence than whites while being equal, or perhaps slightly lower, in verbal intelligence.

The difference in test scores between African-Americans and European-Americans as measured in dozens of reputable studies has converged on approximately a one standard deviation difference for several decades. Translated into centiles, this means that the average white person tests higher than about 84 percent of the population of blacks and that the average black person tests higher than about 16 percent of the population of whites.

The average black and white differ in IQ at every level of socioeconomic status (SES), but they differ more at high levels of SES than at low levels. Attempts to explain the difference in terms of test bias have failed. The tests have approximately equal predictive force for whites and blacks.

In the past few decades, the gap between blacks and whites narrowed by perhaps three IQ points. The narrowing appears to have been mainly caused by a shrinking number of very low scores in the black population rather than an increasing number of high scores. Improvements in the economic circumstances of blacks, in the quality of the schools they attend, in better public health, and perhaps also diminishing racism may be narrowing the gap.

The debate about whether and how much genes and environment have to do with ethnic differences remains unresolved. The universality of the contrast in nonverbal and verbal skills between East Asians and European whites suggests, without quite proving, genetic roots. Another line of evidence pointing toward a genetic factor in cognitive ethnic differences is that blacks and whites differ most on the tests that are the best measures of g, or general intelligence. On the other hand, the scores on even highly g-loaded tests can be influenced to some extent by changing environmental factors over the course of a decade or less. Beyond that, some social scientists have challenged the premise that intelligence tests have the same meaning for people who live in different cultural settings or whose forebears had very different histories.

Nothing seems more fearsome to many commentators than the possibility that ethnic and race differences have any genetic component at all. This belief is a fundamental error. Even if the differences between races were entirely genetic (which they surely are not), it should make no practical difference in how individuals deal with each other. The real danger is that the elite wisdom on ethnic differences—that such differences cannot exist—will shift to opposite and equally unjustified extremes. Open and informed discussion is the one certain way to protect society from the dangers of one extreme view or the other.

Article 5.2

Culture

Thomas Sowell

Whether in an ethnic context or among peoples and nations in general, much depends on the whole constellation of values, attitudes, skills, and contacts that many call a culture and that economists call "human capital." For more than a century, people have marveled at how quickly some nations recover economically from the utter devastation of war. The so-called German miracle after World War II was only the most recent example of something that has happened before in other places. What war destroys is the tangible physical capital of a nation—its cities, factories, farms, railroads, and highways. What it does not destroy is the human capital that built all these things in the first place—and can build them again. John Stuart Mill pointed out more than a century ago that the physical elements of an advanced economy wear out and are used up in a few years, and would have to be replaced anyway. What war does is speed up this process. But continued progress depends on what people know and will do.

The importance of human capital in an ethnic context is shown in many ways. Groups that arrived in America financially destitute have rapidly risen to affluence, when their cultures stressed the values and behavior required in an industrial and commercial economy. Even when color and racial prejudices confronted them—as in the case of the Chinese and Japanese—this proved to be an impediment but was ultimately unable to stop them. Nor was their human capital even a matter of bringing specific skills with them, such as those of the Jews in clothing production or of the Germans in beer production. The Chinese and Japanese came as unskilled young men working in the fields tending crops—but working harder and more relentlessly than anyone else. Later, the ubiquitous Chinese hand laundry did not require any technical skill not already possessed by the Irish or the black washerwoman of the same era. But the Irish and the blacks never set up laundries, or any other businesses, with the frequency of the Chinese or Japanese, although the two Asian groups were initially hampered by lack of money and lack of English, as well as by a lack of technical skills. Japanese gardeners did not have to master any equipment more technical than a lawnmower. What made these humble occupations avenues to affluence was the effort, thrift, dependability, and foresight that built businesses out of "menial" tasks and turned sweat into capital. In the same way, many Jewish pushcart peddlers eventually became storeowners, and sometimes owners of whole chains of stores.

International comparisons of ethnic group progress reinforce the importance of human capital. In the United States, Canada, Great Britain, and Israel, the same striking pattern emerges: immigrants begin economically below the level of existing members of their own ethnic group already in the country, but eventually rise to not only equal but surpass them.[1] In the United States, native-born Americans of Cuban, Japanese, Mexican, Negro, or Filipino ancestry are overtaken by immigrants of the *same* respective ancestry. Cuban immigrants reached the income level of native-born Cuban Americans after eighteen years and surpassed them thereafter. Mexican immigrants take fifteen years to overtake native-born Mexican Americans. Japanese immigrants take eighteen years to overtake native-born Japanese Americans. Immigrants from the Philippines overtake native-born Filipino Americans in thirteen years, and black West Indian immigrants overtake native black Americans in eleven years.[2]

The lengthy period required to equal the economic level of people of the same race or ethnicity born on American soil suggests something of the amount of human capital needed—not simply the technical skills (which could usually be acquired in much shorter time), but the whole spectrum of experience, contacts, personal and institutional savvy, confidence, and ease. However, the fact that immigrants not only equal but eventually surpass their native-born counterparts also suggests that they brought some advantage in terms of human capital, that migration is a *selective* process, bringing the more ambitious or venturesome or able elements of a population. Once they acquire all the other kinds of human capital they need, this advantage (or these advantages) begin to tell. This also implies a difference between selective immigration and unselective, wholesale refugee flight. The famine Irish of the 1840s were more like refugees, fleeing a national catastrophe in which people were literally dying in the streets. Their slow and difficult adjustment in the United States may in part reflect that. Immigrants from Meiji Japan may have had no more skills in the naïve sense, but were much more selectively chosen for personal qualities, as well as partially acculturated to American norms and goals in Japan itself.

Specific skills are a prerequisite in many kinds of work. But history shows new skills being rather readily acquired in a few years, as compared to the generations—or centuries—required for *attitude* changes. Groups today plagued by absenteeism, tardiness, and a need for constant supervision at work or in school are typically descendants of people with the same habits a century or more ago. The cultural inheritance can be more important than biological inheritance, although the latter stirs more controversy. In special isolated circumstances, where the necessary values and disciplines had developed, among small segments of blacks, for example, the skills and the economic results have followed. Among the more striking examples were the hundreds of small businesses established in the depths of the Great Depression by the very lowest income (and usually ill-educated) followers of Father Divine. The success of their businesses,[3] founded under such wholly unpromising circumstances, contrasts with the massive business failures under the government-sponsored "black capitalism" programs of the 1960s and 1970s.[4] Although the latter have had more financial support and/or "experts" available, the Father Divine cult developed more human capital in terms of both individual discipline and group cooperation. The Black Muslims have also achieved business success while drawing on the least educated and lowest income segments of the black population.[5] The importance of human capital is also shown in areas dealing with education. The most successful black high school, in terms of either student test scores or alumni career successes, was also a school with less absenteeism or tardiness than white schools in the same city.[6] It was not simply that either absenteeism or tardiness, as such, was so important, as that a set of attitudes toward school caused students to be there consistently and on time.

It is sometimes believed that educational success requires that the children come from homes well stocked with books and magazines, and have the benefit of continual parent-child verbal interaction, after the model of Jewish immigrant homes. But Japanese-American homes did not meet any of these specifications,[7] and yet their children's achievements in school were outstanding. One of the great political and legal crusades of the twentieth century—school "integration"—has been based on the theory that the differences between being ethnically concentrated and being mixed with children from other ethnic backgrounds is so crucial as to make the whole educational experience itself inferior without them.[8] However, history shows that ethnic groups with different attitudes toward education perform as differently in the same school as in different schools. The differences between Japanese and Mexican-American children attending the same schools have been as great as differences between blacks and whites attending separate schools in the segregated South. Differences between Jewish and Puerto Rican children attending the same school for decades have been even greater,[9]

Diversities of culture have caused intergroup friction from both substantive differences in values and beliefs and from different forms of social coding to convey the same feelings or attitudes. A look, a gesture, a tone of voice, or a set of casual remarks may mean something very different in one culture than in another—causing continual misunderstandings and senses of uneasiness, affront, or hostility.[10] Moreover, personal clashes in an intergroup setting can readily spread from particular individuals to involve other members of each group in the vicinity. The educational and other social advantages of cultural diversity have varied with whether the association was voluntary or by force. For example, early studies of voluntarily integrated schools showed increased racial amity and educational benefits—providing a basis for *compulsory* integration under court orders, which produced opposite results.[11] Ethnically different families brought together in government housing projects—seeking low rents rather than diversity—have often socially segregated themselves, although statistically "integrated."[12]

Cultures are not "superior" or "inferior." They are better or worse adapted to a particular set of circumstances. The most successful of all American ethnic groups—the Jews—had a succession of utter failures in agriculture.[13] Their centuries of acculturation to urban society were as much a hindrance on the farm as they were an advantage in the city.

Personal blame seems especially out of place in dealing with historic forces beyond the control of any individual. It would be fatuous to blame emigrants from Mexico for not bringing with them the skills or other traits brought by emigrants from Germany. It seems equally fatuous to blame employers for not having Mexicans and Germans proportionally represented in jobs requiring such skills or traits.[14]

Acculturation has sometimes been depicted as a one-way process, in which racial and ethnic groups have been forced to surrender their respective cultures and conform to Anglo-Saxon practices. In reality, the American culture is built on the food, the language, the attitudes, and the skills from numerous groups. The old Anglo-Saxon Puritan resistance to social recreation was long ago overwhelmed by the German easygoing attitude of good clean fun, which is now considered the hallmark of Americans in general. American popular music has its roots in the black musical tradition that produced jazz and the blues. American political machines have been predominantly Irish political machines. Nothing is more American than hamburgers or frankfurters, although both names derive from German cities. Pizza and tacos are not far behind. None of these features of American culture is descended from the British settlers. They are a common heritage, despite ethnic diversities that still exist. Budweiser is drunk in Harlem, Jews eat pizza, and Chinese restaurants are patronized by customers who are obviously not Chinese.

Groups that have the skills and entrepreneurship to be self-employed, or to employ one another, have not even had to learn English in order to prosper. The German farmers and Jewish garment industry workers of nineteenth-century America, or the Japanese-American farmers of the early twentieth century, were able to rise economically with little acculturation, and despite varying degrees of hostility. It is the groups that *lack* such skills and entrepreneurship that are dependent on others for employment and that have had to learn to speak their language and know enough of their culture to make working together reasonably comfortable.

The "melting pot" was once a popular image of American assimilation, but is now a disdained concept. Ironically, there was relatively little intermarriage during the era of "melting pot" theories, but such intermarriage is now much more widespread in the era when the concept is rejected by intellectuals. More than half of all marriages among Americans of German, Irish, British, or Polish ancestry are with people of different ethnicity, and Italian and Japanese Americans are not far behind. Even groups with low rates of intermarriage—blacks, Jews, Hispanics—nevertheless have rising levels of intermarriage.

Notes

1. See the path-breaking research of Barry Chiswick, "The Economic Progress of Immigrants: Some Apparently Universal Patterns," in *Contemporary Economic Problems, 1979*, ed. William Fellner (Washington, D.C.: American Enterprise Institute, 1979), pp. 357–399.

2. Ibid, pp. 333–334.

3. Ivan H. Light, *Ethnic Enterprise in America* (Berkeley: University of California Press, 1972), pp. 141–151.

4. Some of the misconceptions behind this concept are explored in Walter E. Williams, "Some Hard Questions on Minority Business," *Negro Educational Review*, April–July 1974, pp. 123–142.

5. Theodore Draper, *The Rediscovery of Black Nationalism* (New York: The Viking Press, 1970), p. 84.

6. Thomas Sowell, "Patterns of Black Excellence," *The Public Interest*, Spring 1976, p. 51.

7. Harry H. L. Kitano, *Japanese Americans* (Englewood Cliffs, N.J.: Prentice-Hall, 1969), p. 72.

8. *Brown v. Board of Education of Topeka*, 347 VS 483 (1954).

9. Thomas Sowell, "Assumptions Versus History in Ethnic Education," in *The State of American Education*, ed. Diane Ravitch (forthcoming).

10. Gerald D. Suttles, *The Social Order of the Slum* (Chicago: University of Chicago Press, 1973), pp. 62, 63, 66, 103, 128; Stephen Birmingham, *Certain People* (Boston: Little, Brown and Co., 1977), p. 67; Richard Gambino, *Blood of My Blood* (New York: Anchor Books, 1974), pp. 235–236.

11. Norman Miller and H. B. Gerard, "How Busing Failed at Riverside," *Psychology Today*, June 1976, pp. 66–67ff.

12. Suttles, *The Social Order of the Slum*, pp. 28, 56.

13. Maldwyn Allen Jones, *American Immigration* (Chicago: University of Chicago Press, 1960), pp. 212–213.

14. See Thomas Sowell, *"Weber and Bakke* and the Presuppositions of 'Affirmative Action,'" *Wayne Law Review*, July 1980, pp. 1309–1336.

Article 5.3

Education and Ethnic Mobility

Stephen Steinberg

"If our children don't go to school, no harm results. But if the sheep don't eat, they will die. The school can wait but not our sheep."

An Italian peasant, quoted in Leonard Covello,
The Social Background of the Italo-American School Child, 1967.

Horace Mann, the architect of the common school, once described education as "the great equalizer." Implicitly Mann recognized that the schools would function within the context of class inequality, providing the less privileged members of society with opportunities for social and economic advancement. In *Democracy and Education* John Dewey also wrote that "it is the office of the school environment...to see to it that each individual gets an opportunity to escape from the limitations of the social group in which he was born, and to come into living contact with a broader environment."[1] To this day, it is an article of faith in American society that education is the key to material success, and the key to eliminating social inequalities as well.

Consistent with this liberal faith in education, two general assumptions run through the social science literature on education and ethnic mobility. The first is that those ethnic groups that have taken advantage of educational opportunities have, for that reason, enjoyed comparative mobility and success. The second assumption is that the values of some groups have been conducive to intellectual achievement, whereas other groups have been saddled with anti-intellectual values or other cultural traits that discouraged their children from pursuing educational opportunities. This "theory" is thus a variant of the more general theory of ethnic success discussed earlier.

As before, issue arises not with the fact that ethnic groups vary in educational attainment, but with the assumption that this reflects the operation of cultural factors, such as the degree to which education is valued. How do we know that some ethnic groups value education more highly? Because they have a superior record of educational attainment. Obviously, it is incorrect to infer values from the outcome, and then to posit these values as causal factors. To prove the cultural thesis, it is necessary to furnish independent evidence that some groups placed special value on education, and that this factor operated in its own right as a determinant of educational achievement.

Yet a number of writers have claimed such evidence by pointing to the cultural systems of certain ethnic groups that are thought to be compatible or incompatible with the requirements of modern education. This argument is commonly made with respect to Asians and Jews, both of whom have in fact achieved higher levels of education than most other groups in American society.

For example, in his book on Japanese-Americans William Petersen begins with the factual observation that "since 1940, the Japanese have had more schooling than any other race in the American population, including whites."[2] He then proceeds to explain the high educational levels of Japanese-Americans as an outgrowth of a particular set of cultural values. On the basis of his examination of the records of Japanese students at Berkeley during the late 1950s and early 1960s, Petersen writes: "Their education had been conducted like a military campaign against a hostile world, with intelligent planning and tenacity....In a word, these young men and women were squares."[3] Irrespective of Petersen's questionable metaphor (would enterprising Jewish or Italian students be described as waging a military campaign, or is this imagery reserved for the Japanese?), his characterization of such students as "squares" is most revealing. According to Petersen, the "cultural traditions" of Japanese produced diligent, persevering, and industrious students who eschewed the pleasures of the moment in their dogged pursuit of long-range goals. Like the "old-fashioned boys" in Horatio Alger's novels, it is the squares who ultimately triumph.

In her praise of Chinese educational achievement, Betty Sung is even more explicit in tracing this to a specific "cultural heritage." According to Sung:

> Chinese respect for learning and for the scholar is a cultural heritage. Even when a college degree led to no more than a waiter's job, the Chinese continued to pursue the best education they could get, so that when opportunities developed, the Chinese were qualified and capable of handling their jobs. Other minorities have not had the benefit of this reverence for learning.[4]

For Sung, the Chinese reverence for learning is not merely characteristic of Chinese-Americans, but is a product of a cultural heritage rooted in centuries of history.

Of course, it is the Jews who are most often acclaimed, in folklore and social science alike, as a "people of the book." The implication here is that Jews owe their intellectual prominence to a reverence for learning that is rooted in their religious culture and that has been passed down through the ages. There is hardly a study of Jews in America that does not cite a "Jewish passion for education" as a major factor, if not *the* major factor, in explaining Jewish mobility. A typical exposition of this idea is found in Marshall Sklare's 1971 book on *America's Jews*:

> Jewish culture embraced a different attitude toward learning from that which characterized the dominant societies of eastern Europe. This Jewish attitude was part of the value-system of the immigrants. It pertains to learning in general, though in the traditional framework it is most apparent with respect to the study of religious subjects.[5]

According to Sklare and numerous others, the high valuation that Jews traditionally placed on religious learning was, in the New World, transferred to secular learning, and with this cultural head start, the children of Jewish immigrants were quick to climb the educational ladder.

A large number of empirical studies have documented Jewish intellectual achievements. It is known that, compared with most other groups, Jews are more likely to go to college, especially highly competitive colleges, to excel once they are there, and to go on to graduate and professional schools. Studies have also shown that Jews are disproportionately represented among the teaching faculties of the nation's colleges and universities and this is especially so in the leading research institutions.[6] Still other studies have shown that Jews have produced more than their share of eminent scholars and scientists, and of course there has been much preoccupation with the fact that Marx, Freud, and Einstein, three of the towering figures of modern history, have been Jewish.[7] As in the case of Jewish economic success, the fact of Jewish intellectual prominence can hardly be disputed. Rather it is the interpretation of this fact—specifically, the notion that Jewish educational achievements result from a reverence for learning embedded in Jewish history and culture—that is problematic.

An alternative to this cultural theory is a social class theory that does not deny the operation of cultural factors, but sees them as conditional on preexisting class factors. Whereas the cultural theory holds that certain groups placed unusually high value on education, which resulted in greater mobility, the class theory turns this proposition around, and holds that economic mobility occurred first, and that this opened up channels of educational opportunity and engendered a corresponding set of values and aspirations favorable to education. Obviously, education allowed these groups to consolidate and extend their economic gains, but these were gains that initially occurred in the occupational marketplace without the benefit of extensive education.

This is not to deny the well-documented fact that Japanese, Chinese, and Jews all placed high value on education; nor does the class theory deny that reverence for education may be rooted in the traditional belief systems of these groups. Where the class theory differs from the cultural theory is in its emphasis on the *primacy* of class factors. That is to say, it is held that cultural factors have little independent effect on educational outcomes, but are influential only as they interact with class factors. Thus, to whatever extent a reverence for learning was part of the religious and cultural heritage of Asians and Jews, it was activated and given existential significance by their social class circumstances. Without this congruence between culture and circumstance, it is hardly conceivable that these groups could have sustained their traditional value on education, or that it would have actually resulted in higher levels of educational achievement.

Notes

1. Quoted in Samuel Bowles and Herbert Gintis, *Schooling in Capitalist America* (New York: Basic Books, 1976), p. 21.

2. William Petersen, *Japanese Americans* (New York: Random House, 1971), p. 113.

3. Ibid., pp. 115–16.

4. Betty Sue Sung, *The Story of the Chinese in America* (New York: Macmillan, 1967), pp. 124–25.

5. Marshall Sklare, *America's Jews* (New York: Random House, 1971), p. 58.

6. Stephen Steinberg, *The Academic Melting Pot* (New York: McGraw-Hill, 1974), chap. 5.

7. Tina Levitan, *The Laureates: Jewish Winners of the Nobel Prize* (New York: Twayne Publishers, Inc., 1960); Nathaniel Weyl and Stefan Possony, *The Geography of Intellect* (Chicago: Henry Regnery, 1913), pp. 123–28.

Article 5.4

Making It in America

Alejandro Portes and Rubén G. Rumbaut

Explaining the Differences: Modes of Incorporation

There are two ways to "make it" in America, at least legally. The first is the salaried professional/managerial route; the other is independent entrepreneurship. There is no doubt that what immigrants "bring with them"—motivation, knowledge, and resources—is a decisive feature affecting whether they will gain entry into one or another path of economic mobility. The typology of immigration is essentially a qualitative summary of basic resource endowments. For example, manual immigration is generally characterized by low levels of education and occupational skills and an absence of prior entrepreneurial experience. This scarcity of human capital, characterizing immigrants of modest origin, makes raw physical power their principal marketable asset in the American labor market.

Professional immigration is characterized by high levels of education and skill. These resources may not translate immediately into highly paid positions because of language difficulties and lack of job-seeking experience. Over time, however, education and professional training tend to give these immigrants a significant edge in gaining access to better-paid positions. Similarly, entrepreneurial flows are distinguished by a substantial number of immigrants with prior business experience. These skills may remain dormant for a while, as new arrivals struggle with language and customs at the receiving end. However, with increasing time and familiarity with the host economy, many are able to reenact past experience by eventually moving into self-employment.

Hence, time is an important variable influencing socioeconomic achievement, but it is so for some groups more than for others. As the previously discussed research shows, earnings tend to increase with number of years since arrival. However, the process is likely to be more accelerated for those who possess skills and resources than for those who must rely on their physical energy. Among refugee groups, time has a different meaning because it is often associated with a declining socioeconomic background. Earlier refugees tend to come from the elite and middle classes; later cohorts increasingly resemble the mass of the sending country's population. The fate of these late arrivals depends, to a large extent, on the kind of community created by their co-nationals. This contingent outcome already calls attention to the significance of the contexts of reception met by newcomers.

An emphasis on the different modes in which immigrants can become incorporated into the host society is a way to overcome the limitations of exclusively individualistic models of immigrant achievement. The basic idea is simple: Individuals with similar background skills may be channeled toward very different positions in the stratification system, depending on the type of community and labor market in which they become incorporated. This process can help explain differences in occupation, business ownership, and income among immigrants who are statistically "equal" in a host of individual characteristics. However, it is not sufficient to point to the importance of context, just as it is not enough to attribute persistent income differences to an "ethnic group effect." We must move beyond this level of generalization to specify at least what some of these contextual factors are and how they operate.

Contexts of Reception

For immigrants, the most relevant contexts of reception are defined by the policies of the receiving government, the conditions of the host labor market, and the characteristics of their own ethnic communities. The combination of positive and negative features encountered at each of these levels determines the distinct mode of newcomers' incorporation. Governments are important because their policies determine whether sizable immigration flows can begin at all and, once under way, the forms they will take. Although occasional surreptitious immigrants may filter in, regular migration flows of predictable size and direction emerge only with the consent of governments. This consent need not be explicit, however. Underground labor flows may be tacitly permitted, as has been the case in the United States at least until the 1980s.[1] In every instance, governmental policy represents the first stage of the process of incorporation because it affects the probability of successful immigration and the legal framework in which it is to take place.

Although a continuum of possible governmental responses toward foreign groups exists, basic options are only three: exclusion, passive acceptance, or active encouragement. When enforced, exclusion precludes immigration or forces immigrants into a wholly underground existence. The second alternative is defined by the act of granting access, explicitly or implicitly, without any additional effort to facilitate or impede the process. Most economically motivated immigration to the United States in recent years has taken place under this alternative. The third governmental option occurs when authorities take active steps to encourage a particular inflow or to facilitate its resettlement. At various times during the nineteenth and twentieth centuries, the U.S. government was directly involved in recruiting laborers or skilled workers deemed to be in short supply domestically.[2]

During the last three decades, active governmental intervention to stimulate migration or facilitate its resettlement has been restricted to selected refugee inflows. Governmental support is important because it gives newcomers access to an array of resources that do not exist for other immigrants. However, the interaction of this contextual dimension with individual characteristics can lead to very different outcomes. If for refugees with professional or business skills, governmental assistance is a means to accelerate social integration and economic mobility; for those lacking these resources, it can be a means to perpetuate social dependence and economic marginalization.[3]

Labor markets represent the second dimension in contexts of reception. Clearly, several features affect the economic prospects for immigrants. These features—such as stage in the business cycle, demand for specific kinds of labor, and regional wage differentials—have been discussed at length in the economic literature as potential determinants of earnings. However, there is a sociological aspect of labor markets that is perhaps more significant, namely, the manner in which particular immigrant groups are typified. Employers as a whole may be indifferent toward a particular group, or they may have a positive or negative view of it. Positive or negative typification of a specific minority can take, in turn, different forms. For example, widespread discrimination may hold that certain groups should be confined to low-wage menial labor ("Mexican work" or, in an earlier time, "coolie labor") or it can hold that they are simply too incompetent to be employable at all. In the first instance, discrimination contributes to confinement of the group to the low-wage segment of the labor market; in the second, it contributes to its exclusion and hence unemployment.[4]

Positive typification, as opposed to mere neutrality, has been far less common. Preferential hiring of immigrants as workers tends to occur only when employers are of the same nationality. Hence, when a segment of the local labor market is composed of ethnic firms, immigrants of the same origin often gravitate toward them in search of employment opportunities unavailable elsewhere.[5]

These various labor market situations interact, of course, with individual skills and resources, leading to a plurality of outcomes. The main difference lies in the ability of different types of immigrants to neutralize labor market discrimination. Lack of resources and information makes discrimination most serious for immigrant laborers who are generally trapped in positions held to be "appropriate" for their group. Professionals and business people can escape discrimination either by moving to other parts of the country or by disguising their nationality, a strategy that explains the frequent reluctance of high-status members of stereotyped minorities to identify with their own group.[6]

The ethnic community itself represents the third and most immediate dimension of the context of reception. A first option is that no such community exists, in which case immigrants must confront the host labor market directly. If employers do not discriminate against the newcomers, the situation approaches the ideal one assumed by individualistic human capital models, because presumably only the person's education and other resources will affect his or her earnings. Among present-day immigrants, this situation is most closely approximated by professionals, who frequently accept jobs away from areas of ethnic concentration, and by refugees, resettled by government or voluntary agencies outside the same areas.

Most common, however, is the arrival of immigrants into places where an ethnic community already exists. A common sociological observation is that such communities cushion the impact of cultural change and protect immigrants against outside prejudice and initial economic difficulties. As important as this observation is the fact that the process of socioeconomic attainment in this context is entirely network driven. Ethnic networks provide sources of information about outside employment, sources of jobs inside the community, and sources of credit and support for entrepreneurial ventures. Because subtracting themselves from the influence of kin and friends is difficult for newcomers in the early stages of adaptation, the characteristics of the ethnic community acquire decisive importance in molding their entry into the labor market and hence their prospects for future mobility.[7]

Ethnic communities vary widely in a number of dimensions, but from the perspective of economic achievement, the central difference is whether they are composed primarily of manual workers or contain a significant professional or business element. All ethnic groups promote their own, but how they do so varies significantly across these situations. For new immigrants in working-class communities, the natural path is to follow the course of earlier arrivals. The help that ethnic networks can provide for securing employment in this situation tends to be constrained by the kind of jobs already held by more established members of the community. In addition, there is often a kind of collective expectation that new arrivals should not be "uppity" and should not try to surpass, at least at the start, the collective status of their elders.

In this fashion, immigrants of above-average ability and motivation find themselves in low-status manual jobs and restricted in their chances for future mobility. Ethnic-network assistance comes at the cost of ethnic pressures for conformity, and the latter often reinforce employer's expectations about the "natural" position of the minority in the labor market. These dynamics help explain the self-perpetuating character of working-class immigrant communities and the frequent tendency among their members to receive lower than average rewards for their past human capital.[8]

The dominant feature of the opposite situation—where a substantial number of community members hold higher-status occupations—is that the support of ethnic networks is not contingent on acceptance of a working-class life-style or outlook. Hence, newcomers, dependent as always on the assistance of kin and friends, may be introduced from the start to the whole range of opportunities available in the host labor market. Within this general pattern, entrepreneurial communities have the additional advantage of being not only sources of information about outside jobs, but sources of employment opportunities themselves. Immigrant firms tend to hire and promote their own; and, as seen previously, they often represent the only segment of the labor market in which newcomers can find employment.

In the past, there was a common belief that jobs in co-ethnic firms were equivalent to those in the lower tier of the outside labor market, insofar as both constrained future mobility opportunities. However, more recent research indicates that this is not the case, because employment within an ethnic enclave is often the best route for promotion into supervisory and managerial positions and for business ownership. These studies have found that education brought from the home country can have a greater economic payoff in ethnic firms than in outside ones and that a key factor promoting business ownership is prior employment in firms owned by persons of the same nationality.[9]

The complexity of modes of incorporation for recent immigrants is more fully appreciated when we combine the three dimensions discussed previously. Figure 1 portrays this diversity. It is a highly simplified portrait because it brings together several of the previously discussed alternatives that are themselves simplifications of real-life situations. Nonetheless, the twelve alternative contexts of incorporation outlined in the figure provide a summary statement of the variety of conditions that newcomers can find on arrival.

I. U.S. Government Policy:	II. Labor Market Reception:	III. Ethnic Community:		
		None[d]	Working Class	Entrepreneurial/ Professional
Passive acceptance	Neutral or positive[b]	Argentines 92,563 30.9 $35,000 11.3	Italians 580,592 8.6 $29,369 8.0	Greeks 177,398 14.8 $33,500 9.1
	Discriminatory[c]	Nigerians 55,350 64.2 $25,500 13.6	Mexicans 4,298,014 3.5 $21,926 29.7	Jamaicans 334,140 14.9 $30,599 12.1
Active support[a]	Neutral or positive[b]	Romanians 91,106 28.8 $35,000 15.8	Polish 388,328 16.3 $29,948 9.7	Cubans 736,971 15.6 $27,292 14.7
	Discriminatory[c]	Ethiopians 34,805 29.3 $26,000 27.2	Laotians 171,577 5.1 $19,671 40.3	Vietnamese 543,262 15.9 $30,039 25.5

Figure 1.   Contexts of reception of recent immigrant groups in the United States, 1990.

SOURCE: U.S. Bureau of the Census, *The Foreigh Born Population in the United States*, CP-3-1 (Washington, D.C.: U.S. Department of Commerce, July 1993), Tables 1, 3, 5; and data drawn from 5% Public Use Microdata Sample (PUMS) of the 1990 U.S. Census, subject to sample variability.

NOTE: The four figures for each nationality are absolute numbers of foreign-born persons from that nationality in 1990, followed by the percentage of adults who completed four years or more of college, the median household income in 1989 dollars, and the poverty rate.

[a] Accorded in recent years only to legal refugee groups.
[b] Accorded primarily to white immigrants.
[c] Experienced primarily by nonwhite immigrants.
[d] Foreigh-born groups of fewer than 100,000 not concentrated in a particular location.

The nationalities in each cell are instances of each context of reception as new immigrants from the respective country would have found it at the beginning of the 1990s. To illustrate, recent Argentine immigrants arrive in a situation in which their co-nationals—a relatively small group to begin with—are highly dispersed. Absence of a sizable ethnic community is compensated for in this case by the lack of widespread discrimination because of these immigrants' generally high educations and white features.

Mexicans face a situation in which a concatenation of historical and geographical circumstances has led to the identification of their group as a source of manual wage labor in many regions of the country. Mostly mestizo, new immigrants face stereotypes about what is suitable "Mexican work" and join working-class communities likely to channel them into this type of occupation. Such contexts help explain the consistent labor market disadvantage experienced by Mexicans and their persistent gap in earnings, after controlling for education and work experience.[10]

Another significant contrast in figure 3 is between Jamaican and certain African immigrants, exemplified by the Nigerians. Both are black minorities that face generalized race prejudice in the American labor market. Over the years, however, Jamaicans and other black West Indians have constituted communities with a relatively high proportion of professionals and entrepreneurs. Fifty percent of the U.S. Jamaican population concentrates in New York City; and its rate of self-employment, although still low by U.S. standards, exceeds significantly those of other Caribbean groups such as Dominicans, Haitians, and Puerto Ricans. In 1989, Jamaican household earnings were on a par with the national median.

Nigerians are a much smaller and more recently arrived group that lacks an established ethnic base and must therefore confront U.S. labor market conditions directly. This situation may help explain why, despite very high levels of educational attainment and high proportions in declared professional occupations, Nigerian household incomes are significantly lower than Jamaican and amounted to only 80 percent of the national median in 1989.[11]

Among nationalities formed by recent political inflows and thus eligible for governmental assistance, Ethiopians represent a similar case of a small and recently arrived group. Unlike refugees from Eastern European countries, racial and cultural markers identify Ethiopians as potential targets of labor market discrimination, a disadvantage that cannot be neutralized through participation in a weak ethnic economy. This situation helps explain the high poverty and low median earnings of Ethiopian households in 1989, despite high levels of education and declared professional backgrounds.

This mode of incorporation may be contrasted with that confronting recent Cuban refugees, where an older community has created a fairly stable ethnic economy. In 1989, Cuban household earnings were closer to the national median, despite educational achievements much lower than those of the Ethiopians and other recently arrived groups. The Cuban ethnic economy helps explain why, according to recent evidence, about half the refugees who arrived during the 1980 Mariel exodus were employed in firms owned by co-nationals, and close to 20 percent had become self-employed after only six years of U.S. residence.[12]

Among Southeast Asian refugees, the Vietnamese have started following a similar path, characterized by increasing spatial concentration and an emerging business enclave. Although the Vietnamese are still far below older entrepreneurial groups, their rates of business participation appear to be increasing. This trend contrasts with the situation of other Southeast Asian refugees, best represented by the Laotians, who are far more dispersed and have low rates of business ownership. Existing Laotian communities remain highly dependent on public assistance and on manual wage labor. Hence, despite their comparable lengths of residence in the United States, Vietnamese median incomes in 1989 were far above those of Laotian households. The latter represented about 65 percent of the national figure.

In conclusion, making it in America is a complex process, dependent only partially on the motivation and abilities that immigrants bring with them. How they use these personal resources often depends on international political factors, over which individuals have no control, and on the history of earlier arrivals and the types of communities they have created, about which newcomers also have little say. These complex and involuntary forces confront the foreign born as an objective reality that channels them in different directions.

Afterwards, apologists of successful groups will make necessities out of contingencies and uncover those "unique" traits underlying their achievements; detractors of impoverished minorities will describe those cultural shortcomings or even genetic limitations accounting for their condition. Both are likely to affirm that, in the end, "if there is a will, there is a way."

Greater knowledge of the contexts immigrants face at present gives a lie to such assertions because it demonstrates the importance of the modes in which they are incorporated and the resulting material and moral resources made available by governments, employers, and their own communities. The most hardworking individuals may thus end up in poor jobs simply because they perceive no alternatives or none are available; others may rise to the top, riding in the wake of a lucky set of circumstances. Social context renders individualistic models insufficient because it can alter, in decisive ways, the link between individual skills and their expected rewards.

Notes

1. See Bustamante, "The Historical Context"; Cornelius, "Mexican Migration to the United States: Causes"; Bach, "Mexican Immigration"; Portes, "Illegal Immigration."

2. On manual labor recruitment, see Grebler, Moore, and Guzman, *The Mexican-American People*; Bach, "Mexican Immigration"; Wood, "Caribbean Cane Cutters." On professional recruitment, see Stevens, Goodman, and Mick, *The Alien Doctors*; Portes, "Determinants of the Brain Drain"; Glaser and Habers, "The Migration and Return"; Rumbaut, "Passages to America."

3. The case of recently arrived Afghan refugees is particularly telling in this respect. See Cichon, Gozdziak, and Grover, "The Economic and Social Adjustment." See also Rumbaut, "The Structure of Refuge."

4. See Bonacich, "Advanced Capitalism"; Barrera, *Race and Class*; Portes and Bach, Latin Journey, chap. 7.

5. Light, "Immigrant and Ethnic Enterprise"; Wilson and Martin, "Ethnic Enclaves."

6. See Geschwender, *Racial Stratification in America*; Grebler, Moore, and Guzman, *The Mexican-American People*, part 3.

7. See Anderson, *Networks of Contact*; Samora, *Los Mojados*; Sassen-Koob, "Formal and Informal Associations"; Kim, *New Urban Immigrants*.

8. Anderson, *Networks of Contact*; Rumbaut, "The Structure of Refuge"; Tilly, "Migration in Modern European History"; Vecoli, "The Italian Americans."

9. See Portes and Bach, *Latin Journey*, chap. 6.

10. See Browning and Rodriguez, "The Migration"; Nelson and Tienda, "The Structuring of Hispanic Ethnicity"; Bean and Tienda, *The Hispanic Population*.

11. U.S. Bureau of the Census, "The Foreign-Born Population," table 5.

12. Portes and Clark, "Mariel Refugees," 15.

CHAPTER 6

Racism

Racism has been an important subject in the ethnic studies curriculum and is a key issue in the current national dialogue. The readings in this chapter deal with various dimensions of racism, such as the forms and effects of racism, racism in the English language, and the development of racial consciousness and prejudice. Dexter Lopina and Stanley Vickers discuss racial slurs in the English language and their differential effects on people of different races. Racism is not just the use of racial epithets, the Ku Klux Klan, white separatist militias, and bigots in the Deep South, and today racism takes subtle forms such as insensitive racist talks, de facto segregation, continuing racial disparity in employment and income, and racial prejudice and discrimination. A perfect illustration of subtle racism, Elijah Anderson's article reveals how the different perceptions of the police toward black males and whites translated into their harsher treatment of black men than the treatment of whites. The story of Melissa Eastham shows that unlike young kids our society is so color-conscious and that all it should matter is the recognition of a human being, not his or her color. The last selection "The Ages of Intolerance" describes the development of racial awareness and racial prejudice from infantry to adolescence and emphasizes the role of social learning in this process.

1.   Verbal Race Wars
     Dexter Lopina and Stanley Vickers

2.   The Police and the Black Male
     Elijah Anderson

3.   What Color Are You?
     Melissa Eastham

4.   The Ages of Intolerance
     Jose Estorga

Article 6.1

Verbal Race Wars

Dexter Lopina and Stanley Vickers

"Nigger!" This word makes many people angry, especially when it is said by the wrong person. A white person can say this term to a black man he does not know and a big fight can break out. A black person can say this to another black person and it will not be that big of a deal. Black people do like it when some people call them "niggers," and white people do not like it when some call them "honkies." Terms that deal with race cause a lot of conflicts because they are very controversial. Some words hurt some people of a particular race and some people are not affected. The problem is that the words that offend many people are common in today's language and it is hard to get these words out of our vocabulary.

A few weeks ago, a basketball commentator named Billy Packer made a remark about Allen Iverson that offended many people. Iverson, Georgetown University's star player, made an acrobatic move in an attempt to score against Villanova. Upon seeing this, Packer referred to Iverson as one "tough monkey." After the game there was a great amount of tension. Packer was questioned about the remark he had made and he replied, "I apologize and I did not mean it that way. People just took it the wrong way." Although Packer claims he did not "mean it that way," it still hurt many people.

Similar to Packer, a psychiatrist named Frederick K. Goodwin let his mouth get him into a hot situation. Goodwin resigned as head of the Alcohol, Drug Abuse, and Mental Health Administration after being attacked by twenty-six black congressmen, Representative John Dingell, and Senator Edward Kennedy for making comments comparing inner-city youth to monkeys. In the article entitled, "Health Official Falls, Lands in NIMH," Goodwin commented during a public meeting, "If you look at male monkeys, especially in the wild, roughly half of them live to adulthood. The rest of them die by violence." He later compared these male primates to inner-city youth. He formally apologized for his insensitivity after being reprimanded by several government officials. He was then forced to resign.

Racial slurs and political correctness is not a new idea. Although this term seems new in American usage, an article in *Science* entitled, "Political Correctness and American Academe," states that the Stalinists tried to push this idea on American society back in the 1940s. Political correctness is now used so that any one group in any society is not disrespected or spoken of in an improper manner. This includes racial slurs. In a politically correct world, there would be no terms like "honkies," "crackers," "rednecks," "whitetrash," and "snowflakes" used when talking about white people. "Spics" and "wetbacks" would not be used when describing people of Hispanic descent. Words including "monkey" or "nigger" would no longer be said when referring to a person of African descent. "Gooks" and "chinks" would stop being used to describe Asians, and American Indians would not be called "Geronimo" or "Tonto." People in this politically correct society would be called by their name or described by their nationality, not stereotypes of their culture.

Chris Alabarracin, a junior at Roselle Catholic said, "I experienced a lot of racism in my life. I am the 'odd ball' out of my friends because they are all black and I am Filipino. They call me 'gook' and 'chink' sometimes. I know they are only playing around but sometimes it gets to me." This is one instance where certain people can call you names and it will not make you mad, but sometimes, as Chris said, it can hurt. We asked Chris if white or black people have the right to use racial names for each other and he said, "No one has the right to call anyone names. People use racial slurs because it makes them feel 'rough' (which means barbaric). It could also be because they hate another person's race, but that still does not give them the right to call them names." Chris shares what any other person would feel if they were in that type of predicament, which is that nobody should use racial comments because they are disrespectful.

Yohance Warrick, a senior at St. Benedict's Prep in downtown Newark, stated, "I think racial slurs are demoralizing and are used by others to make their race superior to other races." This is very true and the main reason that racial slurs are very controversial and cause a lot of conflicts. When asked how he felt when others call him racial names, he answered, "It really does not bother me because I do not know that person that is saying it and he usually does not know me or anything about me. That person is usually ignorant." Ignorance is the main cause of the racial conflict that is going on in America's society. Yohance, unlike most people, does not care when other people call him any racial names because he knows the only reason the person disrespects him is because that person is ignorant.

Matt Kaelin, a sophomore at Benedict's, said, "I feel it is wrong to make fun of a person's race. People who do so are only showing that they are only insecure about themselves. I never call others racial terms in a serious manner. If I do, I always make sure that they know it's a joke." We asked him how he felt when others called him any names and he said, "It all depends on who said it and in what context. If a friend called me a name it would not matter…" This is a problem for America's youth because they accept being called derogatory terms from their friends and colleagues. Even though it is not meant in a wrong way, it is still an insult and degrading to the person's heritage.

Racial slurs show that you have no respect for another person's ethnic background. They are insulting, derogatory, and demoralizing. It creates negative feelings toward persons that are different. Although it is accepted among friends, racial slurs are wrong. No one has the right to use them. America needs to know that racial slurs offend many people and the use of them has dire consequences. America and the world alike need to start showing respect toward one another by stopping the use of racial slurs.

Article 6.2

The Police and the Black Male

Elijah Anderson

The police, in the Village-Northton [neighborhood] as elsewhere, represent society's formal, legitimate means of social control. Their role includes protecting law-abiding citizens from those who are not law-abiding by preventing crime and by apprehending likely criminals. Precisely how the police fulfill the public's expectations is strongly related to how they view the neighborhood and the people who live there. On the streets, color-coding often works to confuse race, age, class, gender, incivility, and criminality, and it expresses itself most concretely in the person of the anonymous black male. In doing their job, the police often become willing parties to this general color-coding of the public environment, and related distinctions, particularly those of skin color and gender, come to convey definite meanings. Although such coding may make the work of the police more manageable, it may also fit well with their own presuppositions regarding race and class relations, thus shaping officers' perceptions of crime "in the city." Moreover, the anonymous black male is usually an ambiguous figure who arouses the utmost caution and is generally considered dangerous until he proves he is not....

To be white is to be seen by the police—at least superficially—as an ally, eligible for consideration and for much more deferential treatment than that accorded to blacks in general. This attitude may be grounded in the backgrounds of the police themselves. Many have grown up in…"ethnic" neighborhoods. They may serve what they perceive as their own class and neighborhood interests, which often translates as keeping blacks "in their place"—away from neighborhoods that are socially defined as "white." In trying to do their job, the police appear to engage in an informal policy of monitoring young black men as a means of controlling crime, and often they seem to go beyond the bounds of duty....

On the streets late at night, the average young black man is suspicious of others he encounters, and he is particularly wary of the police. If he is dressed in the uniform of the "gangster," such as a black leather jacket, sneakers, and a "gangster cap," if he is carrying a radio or suspicious bag (which may be confiscated), or if he is moving too fast or too slow, the police may stop him. As part of the routine, they search him and make him sit in the police car while they run a check to see whether there is a "detainer" on him. If there is nothing, he is allowed to go on his way. After this ordeal the youth is often left afraid, sometimes shaking, and uncertain about the area he had previously taken for granted. He is upset in part because he is painfully aware of how close he has come to being in "big trouble." He knows of other youths who have gotten into a "world of trouble" simply by being on the streets at the wrong time or when the police were pursuing a criminal. In these circumstances, particularly at night, it is relatively easy for one black man to be mistaken for another. Over the years, while walking through the neighborhood I have on occasion been stopped and questioned by police chasing a mugger, but after explaining myself I was released.

Many youths, however, have reason to fear such mistaken identity or harassment, since they might be jailed, if only for a short time, and would have to post bail money and pay legal fees to extricate themselves from the mess....When law-abiding blacks are ensnared by the criminal justice system, the scenario may proceed as follows. A young man is arbitrarily stopped by the police and questioned. If he cannot effectively negotiate with the officer(s), he may be accused of a crime and arrested. To resolve this situation he needs financial resources, which for him are in short supply. If he does not have money for any attorney, which often happens, he is left to a public defender who may be more interested in going along with the court system than in fighting for a poor black person. Without legal support, he may well wind up "doing time" even if he is innocent of the charges brought against him. The next time he is stopped for questioning he will have a record, which will make detention all the more likely.

Because the young black man is aware of many cases when an "innocent" black person was wrongly accused and detained, he develops an "attitude" toward the police. The street word for police is "the man," signifying a certain machismo, power, and authority. He becomes concerned when he notices "the man" in the community or when the police focus on him because he is outside his own neighborhood. The youth knows, or soon finds out, that he exists in a legally precarious state. Hence he is motivated to avoid the police, and his public life becomes severely circumscribed....

Such scrutiny and harassment by local police make black youths see them as a problem to get beyond, to deal with, and their attempts affect their overall behavior. To avoid encounters with the man, some streetwise young men camouflage themselves, giving up the urban uniform and emblems that identify them as "legitimate" objects of police attention. They may adopt a more conventional presentation of self, wearing chinos, sweat suits, and generally more conservative dress. Some youths have been known to "ditch" a favorite jacket if they see others wearing one like it, because wearing it increases their chances of being mistaken for someone else who may have committed a crime.

But such strategies do not always work over the long run and must be constantly modified. For instance, because so many young ghetto blacks have begun to wear Fila and Adidas sweat suits as status symbols, such dress has become incorporated into the public image generally associated with young black males. These athletic suits, particularly the more expensive and colorful ones, along with high-priced sneakers, have become the leisure dress of successful drug dealers, and other youths will often mimic their wardrobe to "go for bad" in the quest for local esteem. Hence what was once a "square" mark of distinction approximating the conventions of the wider culture has been adopted by a neighborhood group devalued by that same culture. As we saw earlier, the young black male enjoys a certain power over fashion: whatever the collective peer group embraces can become "hip" in a

manner the wider society may not desire....These same styles then attract the attention of
the agents of social control

The Identification Card

Law-abiding black people, particularly those of the middle class, set out to approximate
middle-class whites in styles of self-presentation in public, including dress and bearing.
Such middle-class emblems, often viewed as "square," are not usually embraced by young
working-class blacks. Instead, their connections with and claims on the institutions of the
wider society seem to be symbolized by the identification card. The common identification
card associates its holder with a firm, a corporation, a school, a union, or some other institution of substance and influence. Such a card, particularly from a prominent establishment,
puts the police and others on notice that the youth is "somebody," thus creating an important
distinction between a black man who can claim a connection with the wider society and one
who is summarily judged as "deviant." Although blacks who are established in the middle
class might take such cards for granted, many lower-class blacks, who continue to find it
necessary to campaign for civil rights denied them because of skin color, believe that carrying an identification card brings them better treatment than is meted out to their less fortunate brothers and sisters. For them this link to the wider society, though often tenuous, is
psychically and socially important....

"Downtown" Police and Local Police

In attempting to manage the police—and by implication to manage themselves—some
black youths have developed a working connection of the police in certain public areas of
the Village-Northton. Those who spend a good amount of their time on these corners, and
thus observing the police, have come to distinguish between the "downtown" police and the
"regular" local police.

The local police are the ones who spend time in the area; normally they drive around in
patrol cars, often one officer to a car. These officers usually make a kind of working peace
with the young men on the streets; for example, they know the names of some of them and
may even befriend a young boy. Thus they offer an image of the police department different
from that displayed by the "downtown" police. The downtown police are distant, impersonal, and often actively looking for "trouble." They are known to swoop down arbitrarily on
gatherings of black youths standing on a street corner; they might punch them around, call
them names, and administer other kinds of abuse, apparently for sport. A young Northton
man gave the following narrative about his experiences with the police.

And I happen to live in a violent part. There's a real difference between the violence
level in the Village and the violence level in Northton. In the nighttime it's more
dangerous over there.

It's so bad now, they got downtown cops over there now. They doin' a good job
bringin' the highway patrol over there. Regular cops don't like that. You can tell
that. They even try to emphasize to us the certain category. Highway patrol come

up, he leave, they say somethin' about it. "We can do our job over here." We call (downtown police) Nazis. They about six feet eight, seven feet. We walkin', they jump out. "You run, and we'll blow your nigger brains out." I hate bein' called a nigger. I want to say somethin' but get myself in trouble.

When a cop do somethin', nothing happen to 'em. They come from downtown. From what I heard some of 'em don't even wear their real badge numbers. So you have to put up with that. Just keep your mouth shut when they stop you, that's all. Forget about questions, get against the wall, just obey 'em. "Put all that out right there"—might get rough with you now. They snatch you by the shirt, throw you against the wall, pat you hard, and grab you by the arms, and say, "Get outta here." They call you nigger this and little black this, and things like that. I take that. Some of the fellas get mad. It's a whole different world....

You call a cop, they don't come. My boy got shot, we have to take him to the hospital ourselves. A cop said, "You know who did it?" We said no. He said, "Well I hope he dies if y'all don't say nothin'." What he say that for? My boy said, "I hope your mother die," he told the cop right to his face. And I was grabbin' another cop, and he made a complaint about that. There were a lot of witnesses. Even the nurse behind the counter said the cop had no business saying nothin' like that. He said it loud, "I hope he dies." Nothin' like that should be comin' from a cop.

Such behavior by formal agents of social control may reduce the crime rate, but it raises questions about social justice and civil rights. Many of the old-time liberal white residents of the Village view the police with some ambivalence. They want their streets and homes defended, but many are convinced that the police manhandle "kids" and mete out an arbitrary form of "justice." These feelings make many of them reluctant to call the police when they are needed, and they may even be less than completely cooperative after a crime has been committed. They know that far too often the police simply "go out and pick up some poor black kid." Yet they do cooperate, if ambivalently, with these agents of social control....

...Stories about police prejudice against blacks are often traded at Village get-togethers. Cynicism about the effectiveness of the police mixed with community suspicion of their behavior toward blacks keeps middle-class Villagers from embracing the notion that they must rely heavily on the formal means of social control to maintain even the minimum freedom of movement they enjoy on the streets.

Many residents of the Village, especially those who see themselves as the "old guard" or "old-timers," who were around during the good old days when antiwar and antiracist protest was a major concern, sigh and turn their heads when they see the criminal justice system operating in the ways described here. They express hope that "things will work out," that tensions will ease, that crime will decrease and police behavior will improve. Yet as incivility and crime become increasing problems in the neighborhood, whites become less tolerant of anonymous blacks and more inclined to embrace the police as their heroes....

Gentrifiers and the local old-timers who join them, and some traditional residents continue to fear, care more for their own safety and well-being than for the rights of young blacks accused of wrong-doing. Yet reliance on the police, even by an increasing number of former liberals, may be traced to a general feeling of oppression at the hands of street criminals, whom many believe are most often black. As these feelings intensify and as more yuppies and students inhabit the area and press the local government for services, especially police protection, the police may be required to "ride herd" more stringently on the youthful black population. Thus young black males are often singled out as the "bad" element in an otherwise healthy diversity, and the tensions between the lower-class black ghetto and the middle and upper-class white community increase rather than diminish.

Article 6.3

What Color Are You?

Melissa Eastham

As a second-grade teacher in an inner-city school, I am often faced with the task of answering questions that really have nothing to do with our course of study for the day-questions that you won't find on any national standardized tests. Some of these questions can be recycled into research for the class ("Mrs. Eastman, why are butterflies all different colors?" "How does the grass die in the winter and then come alive in the spring?") Others are much more ponderous and may not have an exact right or wrong answer.

Since I am not one to squelch curiosity, we often take these opportunities as they arise and have short class discussions on them. I let everyone comment on the subject and then tell them we can each make up our own minds. ("Why do we have homework every night?" "Are there really such things as angels?")

Our discussion on differences started innocently enough. I asked the class if they could tell me whether a very tall man was good or bad. They agreed that you couldn't tell if someone was good or bad just because they were tall. I told them that I knew someone who couldn't walk and so she rode in a wheelchair most of the time. I asked if that person was bad or mean because she uses a wheelchair, and they all agreed that you couldn't tell. We went on for a while in this vein and came to the conclusion that being different doesn't make someone good or bad, it just makes that person different.

I decided to take the discussion to a more personal level and explore our personal differences. We talked about how we are all different from one another, how no two people are exactly alike, how even twins have different personalities or features that define them as individuals. I went on to tell them that I was different from everyone in the room because I was the tallest. I was also different because I lived in Red Oak and everyone else lived in Dallas.

Then I planned to have each of them tell the class how they were different. But before I could call on the first pupil, my quietest student raised his hand and announced, "Mrs. Estham is different because she is a different color."

As I think back now, I realize that if this had been said in a room with fifteen other adults, this simple statement of truth would have laid out on the floor, floundering like a fish out of water, while embarrassed glances waited for someone to break the awkward silence. Not so in a classroom of fifteen second-graders. They jumped on it!

"Yeah, Mrs. Eastham is white."

"No, she's not, she's peach."

"I think she's really just bright brown."

"She's creamy."

"She's kinda yellow."

"She's just really shiny."

Trying to hide my grin, I told the class they could have small group discussions on it while I turned the attendance report into the office. I barely made it out of the room before my smirk turned into a full belly laugh. I chuckled all the way to the office and related the story to a fellow teacher while there. I couldn't wait to get back to the room to hear them discuss this!

When I opened the door, they were already back in their seats. They had finished their discussion. (Darn, I had missed it!) I picked a spokesperson for the group, and he said that they knew what color I was but they wanted me to tell them if they were right or not. I said that since this question had only one right answer, I would tell them if they had guessed right or not. Then he told me that the class decided that I was clear.

Clear? Somehow I was able to suppress my laughter. How did they come up with that? I was saved by the bell, as it was time for them to go to the gym. I told them we could talk about it after gym and sent them on their way. Looking back now, I know someone was looking out for me.

While grading papers, I began to muse over our morning again. I was reminded of the times I had been at conferences and workshops and even dinner parties and had been asked, "How many of your students are black? How many white children are in your class? Do you teach many Hispanics?" So many times I have had to stop and try to count out the answers. "How many black students do I have? I know I have fifteen kids. Is it ten black and five Hispanic, or eleven and four?"

The person posing the question is very often amazed and perplexed that I don't know the ethnic makeup of my classroom. I guess it's because when I am teaching, I am teaching children, not colors. I began to realize that it was the same for my kids. They don't see me as black or white or Hispanic; they see me as a person, someone who cares about them, encourages them to do their best and works hard with them every day.

When my students got back to the room, they were all still abuzz about our morning discussion and begged me to tell them if they were right or wrong. I had to tell them the truth. They were exactly right. I am clear!

Now when I am asked that inevitable question at dinner parties or conventions or workshops—"How many black and Hispanic and white children do you have?"—I have a pat answer that works every time, with no fumbling or counting. I look the person straight in the eye and say, "None. They are all clear."

Article 6.4

The Ages of Intolerance

Jose Estorga

In *The Nature of Prejudice*, first published in 1954, social scientist Gordon Allport developed a powerful explanation of the psychological roots of prejudice.

Allport says that from a startlingly young age children begin learning the lessons of tolerance or intolerance—recognizing certain differences, for example, while still in diapers. There's nothing intrinsically worrisome about this. The 10- or 12-month-old baby who cries at the approach of a stranger is doing exactly what he or she is biologically programmed to do: alert Mom or Dad to the presence of a potential source of danger.

But if the parents are themselves prejudiced, the infant's reaction to a stranger of a different skin color or different physical features may be subtly reinforced, generating an apparently seamless education in bigotry that justifies itself as "natural." "My baby just doesn't like people of such and such a color," some parent may report, oblivious of their own role in shaping the child's perceptions.

By age 3 or 4, children begin to pick up on more explicit clues about in-groups and out-groups from their own family, the media and their peers. Children at this age are at the cusp of racial awareness and may be extremely curious about physical differences. Although they may use derogatory remarks, they often have little idea what they mean. And while they may utter racist sentiments, and even use race and gender to exclude others, their opinions and attitudes haven't yet gelled.

Of all influences on the child's ideas at this age, the family is clearly the most important. "The family," wrote Allport, "supplies a constant undertone of acceptance or rejection, anxiety or security." Even parents who avoid making overt racist comments may teach their kids negative racial values. The parent's tightening grip around the child's hand or the sound of the car doors being locked shut when a group of teenage males of a different race or ethnicity passes by—these communicate the parent's attitudes about others as clearly as words do.

By age 6 or 7, children have begun to recognize that there are distinct categories of people—that the janitor belongs to a different social class from the doctor, for example. And they've also begun to understand that many of these identities, such as race, gender and ethnicity, are fixed. They recognize that social status and positive or negative qualities can be ascribed to people based on their affiliation within these groups. And they've begun to make the connections between their individual identity and their group identity.

   Often the lessons children learn at this age are as much about societal hypocrisy as they are about race. Parents who mutter something about the "wrong section of town" and then deflect their child's questions about what they meant aren't teaching their child that racism is bad; they are teaching the child to be cautious about speaking his or her mind on issues of race.

   By age 10 or so children may start consistently excluding others who belong to an out-group, or, if they are themselves members of a minority, to develop a complex of attitudes that include defiance, self-doubt and hostility. Children this age are an excellent barometer of societal attitudes, for, in contrast to their elders, they tend to voice racial stereotypes quite freely.

   A final stage comes in the teenage years, when the child learns those subtler rules of etiquette that govern relations between people. They've learned that "prejudiced talk and democratic talk are reserved for the appropriate occasions," Allport writes. What is said between friends in the mall may never be voiced in an official forum like a classroom. "It takes the entire period of childhood and much of adolescence to master the art of ethnocentrism," Allport concludes.

CHAPTER 7

Ethnic Segregation

Ethnic segregation can be defined as the separation of ethnic groups in spatial, social, economic, political, and cultural lives. Although public segregation and military segregation are history, residential segregation is still prevalent in American life, and school segregation still lingers on to some extent and even resurrects. Hence, the selections of this chapter center on these last two dimensions of segregation.

Reynolds Farley and William Frey summarize the complex causes of residential segregation in America, including group economic status, prejudice and discrimination, historical factors, and structural factors. Data sheet provided by the Applied Research Center highlights the current status of segregation in American public schools. Jeanne Weiler's article outlines several trends in school desegregation and alerts us the rise of school resegregation in the 1990s.

1. Changes in the segregation of Whites from Blacks during the 1980s: Small Steps toward a More Integrated Society
   Reynolds Farley and William Frey

2. Public Schools in the United States: Still Separate, Still Unequal
   Applied Research Center

3. Recent Changes in School Desegregation
   Jeanne Weiler

Article 7.1

Changes in the Segregation of Whites from Blacks during the 1980s: Small Steps toward a More Integrated Society

Reynolds Farley and William Frey

Explanation of variation among metropolitan areas in the percent change in segregation scores during the 1980s must consider local area conditions as well as three national-level factors. First, the heavy hand of the past maintains segregation in old metropolitan areas, i.e., functional specialization, suburban patterns, and housing stock of these areas discourages integration, especially in the Northeast and Midwest (Hershberg, Burstein, Erickson, Greenberg, and Yancy 1981). Second, a high percentage of new housing is linked to declines in segregation. Presumably, new housing developments are less segregated than the old ethnic ghettos. Also, a high rate of housing construction may encourage residential mobility throughout a metropolitan area. Finally, the racial attitudes of whites may limit integration. As Massey and Gross (1991) observed, reductions in segregation in the 1970s were confined to metropolises in which blacks were so few they could be accommodated in white neighborhoods without threatening whites. In the 1980s, declines in segregation were not limited to areas with relatively small black populations, but the largest decreases in segregation occurred in metropolitan areas in which blacks made up a small percentage of the neighborhood of the typical white.

This analysis of the forces affecting the residential segregation of blacks and whites suggest the following characteristics of segregation for the 1990s.

(1) *A gap between attitude and behavior.* Racial attitudes have changed—most whites now endorse the *principle* of equal opportunities for blacks in the housing market. However, the evidence from the Detroit study and our analysis of the percent change in segregation in 232 metropolitan areas suggest that most whites are uncomfortable when numerous blacks enter their neighborhoods. Also, few whites will move into neighborhoods with many black residents. The conservative attitudes of whites and their fear of becoming a minority in a neighborhood limit the desegregation that can occur. Presumably, attitudes toward Latinos and Asians are not so restrictive.

From *American Sociological Review*, February 1994. Reprinted with permission of American Sociological Association.

(2) *A stronger link between the economic status of blacks and integration.* Studies of the residential segregation of European ethnic groups and other racial minorities, including Latinos and Asians, report that economic assimilation was associated with lessened segregation from native-born whites (Lieberson 1963:chap. 5). This association is not true for blacks, because Jim Crow laws applied to all blacks regardless of economic status (Denton and Massey 1988; Farley and Allen 1987: table 5.10; Massey 1979, 1981; Massey and Denton 1987; Taeuber 1965). This situation may have changed. A substantial and rapid growth of the black middle class should lead many members to seek high quality housing. Some metropolitan areas may have enough middle-class blacks that prosperous, largely black suburbs will emerge (Dent 1992; Garreau 1991). In others, middle and upper-class blacks may choose to live in integrated areas where their status should elicit greater acceptance by white neighbors. With declining employment opportunities in the industrial North, many middle class blacks will follow new migration paths, leading to black gains in areas in the West and "New South," where segregation is not so entrenched (Frey 1993).

(3) *Differences among metropolitan areas in segregation.* Institutionalized discrimination that denied blacks equal treatment in the housing market will persist in the old metropolitan areas of the industrial North and some portions of the Old South. However, in developing parts of the West and South, such practices may be less firmly established and many of these areas now have relatively more Hispanics and Asians than blacks. These areas, which initially did not attract black migrants, have low segregation levels and registered the biggest percent decline in segregation during the 1980s.

In an analysis of residential segregation in large metropolitan areas during the 1970s, Massey and Denton (1987) concluded:

> If black residential integration has occurred at all, it has not been within metropolitan areas where the vast majority of blacks live, but through movement to small and mid-size cities that presently contain few black residents. Perhaps the growth of black populations in these smaller metropolitan areas will be the means by which residential integration will finally occur in the United States. (p. 823)

Our analysis suggests that this scenario may become reality during the 1990s. The 25 percent of metropolitan areas with the largest decreases in segregation in the 1980-1990 decade had the lowest average percent black, exhibited the highest average annual growth rate for blacks over the 1980s, and the highest average annual growth rate in mean household income of blacks, suggesting that segregation may remain low in these areas. However, the American apartheid system may break down slowly, if at all, in the old, large metropolitan areas.

Article 7.2

Public Schools in the United States: Still Separate, Still Unequal

Applied Research Center

It's been 34 years since the Supreme Court ordered U.S. schools desegregated in the case of Brown v. Board of Education. So why is there still school segregation in 1998? And how do the schools attended by students of color compare to the ones white kids go to? ARC's Just Facts project prepared this fact sheet on school segregation and inequality.

Who goes to public school in this country? Almost everyone. The vast majority of U.S. kids attend public school.

- 95% of all elementary school students and 92% of all high school student go to public school.
- Public high schools serve 97% of African-Americans, 95% of Latinos and even 92% of whites.

Who goes to private schools? Hardly anyone.

- Even 7 out of 8 wealthy white families send their kids to public high schools.

How many kids do the public schools serve? There are approximately 46 million students at public schools in around 16,000 separate school districts. A higher proportion of

Of these,
- 16% are African-American;
- 9% are Latino:
- 3% are Asian-American;
- 1% are Native-American; and
- 72% are white.

And who teaches in our public schools? The vast majority of teachers are white. The proportion of black students is twice as high as the proportion of black teachers. And the proportion of Latino students is three times that of Latino teachers. Here's how our teaching corps breaks down by race:

- 8% African-American
- 3% are Latino.
- 1% Asian-American.
- 1% Native-American
- 88% white

So almost everyone goes to public school. But do students of different races attend the same schools? Most often they do not. In fact, the schools are more segregated today than they were twenty years ago.

School segregation? Didn't the Supreme Court outlaw that in 1954? It's true that the Supreme Court's decision in the famous Brown v. Board of Education case declared that government-imposed school segregation is illegal? This decision struck down the hundred-year old Plessy v. Ferguson decision that said that segregation is allowable as long as facilities—like train cars or schools—are "separate but equal." According to the Court, "Separate educational facilities are inherently unequal."

A lot has happened since 1954. It took another ten years and a national Civil Rights movement to force Congress to pass the 1964 Civil Rights act, which put some teeth in Brown v. Board of Education.

But just 10 years later, beginning in 1974—and accelerating in the 1990s—a series of Supreme Court decisions made it much more difficult again for communities to get and enforce desegregation orders.

- In the 1974 Milliken v. Bradley decision the Court said that if a school district only covers an inner city area, a desegregation plan cannot include the suburban area surrounding the school district. This makes it impossible to desegregate a metropolitan area where most people of color live in inner cities and most white people live in suburbs—unless it can be proved that the government itself intentionally created that residential segregation.
- In several other decisions during the Reagan Administration, the Court said that once a school system has been declared even partially desegregated, it can dismantle all its desegregation programs, essentially returning to segregated schools.

But aren't today's schools more desegregated than they were 20 years ago?

Actually, public schools are being quietly re-segregated. This process began in the 70s and accelerated during the 1980s and 90s. For example:

- Since 1986, the proportion of African-American students who attend schools with majorities of people of color has been rising, not falling.
- In 1991, that proportion returned to the same level as in 1971, when the Supreme Court issued its first school desegregation busing decision.
- By 1986, the proportion of African-American students in intensely segregated (90 to 100 percent students of color) schools, which had been falling during the early 80s, started to climb again.

- Latino students never experienced any decrease in segregation at all. In fact, segregation of Latino students only increases as time goes on.
- And 63 percent of all white students go to schools that are 90 to 100 percent white.

Isn't school segregation mostly a problem in the South? Actually, for historical reasons, schools in the South are less segregated today than their northern counterparts.

- Black students in the South are only half as likely to attend intensely segregated schools as those who live in the Northeast.
- Desegregation measures had a lot of effect in the South. In 1960, only 1/10th of one percent of the students attending majority-white schools in the South were African-American. By 1970, southern majority-white schools were 33 percent African-American.

But recently the South has begun catching up with the North in the race to re-segregate.

What causes school segregation? There are many answers to that question, but one key cause is housing discrimination. Because people go to school near where they live, it's not surprising that school segregation patterns follows housing segregation. This is especially true in large northern metropolitan areas with white suburbs and inner cities inhabited mostly by people of color.

- The most intense school segregation happens in large central cities. Students of color in rural areas and small towns are much more likely to attend integrated schools than those who live in large cities.
- Big metropolitan areas maintain school segregation by having smaller school districts. The Milliken decision forbids desegregation plans that cross school district lines, so if the suburbs and the city have separate districts, their students won't be able to attend the same schools.
- New York, Illinois, Michigan and New Jersey—the four states with the highest rate of school segregation for African-Americans—have many small school districts.
- Southern states, on the other hand, where school desegregation has been more successful, usually have county-wide school districts, which cover urban cities and their suburbs.

Is "separate but equal" really such a bad thing? It's impossible to answer that question, because separate but equal schools do not exist. Schools in this country are both separate and profoundly unequal.

White suburban schools have vastly more money than inner city schools, whose students are often 90 to 100 percent children of color.? Here are some figures from the 1992-93 school year. That's because almost half of school funding comes from local property taxes.

- In New York state, the richest school district spent $38,572 per student in 1992. That's 7 times what the poorest district spent—$5,423.

- In Texas, per-student spending ranged from $3,098 to more than 10 times as much—$42,000.
- In Illinois, the ratio was 8 to 1, $16,700 to $2,276.

Less money means fewer resources:

- In New York City, for example, there are second grade classes meeting in stairwells, science classes taught in hallways, and 1 out of every 11 kids doesn't even have a desk.
- Poor schools often have textbooks that are decades out of date—and rarely have enough to go around.
- Rich schools have computers and Internet access. Poor schools can have televisions, if they agree to expose their students to advertising every day through a program called Channel One.
- Teachers in poor schools earn much less—on average 28% less—than teachers in rich schools.

Students of color have higher dropout rates. Nationwide Latinos and African-Americans are more likely to drop out of high school than whites.

- Ninety-two percent of whites, 86% of African-Americans and only 61% of Latinos finish high school.
- For example, in metropolitan Philadelphia, inner city drop-out rates are four times as high as those of suburban schools.
- Some inner city New Jersey school districts lose 60 percent of their students by 12th grade.

White High school graduates are much more likely to go to college, and to finish college, than African-Americans or Latinos. Here's how it breaks down:

	Some College	B.A. Degree
Whites	67%	34%
Blacks	56%	17%
Latino's	54%	16%

In this period of intense national focus on education, it's time to shed some light on how racism continues to define the public schools.

Sources: U.S. Department of Education, National Center for Educational Statistics; Rethinking Schools, Funding for Justice: Milwaukee, WI, 1997; Orfield and Eaton, Dismantling Desegregation: The Quiet Reversal of Brown V. Board of Education: New Press, 1997

Article 7.3

Recent Changes in School Desegregation

Jeanne Weiler

This digest presents some of the major trends and changes that are taking place in school desegregation in the 1990s. One of the most prominent current trends is the increasing number of court cases which release school districts from court supervision of their desegregation efforts (known as granting "unitary" status). The result has been that many urban school districts are moving toward increasing resegregation of their schools as students return to neighborhood schools (*Orfield, 1996*).

A second important trend in school desegregation is increased attention to access to education and academic performance of minority student (*Willis, 1994*). Both school districts involved in court cases and those involved in desegregation planning have shifted attention away from a focus on desegregation efforts, which primarily concern student assignment to achieve racial integration, and toward increased attention to issues related to within-school equity and integration. But, as educators and parents are discovering, barriers to minority participation and learning in school are proving to be as difficult to remove as is deliberate segregation.

During the 1970s and 1980s, the focus of desegregation was on the physical integration of African American and white students through such measures as busing, school choice, magnet schools, use of ratios, redrawn school district boundaries, mandatory and voluntary intra- and interdistrict transfers, and consolidation of city districts with suburban districts (*Willis, 1994*). While many of these efforts are continuing in school districts across the nation, courts are declaring more and more large urban districts unitary (e.g., Denver, CO; Wilmington, DE; Savannah, GA; Kansas City, KS; Cincinnati and Cleveland, OH; Oklahoma City, OK; buffalo, NY; and Austin, TX).

In particular, there have been several pivotal Supreme Court cases during the 1990s that have spelled out procedures for court approval of the dismantling of school desegregation plans (*Orfield, 1996*). Rulings from these cases have provided the legal standards to determine when a local school district could be released from its obligation to maintain desegregated schools. The significance of these pivotal cases, *Board of Education of Oklahoma v. Dowell* (1991), *Freeman v. Pitts* (1992), *Missouri v. Jenkins* (1995), and of a state case, *Sheff v. O'Neill* (1996), is discussed below.

Published by the ERIC Clearinghouse on Urban Education, Teachers College, Columbia University. Reprinted by permission.

Recent Desegregation Cases

The U.S. Supreme Court

In *Board of Education of Oklahoma v. Dowell* (1991), the U.S. Supreme Court ruled that formerly segregated school districts could be released from court-ordered busing once they have taken all "practicable" steps to eliminate the legacy of segregation. This meant that districts could be freed from court oversight if they had desegregated their students and faculty and met the other requirements of mandatory desegregation, such as transportation and facilities. The court further ruled that school districts are not responsible for remedying local conditions, such as segregated housing patterns *(Fife, 1996)*. In essence, with this ruling, the Supreme Court made it easier for districts to be declared unitary, or to be released from desegregation orders *(Orfield, 1996)*.

In the case of *Freeman v. Pitts*, the 1992 Supreme Court ruling held that Federal district courts can have discretion to order incremental withdrawal of court supervision over school districts *(Fife, 1996)*. In other words, a school district does not need to achieve unitary status in all six of the "Green factors"-student assignment, faculty, staff, transportation, extracurricular activities, and facilities-before being released from court supervision. The Green factors, codified by the Supreme Court decision in *Green v School Board of New Kent County*, are typical components of a school system where desegregation is mandatory. Thus, the *Freeman* decision effectively weakened the Green standards by allowing schools to desegregate incrementally, although it did not release districts from their obligation to desegregate *(Fife, 1996)*.

Missouri v. Jenkins is one of the most complex desegregation cases to date in the United States. Since 1985, the state of Missouri has spent $1.4 billion on the court-ordered desegregation plan for the Kansas City school district. In 1995, however, the U.S. Supreme Court ruled that a desegregation plan does not have to continue just because minority student achievement scores remain below the national average. The state of Missouri could not be required to provide funding for programs and various kinds of school improvement activities, or to pay for a plan aimed at attracting white students from suburban districts for an undetermined amount of time, simply because minority student achievement scores remained below the national average. The state could only be required to do what is practicable for remedying the vestiges of past discrimination; it was not responsible for remedying inequities that may exist between students within schools *(Fife, 1996)*. Recently, a Federal judge ruled that the state be freed from financial responsibility by approving a settlement paying $315 million that would cut out $100 million in annual state subsidy for school desegregation efforts after 1999. The court ordered that the district narrow the gap in test scores between black and white students by the end of 1998–99. *(Hendrie, 1997)*.

The Connecticut Supreme Court

In a ruling that has been hailed by civil rights advocates, the Connecticut Supreme Court, in the 1996 case, *Sheff v. O'Neill,* found that the racial and ethnic isolation in the Hartford school district was a violation of the state constitution's protection against segregation, and that the extreme racial and ethnic isolation in and around Hartford schools denied students their constitutionally guaranteed rights to an education. The court ordered state officials to desegregate the schools *(Archer, 1996)*. The state legislature then approved a plan that would allow students to transfer between public school districts throughout Connecticut and enhance the urban schools with magnet and charter schools *(Archer, 1997)*. Although this case is clearly a victory for desegregation advocates, plaintiffs in the case argue that a statewide interdistrict transfer plan will still not integrate Hartford's schools.

Impact of Court Decisions

Many educators, parents, community members, and politicians are relieved to see an end to the desegregation orders that for years heavily influenced decisions about educational and fiscal policies. Conversely, critics and civil rights advocates argue that the current trend toward dismantling court-ordered desegregation in many school districts is a step backwards toward segregated schooling. Recent studies indicate that school segregation and the creation of school districts with numerous poor students, which have been increasing during the 1990s, are also affecting Latino students. Latino students are increasingly isolated from whites, and are more highly concentrated in high poverty schools, than any other group of students *(Orfield, Bachmeier, James, & Eitle, 1997)*.

The Return to Neighborhood Schools

When a school district is released from court supervision, it is often free to send students back to their neighborhood schools. Community members, parents, and educators often support a return to neighborhood schools because they believe that desegregation is costly, that it has not accomplished what it was intended to do many years ago, and that it has resulted in meager improvements *(Neuborne, 1995)*. They also hope that whites and middle-class residents who fled during desegregation will return to the schools closer to their homes *(Orfield, 1996)*. Other people claim that African American children would be better off staying in neighborhood schools rather than being transferred out of their communities to unfamiliar and often unwelcoming places. In fact, many minority parents, having lost confidence in the ability of their child's desegregated school to provide an equitable education of high quality, demand a return to neighborhood schools.

Despite this belief in the value of neighborhood schools, the reality is that many urban students return to schools that are segregated and inferior. Often new funding for upgrading school facilities and educational programs is promised but not delivered. However, as is the case with many large urban schools, even an infusion of extra funds is often not enough to transform a school, as schools must struggle with the profound and increasing poverty and joblessness in their local communities. Moreover, in cities that previously used busing measures to desegregate their schools, costs to create new schools and classrooms that had been underutilized for years can run as high as hundreds of million dollars.

School Resegregation

Gary Orfield and his colleagues at the Harvard Project on School Desegregation have reported that school segregation has increased steadily over the past 15 years, particularly in non southern states. The increase in school segregation has profound consequences for urban minority students. For example, while only 5 percent of segregated white schools face conditions of poverty among their students, more than 80 percent of segregated African American and Latino schools do *(Orfield et al., 1997)*.

This means that a student who moves from an integrated school back to a segregated neighborhood school will most likely exchange the resources of a middle-class school for a poverty-stricken one, the result of the end of court-mandated busing or desegregation choice plans. High poverty schools have generally lower levels of educational performance and are less likely to prepare students for college than more affluent schools. Researchers such as *Wells and Crain (1997)* argue that the gradual undoing of desegregation and increasing con-centration of urban minority students in high poverty schools cut off access to the full range of middle-class opportunities-impacting on higher education, employment, and future choice of residential community- that a more affluent integrated school would provide.

Impact on Academic Performance

It is clear that desegregation has little relevance for many of the nation's largest cities: a number of the biggest urban districts are one-sixth or less white, and thus lack a sufficient number of white students to meaningfully desegregate. Desegregation plans in many smaller cities are becoming increasingly ineffective with the tremendous growth of white suburbs and the expansion of inner-city neighborhoods without adjustments to racial balance man-dates. Even within desegregated schools, claims persist that segregation still continues under the guise of school tracking and grouping practices. Because of these trends in the 1990s, desegregation planners across the country are increasingly turning their attention from de-segregation remedies such as student transfer and reassignment to achieve racial balance to a focus on access, equity, and the academic performance of minority students *(Willis, 1994)*.

As more school districts have fulfilled their responsibilities insofar as the above-described Green factors are concerned, plaintiffs in desegregation cases have shifted their focus to what are sometimes referred to as "educational vestiges." They argue that the edu-cational achievement of racial and ethnic minority students continues to lag behind that of white students in the school district, and that this achievement gap, a vestige of legalized segregation, must be eliminated before a school district can be released from court orders *(Lindseth, 1997)*. This argument is critical, and it will most likely be the subject of further Supreme Court decisions. The gap in performance on standardized test scores between white students and African American and Latino students, and differences in the choice of courses and curriculum available to different groups of students, is leading to serious exami-nation of what happens to minority students within individual schools and classrooms. It will most likely lead to an era of desegregation cases that focus on within-school integration *(Willis, 1994)*.

Within-School Integration

Currently, several school districts across the country are engaged in desegregation plan-ning and are focusing on provisions that address internal integration rather than the more conventional desegregation measure such as student assignment. *Willis (1994)* uses the term "within-school integration" to mean "the elimination of all vestiges of segregation from all policies, practices, programs, and activities *within* a district's school" (p.7). The focus of within-school integration is provision of the greatest possible integration and interaction among students and staff regardless of the student composition of the school. Although a school's racial/ethnic enrollment may reflect integration, the school can often engage in segregative practices that negate the benefits of a well integrated school *(Willis, 1994)*.

Such a situation sparked a desegregation case in Rockford, IL, *People Who Care, et al. v. Rockford Board of Education* (1993). The school district was under District Court order to address within-school integration in its high schools, all of which are racially balanced. The district was also ordered to implement a student assignment plan utilizing controlled choice; to develop programs for significant improvement in instruction and achievement in a subset of elementary schools that for a short period of time will remain minority, racially identifiable; and to integrate all courses and other educational services offered in middle and high school. The court had found the level of internal segregation within racially integrated schools severe, as the district had maintained separation of white and minority students in most courses and in extracurricular activities.

For many school districts engaged in desegregation planning, the emphasis on within school integration addresses both integrated schools and racially identifiable schools (segregated schools) since a school district often has a combination of both schools. For integrated or racially balanced schools, plans are developed to address equitable participation and performance of minority students compared to white students attending the same schools. In racially identifiable schools, plans are developed to address the quality of education and performance of minority students.

Monitoring equity within schools in the implementation of desegregation plans has often been difficult, in part because of the reliance on inadequate data from schools districts. In the past, school districts were not required by the courts to provide discrete information on different groups of students. At best, statistical indicators such as achievement and attendance data were provided for only two student categories: white and minority. More recently, this limited categorization has been considered inadequate as the demographics in school districts change, and as school officials, plaintiffs, and court monitors ask for a more extensive breakdown of data. Going beyond simple separation by race, they seek data disaggregated by poverty status and fluency of English, and equity indicators such as information on enrollment levels in special education, extent of mainstreaming, courses and grades of students, grade retention rates, graduation rates, access to services, participation of parents, etc. (For a complete list of equity indicators developed by the Southwest Center for Educational Equity, see *Willis, 1994.)*

Racial Diversity as an Educational Goal

As desegregation cases come to a close, many educators are questioning the extent to which they should attempt to promote racial and ethnic integration without court orders to do so*(Hendrie, 1997)*. As the nation becomes more multicultural, educators argue that public school diversity is more important than ever, since many school districts have retained or implemented school policies, such as the institution of selective admissions criteria to special schools or magnet programs, which sometimes adversely impact minority students.

It is, however, unclear how the judicial system will respond to desegregation efforts, as advocates argue that diversity policies are in the national interest and critics respond that they are unnecessary unless there are specific wrongs to be righted. Legal challenges have already been brought against two top high schools in the nation: Lowell High School in San Francisco and Boston Latin School in Massachusetts. In San Francisco, Chinese American students who were denied admission brought a lawsuit against the school district, particularly centered on Lowell High School, challenging the 40 percent cap on Chinese American students. Before the court could rule, the school changed its quota policy. Subsequently, a judge upheld the cap but left open the possibility that it might be time to end the policy *(Reinhard, 1997)*. At the Boston Latin School, a suit was brought by a white student who was not admitted despite having higher test scores than African Americans and Latinos who were accepted. A judge ruled in the white student's favor, thus ending over 20 years of racial set-asides at the school.

Conclusion

The barriers to school desegregation are mounting. The Supreme Court rulings of the 1990s have encouraged more and more school districts to seek unitary status and have "signaled a reluctance by the courts to indefinitely continue Federal court supervision of school districts" *(Orfield, 1997)*. Plaintiffs' best hope for continuing under desegregation orders center on the issue of "educational vestiges," such as within-school segregation, differential course availability, and the educational performance gap between white and minority students. The growing number of poor students of color in inner-city areas makes racial balance plans difficult if not implausible. Thus, efforts to improve the education of students of color must be focused on effective school reform regardless of whether a school or district is physically desegregated or not.

References

Archer, J. (1996, December 4). Student Transfers proposed on Conn. desegregation plan. *Education Week, XVI*(14), p.9.

Archer, J. (1997, April 23) Conn. bill to seize Hartford school passes. *Education Week, XVI*(30), p.1, 30.

Fife, B.L. (1996, September). The Supreme Court and school desegregation since 1896. *Equity and Excellence in Education, 29(2), 46–55.* *(ERIC Abstract)*

Hendrie, C. (1997, April 2). Judge decides state funds for desegregation to end in K.C. *Education Week, XVI*(27), pp.1, 30.

Hendrie, C. (1997, April 30). Without court orders, schools ponder how to pursue diversity. *Education Week, XVI*(31).

Kunen, J.S.(1996, April 29). The end of integration. *Time Magazine,* 147(18).

Lindseth, A.A. (1997, April). *The changing face of school desegregation.* Paper prepared for the Conference on Civil Rights and Equal Opportunity in Public Schools, Atlanta, GA.

Neuborne, B. (1995). *Brown* at forty: Six visions. *Teachers College Record,* 96(4), 799–805. *ERIC Abstract)*

Orfield, G. (1996). Turning back to segregation. In G. Orfield, S. Eaton, & The Harvard Project on Desegregation (Eds.), *Dismantling desegregation: The quiet reversal* of Brown v. Board of Education (pp. 1–22). New York: The New Press. *(ERIC Abstract)*

Orfield, G. Bachmeier, M.D., James, D.R., & Eitle, T. (1997, September). Deepening segregation in American public schools: A special report from the Harvard Project on School Desegregation. *Equity and Excellence in Education,*30(2), 5–24.

Reinhard, B.(1997, May 21). Judge blocks bid to ax quotas in S.F. schools. *Education Week, XVI(34),* p.3.

Wells, A.S., & Crain, R. (1997). *Stepping over the color line: African-American students in white suburban schools.* New Haven: Yale University Press. *(ERIC Abstract)*

Willis, H.D. (1994, November 1). *The shifting focus in school desegregation.* Paper presented to the SWRL Board of Directors and The 1995 Equity Conference.

CHAPTER 8

Ethnic Conflict

Ethnic conflict is at the heart of ethnic studies. The readings in this chapter center on the sources of ethnic conflicts observed in recent years. Andrew Ford's report suggests that controversies over issues from Farrakhan to the verdict in the O.J. Simpson murder trial, as well as the disparity in their levels of prosperity and their turn toward inward spiritual and social support in recent years, contributed to the black-Jewish division. From Mike Clary's report, one can also see that the black-Cuban conflict in Miami was caused by the disparity in the two groups' economic status, the dominance of Cubans in local political power, a lack of understanding of each other's histories, and racial divide. Unlike the sociopsychological explanations that stress the role of mutual prejudice, cultural differences, and Koreans' language barriers, Pyong Gap Min emphasizes the structural sources of recent Korean-black conflicts in America's multiethnic cities, such as the poverty and the resulting frustration of inner-city black residents, the scapegoating of Korean middleman merchants, and the role of black nationalist organizations.

1. Blacks, Jews Take New Steps to Heal Divisions
   Andrew Ford

2. Black, Cuban Racial Chasm Splits Miami
   Mike Clary

3. Korean/African-American Conflicts
   Pyong Gap Min

Article 8.1

Blacks, Jews Take New Steps to Heal Divisions

Andrew Ford

It was only a matter of time before Louis Farrakhan's name came up.

The questioner was a Jewish man who shook with anger and hurt as he stood in an audience at the Jewish Student Center at UCLA. Why, he demanded of City Councilman Mark Ridley-Thomas, an African American, didn't blacks condemn the Nation of Islam leader, who many Jews believe is an incorrigible anti-Semite?

Ridley-Thomas' distaste for the question was obvious. He seemed to wince and waited several moments before speaking. His answer, boiled down to its essence, was that he chose not to use his energy to denounce anyone. "I'm not prepared to spend my time dealing with that issue," he said. "I've tried to make it abundantly clear what my political views are. My record speaks for itself. I will not be forced to take some litmus test."

The answer only made the man angrier, but his attempts to engage Ridley-Thomas in debate over the matter were quickly curtailed by Laurie Levenson, a Loyola Law School professor who was moderating the recent panel discussion organized by the Hillel Council at UCLA, a Jewish service group.

The topic? Whether a black-Jewish alliance could be forged at a time when the two communities have drifted into sometimes hostile camps.

It is a question that is increasingly being asked in Los Angeles and across the country.

Eight days before the UCLA panel, the African American/Jewish Leadership Connection sponsored a conference in May at the Wilshire Boulevard Temple, where about 120 black and Jewish community leaders sought to air sometimes unspoken perceptions and pains on both sides.

Nationally, similar dialogues are taking place among academic, clerics and activists who have looked on in alarm in recent years as some members of the two groups—formidable allies at various points in their histories, most notably during the civil rights movement—have become bitterly estranged over issues from Farrakhan to the verdict in the O.J. Simpson murder trial.

In an attempt to cool the fires, the historically black Howard University and the American Jewish Committee last month jointly published the first issue of CommonQuest, a magazine whose purpose is to provide a forum for discussion of black-Jewish relations in an atmosphere "beyond frenzy and accusation."

From *Time*, June 10, 1996. Reprinted by permission.

Later this year, the NAACP, the Hillel Foundation and other groups plan to host a national summit on the issue in Washington.

In Los Angeles, where divisiveness between the two groups has flared and ebbed repeatedly over the last decade, old allies are attempting to breach the divide by talking honestly to each other, agreeing to disagree on some issues and joining forces on those on which they can agree.

Farrakhan, one participant in the dialogues said, is an example of a topic that probably won't be agreed on any time soon, if ever.

He is a difficult "knot," said Raphael Sonenshein, a political science professor at Cal State Fullerton who was on the UCLA panel with Ridley-Thomas.

"A knot should be untied or cut, but not necessarily settled," he said. "To expect all Jews to accept Farrakhan and all blacks to reject him is unrealistic."

Most of those involved in the dialogues, however, are optimistic that they will bear fruit in other areas. If reconciliation between blacks and Jews is possible anywhere, they contend, it is in Los Angeles, because the lines of communication between the two groups here have never been completely severed.

Even in the worst of times, said many, individual Jews and blacks have continued to communicate, work, in joint programs and attend each other's places of worship, while more strident members of both communities got the headlines.

"Los Angeles created for about a 15- to 20-year period the most important black-Jewish alliance than probably any major metropolitan area has ever had," said Sonenshein, referring to the political coalition of mostly Westside Jews and South Los Angeles blacks that put Tom Bradley in the mayor's office and kept him there for two decades.

"The question is not why we keep fighting," Sonenshein said. "The question is why are we still talking?"

Rabbi Harvey Fields, chairman of the Community Relations Committee of the Jewish Federation, an umbrella organization of Jewish groups, cited the shared history of blacks and Jews as persecuted people and civil rights champions.

"This is a relationship with roots back in the 19th century," Field said. "Jews and African Americans have been partners in the battle for civil rights for our communities and everyone else. This is a valued partnership."

Ridley-Thomas agreed.

"There is an almost unquenchable thirst on the part of the two communities to remain in communication," he said, "because we do see ourselves as important in this experiment called Los Angeles."

Sonenshein agreed with both men but warned against painting too rosy a picture of the past.

In reality, he said, the two groups have clashed locally and nationally as often as they have worked together since the turn of the century, when progressive Jews, other whites and blacks formed the NAACP.

He told the UCLA audience that he had found a magazine with an article that bemoaned the poor state of the relations between blacks and Jews. The year of its publication? 1944.

In an interview, Sonenshein also cited the rift that occurred between the two communities during the birth of the Black Power movement in the 1960s, when young black activists accused Jewish and other white activists of paternalism and drove them away from their organizations.

Even in Los Angeles during the height of the Bradley coalition, the relationship was not always stable, said Bill Elkins, Bradley's longtime confidant and mayoral aide.

He recalled the anger and hurt feelings among blacks that resulted from Jewish calls for Andrew young's 1978 firing from his post as the U.S. ambassador to the United Nations, after it was revealed that Young had met in secret and without authorization with PLO officials.

A year later, black and Jewish Angelenos were yelling at each other again over involvement of some Jews as leaders of the anti-busing movement. Some blacks demanded they be denounced.

Perhaps the most rancorous dispute, however, was a few years later, when Jews demanded that Bradley denounce Farrakhan over what were seen as disparaging remarks about Judaism that Farrakhan made before a trip to Los Angeles. Bradley finally did criticize Farrakhan, but only after Farrakhan made remarks in Los Angeles that were also seen as inflammatory.

Since then, the public relationship between the two groups has deteriorated as the result of the support many blacks give Farrakhan's Nation of Islam, and also over accusations by some Jews that black youth are anti-Semitic and accusations by some blacks that Jews are racist.

Other factors such as the difference in the two groups' levels of prosperity, the end of the Bradley era, and a general tendency in recent years for both Jewish and black communities to turn inward for spiritual and social sustenance also contributed to the drifting apart, all parties agree.

It was against this backdrop two years ago that Rabbi Fields decided to "jump-start" a dialogue and reach out to John Mack, president of the Los Angeles chapter of the urban League, one of the oldest black civil rights groups in the country.

Fields, who had just been named chairman of the Jewish Federation's Community Relations Committee, and Mack met without fanfare and began quietly bringing leaders of other social, political and religious organizations into the discussions.

The result is the African American/Jewish Leadership Connection.

Before last month, when a few journalists were invited to observe that gathering, the group had gone public only once before, when it called a news conference last fall to announce its opposition to Proposition 187, the measure that seeks to deny public education and other social services to illegal immigrants. Voters eventually approved it.

The news conference got little attention, however, because its organizers had the misfortune of scheduling it Oct. 3—the same day the O.J. Simpson murder trial verdict was announced.

Talk now is centered on whether the group can come up with a consensus on the California ballot measure that would ban affirmative action based on race, gender, ethnicity or national origin in public employment, contracting and public education.

Some Jewish organizations have opposed the measure, others have supported it, and at least one—the Anti-Defamation League, which has come out against affirmative action in the past—has decided to remain publicly neutral on it.

Field, Mack and Rabbi Chaim Seidler-Feller, the organizer of the UCLA forum, say that another task in the reconciliation between blacks and Jews is to bring more young people into the discussion.

"In both communities, youth no longer harbor a commitment to reaching out," Seidler-Feller said.

Nor, he added, do they have the common experience of the civil rights movement or the Bradley years.

Students involved in the UCLA dialogue said the situation on campuses may be worse than in the general population.

"Black students don't see any difference between the average Jewish student and the average white student. Jewish student participation in [causes supported by students of color] is no longer there," said Jioni Palmer, editor of Nommo, a news magazine produced by black UCLA students.

Nevertheless, Palmer, along with a Jewish student who is a former editor of the campus newspaper, the Bruin, agreed that dialogue between black and Jewish students should be pursued.

"Where we can agree, we can. Where we can't, we can't," said Palmer, adopting the vocabulary of his elders. "Let's work on those things we can agree with."

Article 8.2

Black, Cuban Racial Chasm Splits Miami

Mike Clary

Miami—In any other American city, a spitting incident might be dismissed as a silly office tiff between co-workers. But not here. Not now. Especially not when the alleged spitter is Latino and the person spat upon is black.

"We are very much on edge here, and it's getting worse because of the constant elimination of African Americans from jobs and political offices," warned Nathaniel J. Wilcox, executive director of a civil rights group called People United to Lead the Struggle for Equality, or PULSE. "They are becoming the oppressor."

In this case, "they," to Wilcox and many other blacks here, means Cuban Americans, who in the 38 years since the Cuban revolution have infused Miami's soul with an undeniable Latin rhythm while becoming the area's predominant ethnic group.

Throughout Dade County, Cuban Americans now occupy almost every top elected and administrative post. Cuban Americans hold the offices of mayor and city manager in Miami and Metropolitan Dade County, county school superintendent and Metro police chief as well as the presidencies of Florida International University and Miami-Dade Community College.

To many, the story of how penniless Caribbean immigrants found refuge in a new land and in less than two generations realized the American dream is nothing less than a testament to hard work and the virtues of capitalism.

Others, however, read that success story and see little more than a Miami spin on that oldest of American problems: race relation. "Now Cubans are in power and blacks are still second-class citizens," said Miami attorney H.T. Smith, a prominent activist in black causes. "And they have shown no intention of sharing that power."

On the streets of Overtown and Liberty City, this city's predominantly black sections, frustration and anger bubble very near the surface. The ascent of Cuban Americans, coupled with a history of mistrust and the perception that blacks are slipping even further down the economic ladder, have led to public rallies at which speakers decry what one recently called "a sense of isolation, a sense of disenfranchisement, a sense of not being connected to the community in a larger way."

Unemployment is high, welfare benefits are being cut back and many complain that an inability to speak Spanish denies American-born blacks even entry-level jobs. For the first time in more than three decades, there are no blacks—and four Cubans—on the five-member Miami City Commission.

Blacks too young to remember the horror of four bloody riots in the 1980s suggest that another urban uprising may be the only way to get the attention of Latino civic leaders. With a climate of resentment that some black leaders say is a flash point, even a rude joke that backfires could spark an explosion.

Take the spitting incident, for example.

According to local press reports, Eileen Valdes, who works in the Dade County clerk's office, walked by the desk of Nekesia Paschal and blew her a raspberry, also called a Bronx cheer. Paschal says spittle landed on her cheek.

The day before that Feb. 25 exchange, Paschal skipped work to take part in Blackout '97, a day of protest designed to call attention to the economic and political plight of blacks in Dade County. That protest had already ignited controversy because it coincided with the first anniversary of the day Cuban MIGS show down two unarmed Cessnas piloted by exiles searching for refugees off the Cuban coast. Four young aviators were killed.

To Cuban Americans, who had a full slate of memorial observances planned, scheduling Blackout for the same day was insensitive and disrespectful.

Paschal said she was spat upon by Valdes in retaliation for taking part in the Blackout protest. Valdes said the gesture was innocent. She apologized.

The spitting incident, which is under investigation by county officials, has become to many blacks just one more straw in a back-breaking load of affronts that has accompanied what they see as a total Cuban takeover.

"Here you have a group of Latinos—Cubans specifically—who have realized in one generation a dream denied to blacks for 300 years," said University of Miami sociologist Max Castro. "So the problems of race—found everywhere in the U.S.—are aggravated here."

Of Dade County's 2 million residents, 55% are Latino, 25% are non-Hispanic white, and 21% are black. (About 1.6% are both black and Latino. Of Latinos, about 60% are Cuban.

To be sure, the traditional power brokers, non-Hispanic whites, retain considerable influence in greater Miami. While assuming a lower profile, white men still predominate in the corporate board rooms and Biscayne Bay-front mansions.

But during three decades of steady immigration to South Florida, Cubans have prospered. While median household income has declined for the 27 million Latinos in the United States, Cuban Americans are the exception. The average median income of the Cuban American is slightly higher than black Americans in Dade County, and Cubans—most of them in South Florida—account for 40% of the 80 people topping Hispanic Business magazine's list of the richest U.S. Latinos.

Over the years, ethnic and racial insults—real and perceived—between African Americans and Cubans have piled up like tinder. Three of Miami's riots in the last decade were touched off by the fatal shootings of black men by Latino police officers. On a long list of other controversies are everything from Cuban American snubs of two visiting dignitaries—South African leader Nelson Mandela and former U.N. Ambassador Andrew Young

—because of their contacts with Cuban leader Fidel Castro, to election day defeats and the closing of a neighborhood swimming pool.

Now even the slightest of slights seems charged with explosive potential.

"Under normal circumstances, something like this would not become a community issue," said civic activist Smith. "But with our history, neither side is prepared to give the other the benefit of the doubt. So instinctively, we are ready to assume the worst. It's a very volatile situation.

"The major problem," Smith said, "is that Cubans have not made the mental transition from poor minority to extremely powerful majority. So we now have a group of people with economic and political power who unfortunately act as if they believe they are entitled to 100% of the power, 100% of the time. That is a formula for ultimate anarchy."

Aggravating the mistrust between Cubans and Blacks is a mutual impression that neither group understands the history of the other. As immigrants, Cubans owe some of their success here to government-backed minority programs brought about by the black-led struggle for civil rights, Smith said.

Now ascendant, Cubans "should not have such short memories," he said. "They have power because of alliances with blacks.

"They are like young ponies trying to find their legs. But while doing so, Cubans have to understand they don't get to eat all the hay. They have to share."

Said Wilcox of PULSE: "There are some Cuban brothers who want to see the right thing happen, so it's unfair to stereotype all. But those in power are abusing their authority. So it won't take a whole lot to reach the flash point."

Race is also a factor. Although 62% of the 11 million people in Cuba today are either black or of mixed race, Cuban Miami is overwhelmingly white. According to the 1990 census, 92% of Cubans in greater Miami describe themselves as white.

Why the disparity? The first wave of people to flee Cuba in the early 1960s came chiefly from the white, well-off middle class whose property was being confiscated by the Castro government, according to historians. Successive migrant waves, driven by family ties, have followed that pattern.

Many Cubans in positions of power admit inequities. Earlier this month, Miami Mayor Joe Carollo announced formation of a panel to study redistricting the city to ensure black representation on the City Commission. And Metro Mayor Alex Penelas has come up with an economic plan that targets urban redevelopment and job creation in the black community.

But Carollo's actions came only after PULSE sued the city for denying blacks adequate representation.

And Penelas made his urban action proposals only after the announcement of Blackout '97 galvanized the black community's outrage over economic and political impotence.

Metro Commissioner Barbara Carey—one of four blacks on the 13-member county governing board—said that blacks must emulate Cuban success. "They understand that in this capitalistic society, power is having the means to economic survival," she said. "I don't fault the Cubans. The Anglos created the model and Hispanics followed it. I just with African Americans had been able to do the same thing."

Article 8.3

Korean/African-American Conflicts

Pyong Gap Min

The central thesis of this book is that Koreans' concentration in small business enhances ethnic solidarity mainly because it increases intergroup conflicts. Intergroup conflict is therefore theoretically important as a variable mediating ethnic business and ethnic solidarity. However, Korean/African-American conflict in itself is a key topic in this book because of its theoretical and policy implications. Korean/African-American tensions over the last ten years have been a major social problem in contemporary urban America, affecting not only the Korean community but also relations among ethnic and racial groups more generally in many cities; Korean community leaders, African-American civil rights leaders, and government agencies have all tried to reduce these tensions.

In discussing Korean/African-American conflicts, we need to distinguish between radical forms of hostility toward Korean merchants, such as boycotts, looting, and arson, and individual disputes between merchants and customers. Korean and African-American community leaders, the mass media, and policy makers have emphasized cultural differences, mutual prejudice, and Koreans' language problems as major sources of friction. Undoubtedly, these sociopsychological factors have contributed to the frequent disputes that have occurred on the individual level in Korean stores in Black neighborhoods.

However, Korean/black conflicts on the collective level, as reflected in blacks' long-term boycotts and sometimes arson of Korean stores and in Koreans' group responses to these actions, result from broad structural forces that cannot be explained by sociopsychological factors. The deteriorating economic conditions and increasing crime rates in the inner city since the early 1970s pushed large chain stores and independent White-owned businesses out of African-American neighborhoods. At the same time, Korean immigrants, who were severely handicapped for employment in the general labor market, were turning to self-employment in small business as an alternative to blue-collar occupations. Despite high crime rates, Korean merchants preferred low-income minority neighborhoods to middle-class White neighborhoods because they could start businesses there with smaller amounts of capital and without competition from large chain stores.

Korean merchants have played a middleman minority role in low-income neighborhoods, distributing the products of White corporations to African-American customers. In that role, they were scapegoated by residents who were frustrated with their inability in improve their economic conditions. Korean merchants were easy targets; as new immigrants they did not have political power. They bore the brunt of Black anger, though the larger system was responsible for Blacks' economic problems. This suggests that Korean-Black conflicts are rooted in racial inequality between Whites and Blacks in general and in the poverty of inner-city black neighborhoods in particular. Korean and Black community leaders and policy makers who emphasize the sociopsychological reasons for Korean/black conflict have not paid enough attention to these structural causes.

Though Korean merchants also ran businesses in low-income Latino neighborhoods in large numbers, there they did not encounter boycotts and other forms of anti-Korean violence. This suggests that simple frustration over deplorable economic conditions is not the sufficient condition for organized movements against Korean merchants in Black neighborhoods. The transformation of Black residents' economic frustrations into concerted anti-Korean actions required leaders and an ideology. Black nationalists have played the leading role in organizing anti-Korean activities, and Black nationalism, emphasizing the economic autonomy of the Black community, has served as the needed ideology. Though the ostensible reason for boycotting Korean stores was merchants' disrespectful attitudes toward customers, Black nationalists who organized boycotts emphasized the need for economic control of the community by Blacks.

Middleman minority theory suggests that middleman merchants become scapegoats of both minority customers and the ruling group. Many Korean Americans, especially young Korean Americans, argued that during the Los Angeles riots Korean merchants were used to shield the White majority from African Americans' hostility toward the system. Without doubt, the biased media coverage of Korean-Black conflicts significantly contributed to the victimization of Korean merchants during the riots. However, there is no evidence that the media or the U.S. government intended to use Korean merchants as scapegoats to mitigate African Americans' hostility toward the "White system." By sensationalizing Korean-Black conflicts, the media were irresponsible and unethical, but not malicious. Indeed, it is important that Black, Korean, and mainstream media should be more sensitive to the practical consequences of their coverage. Fair and objective reporting is essential to the ethical code of journalists. Yet, unfortunately, many journalists do not adhere to this code. Federal and city governments should use symposiums and meetings to help sensitize journalists to community issues. Korean and Black media in particular can play a key role in bridging the two communities. In September 1990, when Korean-African American tensions were growing, Los Angeles City's Human Relations Commission brought together the editors of the city's five major ethnic publications to reverse the growing distance between minority populations. Their meetings led to the formation of the council of Multicultural Publications, an organization comprising twenty publications, in April 1991. Meetings between the editors of ethnic publications contributed to more cautious and objective reporting, particularly by the *Korea Times Los Angeles* (English edition) and the *Los Angeles Sentinel* (Marks 1991). Local governments in New York City and other cities should try to organize similar councils for dialogue.

Much more important than the media in contributing to Korean-Black tensions are the economic conditions of inner-city neighborhoods, which are not likely to substantially improve in the near future. Therefore, Korean merchants in Black neighborhoods will continue to encounter boycotts and other forms of hostility. However, by emphasizing the structural sources of Korean-Black conflicts, I do not intend to suggest that the multifaceted efforts of the Korean community to improve social and cultural ties with the African American community, reviewed in chapter 7, are useless. Black boycotts of Korean stores have generally started with individual disputes between store owners and customers. Therefore, by improving their services to customers and by contributing money and merchandise to African American neighborhoods, Korean merchants can reduce tensions. As noted in chapter 7, Korean merchants in Jamaica, Queens, have maintained close contacts with the Black neighborhood since they experienced a boycott in 1981. As a result, they have been able to avoid another long-term boycott, though Korean merchants in Brooklyn and Harlem have endured several. Moreover, establishing communication channels with the Black community through social and cultural ties helps the Korean community resolve serious conflicts in their early stages. Remember that one reason for the length of the 1990 Brooklyn boycott of two Korean stores—one and a half years—was the lack of any communication and dialogue between the Black community and the Korean community and business leaders.

My stress on Koreans' various efforts to improve relations with the black community as useful and worthwhile is deliberate. Many theoretically oriented scholars and second-generation Korean Americans argue that the "White system" or "U.S. capitalism" is entirely responsible for Korean-Black conflicts and that therefore Koreans and Blacks can do nothing significant to moderate tensions. Such a position is hardly useful to Korean and Black community leaders and policy makers who wish to address these problems. I remember reading a term paper by a second-generation Korean American doctoral student in which she argued that "if Korean merchants exploit Black customers, U.S. capitalism is responsible for Korean merchants' behaviors." I believe this type of deterministic thinking is not only useless but harmful and, therefore, irresponsible. To be sure, many intergroup conflicts in the United States, including Korean-Black conflicts, are inseparably tied to the capitalistic economic structure and White power structure. Nevertheless, community leaders and government agencies can intervene effectively to reduce these conflicts, however limited their interventions might be. We, as social scientists, should provide constructive recommendations rather than pessimistic and cynical conclusions.

In addition, improving relationships with the African American community through cultural and social exchanges is desirable in itself for the future of the Korean American community, regardless of how it affects Korean merchants. Korean immigrants, who are from an ethnically and culturally homogeneous society, are not well prepared to live in a multiethnic society like the United States. They are more isolated from the larger society than any other Asian group. It is an encouraging and positive sign that many Korean individuals and groups have recently participated in the efforts to bridge Korean and Black communities, as described in chapter 7. By learning about other cultures, Koreans will make it possible to live in peace and harmony with other ethnic groups.

CHAPTER 9

Race, Class, and Gender

In recent years, the study of the interrelationship among race, class, and gender has shifted from the margin to the center of scholarship, especially in ethnic studies and women's studies. The selection in this chapter introduces students to this burgeoning subject. Using a typical college basketball game as an example, Margaret Anderson and Patricia Collins explicate the interlocking nature of race, class, and gender.

1. Conceptualizing Race, Class and Gender
    Margaret Anderson and Patricia Hill Collins

Article 9.1

Conceptualizing Race, Class, and Gender

Margaret Anderson and Patricia Hill Collins

Picture a typical college basketball game. It all seems pretty familiar—the players on the court, the cheerleaders arrayed at the side, the band playing, fans cheering, boosters watching from the best seats, and if the team is ranked, perhaps a television crew. Everybody seems to have a place in the game. Everybody seems to be following the rules. But what are the "rules" of this game? What explains the patterns that we see and don't see?

Race clearly matters. The predominance of young African American males on many college basketball teams is noticeable. Why do so many young Black men play basketball? Some argue that African Americans are better in areas requiring physical skills such as sports and are less capable of doing intellectual work in fields such as physics, law, and medicine. Others look to Black culture for explanations, suggesting that African Americans would be perfectly happy just playing ball and partying. But these perspectives fail to take into account the continuing effects of institutional racism. Lack of access to decent jobs, adequate housing, quality education, and adequate health care has resulted in higher rates of poverty for African Americans. For example, in 1991, 33 percent of African Americans were poor, as compared to 9 percent of Whites (O'Hare 1992:6). For young Black men growing up in communities with few opportunities, sports like basketball become attractive as a way out of poverty. But despite the importance of institutionalized racism, does a racial analysis fully explain the "rules" of the game of college basketball?

Not really, because Black men are not the only players. White men also play college basketball, and their backgrounds in some ways mirror those of the Black players. This leads to the significance of social class in explaining a basketball game. Who benefits from college basketball? Some argue that because the players get scholarships and are offered a chance to earn college degrees, the players reap the rewards, but this misses the point of who really benefits. College athletics is big business, and the players make far less from it than we typically believe. As amateur athletes, the players themselves are forbidden to take any payment for their skills. They are offered the hope of an NBA contract when they turn pro, or at least a college degree should they manage to graduate. But, as Messner shows in his "Masculinities and Athletic Careers," few actually turn pro; moreover, 47 percent of male college athletes actually graduate, compared to 54 percent of college students overall (*The Chronicle of Higher Education*, May 26, 1993, p. A33). These trends are accentuated among Black athletes. Interestingly, among women college athletes, 61 percent graduate.

So, who actually benefits from college basketball? The colleges that recruit these athletes certainly benefit. Winning teams garner increased alumni giving, corporate support, and television revenues. In athletics as a business, corporate sponsors want their names and products identified with winning teams and athletes; advertisers want their products promoted by members of winning teams. Even though the athletes themselves are forbidden to promote the products, corporations create and market products that can be sold in conjunction with the excitement about basketball sustained by the players' achievements. Products such as athletic shoes, workout clothing, cars, and beer are all targeted toward the consumer dollars of males who enjoy watching basketball. Also, consider how many full-time jobs are supported by the revenues generated by the enterprise of college basketball. Referees, sports reporters both at the actual games and on local new stations, athletic trainers, coaches, and health personnel all benefit. Unlike the players, these people all get paid for their contributions to college basketball.

Do race and class fully explain the "rules" of basketball? Sometimes what we *don't* see can be just as revealing as what we do see. One other feature of the game on the court may escape attention because it is so familiar and, therefore, so unquestioned. All of the players are men. All of the coaches and support personnel are men. Probably, most of the camera crew and announcers are men. Where are the women? Those closest to the action on the court are probably cheerleaders, tumbling, dancing, and being thrown into the air in support of the exploits of the athletes. Others may be in the band. Some women are in the stands, cheering on the team—many of them accompanied by their husbands, boyfriends, parents, and children. Many work in the concession stands, fulfilling women's traditional roles of serving others. Still others are even more invisible, left to clean the restrooms, locker rooms, and stands after the crowd goes home. Women remain on the sidelines in other ways as well. The treatment of women basketball players is markedly different than that of their male counterparts; women have many fewer opportunities for scholarships and professional careers in athletics. The centrality of men's activities in basketball mirrors the centrality afforded men's activities in the society as a whole; thus, women's seeming invisibility in basketball ironically highlights the salience of gender.

This brief discussion of a college basketball game demonstrates how race, class, and gender each provide an important, yet partial, perspective on the action on the court. Race, class, and gender are so inextricably intertwined that gaining a comprehensive understanding of one basketball game requires that we think inclusively. If something as familiar and widespread as college basketball is embedded in race, class and gender relations, we might ask how other social practices, institutions, relations, and social issues are similarly structured.

Although some people believe that race, gender, and class divisions are relics of the past, we see them as deeply embedded in the structure of social institutions such as work, family, education, the state, and sports. Moreover, the politics of race, class, and gender in turn shape both the social issues that emerge from within and shape these institutional contexts.

CHAPTER 10

Controversial Issues in Ethnic Studies

Currently, there are a number of controversial issues in ethnic studies that occupy the national forum. This chapter highlights three of the most contentious: (1) affirmative action; (2) illegal immigration; and (3) bilingual education.

Three selections represent three different positions on affirmative action. Jesse Jackson argues for the preservation of affirmative action policy (i.e., "keep it"). Arch Puddington strives for its elimination (i.e., "end it"). The prescription of President Bill Clinton to the controversy is "mend it, but don't end it." The articles of Elizabeth Kadetsky and Governor Pete Wilson represent the positions of both sides on the debate over Proposition 187: Kadetsky, against it, and Wilson, for it.

To facilitate class discussions and the understanding of the debates, this chapter also includes the original texts of the three controversial propositions passed by California voters: Proposition 187 (1994), Proposition 209 (1996), and Proposition 227 (1997).

1. Affirming Affirmative Action
   Jesse Jackson

2. What to Do about Affirmative Action
   Arch Puddington

3. Mend It, Don't End it
   Bill Clinton

4. Bashing Illegals in California
   Elizabeth Kadetsky

5. Securing Our Nation's Borders
   Pete Wilson

6. Text of Proposition 187—The Save Our State Initiative

7. Text of Proposition 209—The California Civil Rights Initiative

8. Text of Proposition 227—The English Language Education for Children in Public Schools Initiative

Article 10.1

Affirming Affirmative Action

Jesse Jackson

People of color and white women have traditionally been locked out of the broader economic opportunities available to white males, and they are once again being scapegoated as the American public faces uncertainties about what the future global market will bring. Capitalizing on these fears, long-time critics of affirmative action are attempting to turn public opinion against the programs by claiming they are ineffective and that they discriminate against white males, neither of which is true. Statistics reveal that white males continue to monopolize high status positions in society, proving that discrimination continues to persist and that affirmative action is warranted. Three decades of this policy are an inadequate reparation for 250 years of slavery and discrimination. Therefore, America's commitment to affirmative action must be renewed.

There is great tension in our country today. There are economic fears and insecurities that are real and must be corrected. But there are the hostile voices of fear and demagoguery using the tactic of scapegoating, turning American against American, neighbor against neighbor.

Scapegoating the Disadvantaged

We have a smiling face on our economy—the stock market has hit its all-time high, Wall Street is booming, the top 20% of all Americans are doing very well. But there is beneath that face a nauseous stomach, the underbelly of our economy, that is not as fortunate. Our rank-and-file workers are feeling insecure and with good reason. For the past 20 years, they've been working longer and making less at less stable jobs. America once exported products; we now export jobs and plants.

Workers feel the pain of the globalization of the economy, the impact of competing with cheaper, less secure, more vulnerable workers. When you combine this with the impact of "reinventing" or reducing government, exporting jobs, downsizing corporations, ending the Cold War (there is nobody to fight), closing military bases, plants, and family farms, while increasing the military budget, it is not surprising that we, as a nation, are feeling anxious.

Nike, Reebok, LA Gear, Westinghouse, Smith Corona, and many of our other manufacturing companies have moved offshore. RCA, once symbolized by the dog listening to its master's voice, is an image which no longer applies. Today, the master speaks a language the dog cannot understand.

In the face of this profound structural crisis in our national economy, we need leadership to provide a clear analysis and constructive solutions to appease our anxieties. Instead, women and people of color are being used as scapegoats and objects of vilification.

While we witness congressional attacks on Aid to Families with Dependent Children, Congress blindly embraces Aid for Dependent Corporations. There is an attack on welfare but tiptoeing around S&L thieves, buccaneer bankers, a trillion and one-half dollar military budget to defend Europe, Japan, and South Korea at a time when they are able to share the burden of their own defense.

Instead of identifying these real problems and finding real solutions, many are perpetrating falsehoods and spreading myths blaming the weakest in our society for the excesses of the few. The new Republican congressional majority is using affirmative action to divide our nation for political gain.

Myth Vs. Fact

Affirmative Action is under attack. The Republicans want to rip it. The President wants to review it. We must look at America before Affirmative Action and since Affirmative Action. We must look at the remaining gap in wages between men and women, whites and people of color. We must determine its necessity by data, not by anecdotes.

It is a myth that white males are being hurt and discriminated against because of Affirmative Action programs. White males are 33% of the population, but

- 80% of Tenured Professors
- 80% of the U.S. House of Representatives
- 90% of the U.S. Senate
- 92% of the Forbes 400
- 97% of School Superintendents
- 99.9% of Professional Athletic Team Owners; and
- 100% of U.S. Presidents

Since the inception of this nation, white males were given preferential or deferential treatment—for the right to vote, the right to own land, to apply for loans and institutions of higher education. In the late 1800s white males were given a million acres of oil and soil-rich land under the Homestead Act as a bonus to go west and replace Native Americans. As current statistics show, such preferential treatment carries over to 1995.

It is a myth that Affirmative Action creates preferences for women and people of color. After 250 years of slavery, 100 years of apartheid, and 40 years of discrimination—history, of course, is unbroken continuity—we cannot burn the books, we cannot scorch the Earth. This unbroken record of race and sex discrimination has warranted a conservative remedy—Affirmative Action. Those who have been locked out need the law to protect them from the "tyranny of the majority." That is the genius of our Constitution, with its checks and balances and balance of power. We need not be race neutral, but race inclusive. We need not be color and gender blind, but color- and gender-caring. The Good Samaritan was not blind to a damaged man of another race, another religion, and another language; he was caring.

The conservative remedy of affirmative action seeks to repair the effects of past and *present* discrimination. It creates equal opportunities for people who have been historically and currently discriminated against. Affirmative Action does not mean "quotas"—in point of fact, it is *illegal* for employers to prefer *unqualified* applicants over qualified ones. What Affirmative Action mandates is the use of goals and timetables to diversify our workforce and universities.

It is a myth that Affirmative Action has hurt people of color, women, or the nation. Affirmative Action has benefitted our entire nation. The first beneficiaries are U.S. corporations. We have the strongest, most diversified workforce in the world. We urge the President to convene corporate leaders and let them assume the burden and the obligation to make a statement sharing their experience of the advantages of having a diversified, educated workforce. Affirmative Action has benefitted white women and their families as a result of two-wage earners in their households. It has benefitted blacks, browns, Native Americans, Asians, veterans, and the disabled. It has turned tax consumers into taxpayers and revenue-generators. It has created a new middle class. It has diversified our workforce and has made us a better nation. I literally went to jail to open up building trades unions so that we might become carpenters and brickmasons and glazers and have the right to work with a skill, and earn a livable wage.

Review Must Be Based on Data, Not Myth

As the President pursues his review it must be based on data, not myth. We urge him to convene the Chair of the EEOC [Equal Employment Opportunity Commission], a rather invisible position, the Chair of the Office of Contract Compliance, and indeed the Chair of the U.S. Civil Rights Commission. And let's have a review, not a retreat. A review to renew a commitment to fairness and to complete unfinished business.

The President is calling for a review. When he does his review, he will discover that Department of Labor statistics illustrates clear disparities in the representation of women and people of color in the American workforce as compared to white men.

In the 1994 labor market, while women represented 51.2% of the U.S. adult population, African Americans 12.4%, and Latinos 9.5%.

- 22% of all doctors were women, 4% African American, 5% Latino
- 24% of all lawyers were women, 3% African American, 3% Latino
- 42% of all professors were women, 5% African American, 2% Latino
- 16% of all architects were women, 1% African American, 3% Latino
- 31% of all scientists were women, 3% African American 1% Latino
- 8% of all engineers were women, 4% African American, 3% Latino

In May 1994, the National Rainbow Coalition [a civil rights organization] released a study of the National Broadcast Corporation (NBC) which highlights a pattern of racial and gender discrimination in hiring practices in its New York division. ABC and CBS do not vary very much. We found:

- Out of 645 employees of the News Division, 354 were white males, 261 were white females (a total of 96%), 8 were black males, 8 black females, 7 Latino females, 1 Latino male, 3 Asian males and 3 Asian females, 0 Native Americans.
- Of the key employee positions, 142 were white males, 121 were white females, 3 black males, 2 black females, 1 Latino male, 1 Latino female, 0 Asians, and 0 Native Americans.
- Out of 386 employees in NBC's East Coast Entertainment Division, 237 were white males, 130 white females, 6 black males, 3 black females, 5 Latino males, 1 Latino female, 4 Asian males, 0 Asian females and 0 native Americans.

Patterns of present-day discrimination—of being locked out. This is not a gene factor. This is a pattern based upon cultural, race, and sex bias.

Affirmative Action Is Still Needed

We cannot fall prey to the inane notion that discrimination is an evil of the past. It is today a very painful reality. As the figures above demonstrate, representation of women and people of color in the American workforce has improved, but is hardly sufficient. We still have a long way to go. When Affirmative Action was being enforced, gains were made, but during the Reagan-Bush years, many of the gains were lost. One need look no further than the well-documented disparity in pay between white men, women, and people of color:

- In 1975, median income as a *percentage of white men's salaries* was 74% for African American men, 72% for Latino men, 58% for white women, 55% for African American women, and 49% for Latino women.
- At the height of the Reagan-Bush years in 1985, median income for African American men had dropped to 70%, for Latino men to 68%, rose for white women to 63%, and nominally increased to 57% for African American women and 52% for Latino women.
- In 1993, the figures reflect an increase for African American men to 74%, the rate for Latino men fell to 64%, 70% for white women, and 53% for African American women.

When the President reviews college and professional athletics, he will find great disparities in the positions of power between women, people of color, and white men:

- When the Chargers and the Super Bowl champion 49ers met on Super Bowl Sunday in 1994, there were no people of color or women in positions of power. Yet over 60% of those on the field were African Americans. But beyond the playing field, from coaches to athletic directors, to owners, the same situation is evident in NCAA [National Collegiate Athletic Association] athletic programs. We have effectively gone from picking cotton balls to picking basketballs, baseballs, and footballs. Upward mobility is severely limited.

When the President reviews institutions of higher education, he will find an attack on scholarships and, in effect, the globalization of American doctoral degrees according to a NAFEO (National Association For Equal Opportunity) report:

- Today African Americans comprise only 9.9% of the 12 million students enrollment in two- and four-year undergraduate institutions.
- In 1993, of the 6,496 doctorates awarded in physical sciences only 41 (0.6%) were awarded to African Americans, 89 (1.4%) were awarded to Latinos, and 2,818 (43.3%) were awarded to foreign students (whose countries we subsidize).
- Of all the 39,754 doctorates awarded in 1993, African Americans received 1,106 (2.8%), Latinos received 834 (2.1%), and foreign students received 12,173 (30.6%).

Lest we forget, forms of preferences have traditionally been granted in higher education on non-racial grounds. For example, we have not yet heard the call to deny children of alumnae special consideration in the admissions process.

When the President reviews government contracting practices, he will find empirical proof that when controls are eliminated, we witness a return to pre-Affirmative Action underrepresentation in our economy. Since the *Croson* decision, minority contracting in the city of Richmond, Virginia—a city of about 70% African American—went from 35% to 1%—reverting back to its pre-affirmative Action levels.

When the President reviews lending practices, he will find that access to capital and credit is denied to women and people of color because lending decisions are so arbitrary and subjective. Unless there is a reinvestment plan with goals, targets and timetables, the traditionally locked out will never gain access to capital. The contract is useless without the capital. Women and minorities have often had to joint venture with larger, white male firms in order to obtain the necessary capital.

A Renewed Commitment

Upon completion of his review, we urge the President to renew his commitment to Affirmative Action and enforce Affirmative Action laws as a way of expanding our economy and making us bigger and better and stronger. We hope that he will make the Equal Employment Opportunity Commission and the Office of Contract Compliance and Civil Rights Commission visible agencies and forces for good. The falsely accused need protection, and hope, and opportunity, not scapegoating, and review, and divisiveness, and undue blame.

What to Do about Affirmative Action

Arch Puddington

Affirmative action is simply another name for racial preferences. As a policy, it affronts the most treasured American values—those of fairness and individualism. Most Americans oppose preference policies, which were prohibited—although the prohibitions were subsequently disregarded by political elites—in the original antidiscrimination legislation of the 1960s. Proponents claim that "institutional racism"—racism pervasive in America's social and economic institutions—justifies continued racial preferences. However, rather than achieve equality for minorities and women, the programs have spawned reverse discrimination, which has in turn caused increasing racial disharmony. Moreover, affirmative action has eroded academic and professional standards as schools and employers strive to meet mandated quotas. America's political leaders should eliminate all federal programs that extend racial preferences while retaining antidiscrimination laws for an America that truly offers equal opportunity.

The thinking behind the policy of racial preference which has been followed in America over the past quarter-century under the name of "affirmative action" is best summed up by former Supreme Court Justice Harry Blackmun's famous dictum that, "In order to get beyond racism, we must first take race into account."

A Contradiction in Values

The Orwellian quality of Blackmun's admonition is obvious. Seldom has a democratic government's policy so completely contradicted the core values of its citizenry as racial preference does in violating the universally held American ideals of fairness and individual rights, including the right to be free from discrimination. Not surprisingly, then, where Americans regarded the original civil-rights legislation as representing a long-over-due fulfillment of the country's democratic promise, they overwhelmingly see racial preference as an undemocratic and alien concept, a policy implemented by stealth and subterfuge and defended by duplicity and legalistic tricks.

Americans do not believe that past discrimination against blacks in the workplace justifies present discrimination against whites. Nor do they accept the thesis that tests and standards are tainted, *en masse*, by cultural bias against minorities. Having been taught in high-school civics classes that gerrymandering to ensure party domination represents a de-fect in democracy, Americans are bewildered by the argument that gerrymandering is neces-sary to ensure the political representation of blacks and Hispanics. They are unimpressed by the contention that a university's excellence is enhanced by the mere fact of racial and eth-nic diversity in its student body, especially when entrance requirements must be lowered substantially to achieve that goal.

Americans, in short, oppose racial preference in all its embodiments, and have signified their opposition in opinion poll after opinion poll, usually by margins of three to one or more, with women as strongly opposed as men, and with an impressive proportion of blacks indi-cating opposition as well. The contention, repeatedly advanced by advocates of preferential policies, that a national consensus exists in support of such policies has been true only at the level of political elites. Americans do support what might be called soft affirmative action, entailing special recruitment, training, and outreach efforts, and are willing to accept some short-term compensatory measures to rectify obvious cases of proven discrimination. But at-titudes have, if anything, hardened against the kind of aggressive, numbers-driven preference schemes increasingly encountered in university admissions and civil-service hiring.

Refusing to Let Go

Nonetheless, up until this year [1995], racial preference in its various manifestations has been impressively resistant to calls for reform, much less elimination. In fact, race con-sciousness has begun to insinuate itself into areas which, common sense alone would sug-gest, should be immune to intrusive government social engineering. To cite but one example of this disturbing trend: Congress has mandated that guidelines be established guaranteeing the involvement of minorities (and women) in clinical research—a form of scientific experi-mentation by quota.

There is, furthermore, reason to question whether the advocates of race-conscious social policy continue to take seriously the objective of getting "beyond race," a condition which presumably would warrant the elimination of all preferential programs. The late Thurgood Marshall, an outspoken champion of preference while on the Supreme Court, is reported to have blurted out during an in-chambers discussion that blacks would need affirmative action for a hundred years. A similar opinion has been expressed by Benjamin Hooks, the former director of the National Association for the Advancement of Colored People (NAACP). Hooks contends that affirmative action, in some form should be accepted as one of those permanent, irritating features of American life—he cited as examples speeding laws and the April 15 income-tax deadline—which citizens tolerate as essential to the efficient and just functioning of society.

Neither Marshall nor Hooks is regarded as an extremist on race matters; their advocacy of a permanent regime of affirmative action falls within the mainstream of present-day liberal thought. The promotion of "diversity"—the latest euphemism for preferential representa-tion—is as fundamental to liberal governance as was the protection of labor unions in an earlier era. And until very recently, liberal proponents of preference clearly believed that history was on their side.

Thus, where enforcement agencies were formerly cautious in pressing affirmative action on the medical profession, the Clinton administration was formulating plans for a quota system throughout the health-care workforce. The goal, according to one memo of Hillary Clinton's task force, was nothing less than to ensure that this workforce achieve "sufficient racial, ethnic, gender, geographic, and cultural diversity to be representative of the people it serves." The task force also had plans to guide minority doctors into specialties while tracking other doctors into general practice. To realize this medical-care diversity blueprint, the task force proposed the creation of a bureaucracy with coercive powers to regulate the "geographic" and "cultural" distribution of physicians and other medical practitioners.

The Entrance of Quotas

How did American drift from the ideal of a color-blind society to the current environment of quotas, goals, timetables, race-norming, set-asides, diversity-training, and the like?

Those troubled by this question often refer wistfully to Martin Luther King, Jr.'s declaration that he hoped to see the day when his children would be judged by the content of their character and not by the color of their skin. Yet it must be recognized that even when King uttered those inspirational words at the 1963 March on Washington, they no longer reflected the thinking of crucial segments of the civil-rights movement. Already, increasingly influential black activists and their white supporters were advancing demands for hiring plans based on racial quotas. In pressing for such plans (then called compensatory treatment), the civil-rights movement was being joined by officials from the Kennedy administration, as well as by white intellectuals who, going further, announced that black economic equality could never be attained without a wholesale adjustment of standards and the merit principle.

These ruminations were not lost on the Dixiecrat opponents of desegregation, and the charge was soon made that Title VII of the pending civil-rights bill—the section dealing with discrimination in the workplace—would lead to the widespread practice of reverse discrimination. This in turn provoked a series of statements and speeches by stalwart liberals like Senators Hubert Humphrey, Joseph Clark, and Clifford Case, adamantly and unequivocally denying that the bill could be interpreted to permit racial preference.

In order to dispel lingering doubts, Humphrey and other supporters inserted an amendment to the bill declaring flatly that the law's purpose was to rectify cases of intentional discrimination and that it was not intended to impose sanctions simply because a workplace contained few blacks or because few blacks passed an employment test. Armed with this and similar clauses prohibiting reverse discrimination, Humphrey promised to "start eating the pages [of the civil-rights bill] one after another" if anyone could discover language in it "which provides that an employer will have to hire on the basis of percentage or quota."

Under normal circumstances, the insertion of unambiguous antipreference language, combined with the condemnations of reverse discrimination by the bill's sponsors, would have been sufficient to prevent the subsequent distortion of the law's intent. But these protections turned out to be useless against the determination of the country's elites (in the political system, in the media, in the universities, and in the courts) to override them. Having concluded (especially after the urban riots of the late 60s) that social peace demanded racial preference, political leaders from both parties, along with a growing number of intellectuals and activists, both white and black, began looking upon the antipreference clauses in Title VII as obstacles to be circumvented rather than guides to be followed. The anti-preference language which had been added to ensure passage of the Civil Rights Act of 1964 was now not only ignored but treated as though it did not even exist.

Hence there was no serious effort by either Congress or the courts or anyone else to rein in the civil-rights bureaucracy, which dismissed the anti-preference provisions with contempt from the very outset. A "big zero, a nothing, a nullity," is how these provisions were characterized by an official of the Equal Employment Opportunity Commission (EEOC) at the time. Federal enforcement officials in general, most of whom were white, were more aggressive in pursuing preferences, and less inclined to reflect on the broader implications of affirmative action, than were many mainstream black leaders of that day, some of whom—Toy Wilkins, Bayard Rustin, and Clarence Mitchell, for example—opposed reverse discrimination on moral and political grounds.

The part played by the EEOC in putting together the structure of racial preference cannot be overstated. In blithe and conscious disregard of the anti-preference sections of Title VII, EEOC officials broadened the definition of discrimination to encompass anything which contributed to unequal outcomes. In its most far-reaching move, the EEOC launched an all-out assault on employment testing. The agency's mindset was reflected in comments about "irrelevant and unreasonable standards," "the cult of credentialism," and "artificial barriers."

Yet despite the ingenuity of its lawyers in devising intricate arguments to circumvent the strictures against reverse discrimination—and despite the willingness of activist judges to accept these arguments—the EEOC could never have achieved its aims had it not been for a transformation of elite attitudes toward the problem of race in America.

"Institutional Racism"

In 1964, the year the Civil Rights Act was passed, an optimistic and morally confident America believed that the challenge posed by the "Negro revolution" could be met through a combination of anti-discrimination laws, economic growth, and the voluntary good will of corporations, universities, and other institutions. But by the decade's end, a crucial segment of elite opinion had concluded that America was deeply flawed, even sick, and that racism, conscious or otherwise, permeated every institution and government policy. Where individual prejudice had previously been identified as the chief obstacle to black progress, now a new target, "institutional racism," was seen as the principal villain. And where it was once thought that democratic guarantees against discrimination, plus the inherent fairness of the American people, were sufficient to overcome injustice, the idea now took hold that since racism was built into the social order, coercive measures were required to root it out.

In this view, moreover, the gradualist Great Society [an agenda of social programs designed to fight poverty] approach launched by Lyndon Johnson, which stressed education, training, and the strengthening of black institutions, could not alleviate the misery of the inner-city poor, at least not as effectively as forcing employers to hire them. Even Johnson himself began calling for affirmative action and issued an executive order directing that federal contractors adopt hiring policies which did not discriminate on the basis of race (or gender); in a process that would soon become all too familiar, court decisions and the guidelines of regulators subsequently interpreted the directive as mandating racial balance in the workforce, thus paving the way for demands that companies doing business with the government institute what often amounted to quotas in order to qualify for contracts.

Little noticed at the time—or, for that matter, later—was that black America was in the midst of a period of unprecedented economic progress, during which black poverty declined, the racial income gap substantially narrowed, black college enrollment mushroomed, and black advancement into the professions took a substantial leap forward. All this, it should be stressed, occurred *prior* to the introduction of government-mandated racial preference.

Hiring-by-the-Numbers

Once affirmative action got going, there was no holding it back. The civil-rights movement and those responsible for implementing civil-rights policy simply refused to accept an approach under which preference would be limited to cases of overt discrimination, or applied to a narrow group of crucial institutions, such as urban police departments, where racial integration served a pressing public need. Instead, every precedent was exploited to further the permanent entrenchment of race consciousness.

For example, the Philadelphia Plan, the first preferential policy to enjoy presidential backing (the President being Richard Nixon), was a relatively limited effort calling for racial quotas in the Philadelphia building trades, an industry with a notorious record of racial exclusion. Yet this limited program was seized upon by the EEOC and other agencies as a basis for demanding hiring-by-the-numbers schemes throughout the economy, whether or not prior discrimination could be proved.

Similarly, once a race-conscious doctrine was applied to one institution, it inevitably expanded its reach into other areas. The Supreme Court's decision in *Griggs v. Duke Power, Inc.*—that employment tests could be found to constitute illegal discrimination if blacks failed at a higher rate than whites—was ostensibly confined to hiring and promotion. But *Griggs* was used to legitimize the burgeoning movement against testing and standards in the educational world as well. Tracking by intellectual ability, special classes for high achievers, selective high schools requiring admissions tests, standardized examinations for university admissions—all were accused of perpetuating historic patterns of bias.

The campaign against testing and merit in turn gave rise to a series of myths about the economy, the schools, the workplace, about America itself. Thus, lowering job standards as a means of hiring enough blacks to fill a quota was justified on the grounds that merit had never figured prominently in the American workplace, that the dominant principles had always been nepotism, backscratching, and conformism. To explain the racial gap in Scholastic Assessment Test scores, the concept of cultural bias was advanced, according to which disparities in results derived from the tests' emphasis on events and ideas alien to urban black children. Another theory claimed that poor black children were not accustomed to speaking standard English and were therefore placed at a disadvantage in a normal classroom environment. It was duly proposed that black children be taught much like immigrant children, with bilingual classes in which both standard English and black English would be utilized. A related theory stated that black children retained a distinct learning style which differed in significant respects from the learning styles of other children. As one educator expressed the theory, any test which stressed "logical, analytical methods of problem-solving" would *ipso facto* be biased against blacks.

Affirmative Action Begins to Crumble

Until quite recently, the very idea of abolishing racial preference was unthinkable; the most realistic ambitions for the critics of race-based social policy went no further than trying to limit—limit, not stop—the apparently relentless spread of racial preferences throughout the economy, the schools and universities, and the political system. Yet it now appears not only that the momentum of racial preference has been halted, but that, at a minimum, a part of the imposing affirmative-action edifice will be dismantled. Furthermore, a process has already been set in motion which could conceivably lead to the virtual elimination of race-based programs.

Racial preferences have become vulnerable mainly because of the sudden collapse of the elite consensus which always sustained affirmative action in the face of popular opposition. Where in the past many Republicans could be counted on to support, or at least tolerate, racial preferences, the new congressional majority seems much more inclined to take a sharply critical look at existing racial policies. Equally important is the erosion of support for preference within the Democratic Party. While some newly skeptical Democrats are clearly motivated by worries about reelection, others have welcomed the opportunity to express long-suppressed reservations about policies which they see as having corrupted, divided, and weakened their party.

The revolt against affirmative action has also been heavily influenced by the fact that, as preferential policies have extended throughout the economy, a critical mass of real or perceived victims of reverse discrimination has been reached—white males who have been denied jobs, rejected for promotion, or prevented from attending the college or professional school of their choice because slots were reserved for blacks (or other minorities or women).

There is, no doubt, an inclination on the part of white men to blame affirmative action when they are passed over for jobs or promotions, a tendency which is reinforced by the atmosphere of secrecy surrounding most preference programs. But enough is known about affirmative action in the public sector through information which has come out in the course of litigation to conclude that thousands of whites have indeed been passed over for civil-service jobs and university admissions because of outright quotas for racial minorities. It is also clear that a considerable number of private businesses have been denied government contracts because of minority set-asides.

Another major factor in the change of attitude toward affirmative action is the California Civil Rights Initiative (CCRI), which has already had an incalculable impact. The CCRI was organized by two white, male, and politically moderate professors in the California state-university system. The measure would amend the California constitution to prohibit the state government or any state agency (including the university system) from granting preference on the basis of race, ethnicity, or gender in employment, college admissions, or the awarding of contracts. It would, in other words, effectively ban affirmative-action programs mandated by the state.

Though limited to California, the CCRI is at heart a response to the logical destination of affirmative action everywhere in America: quota systems sustained by the support of elites from both political parties. To be sure, policy by racial classification has grown more pervasive in California than elsewhere in America. White males have been told not to bother applying for positions with the Los Angeles fire department due to the need to fill minority quotas. In San Francisco, Chinese students are denied admission to a selective public high school because of an ethnic cap; for similar reasons, whites, mainly Jews and East European immigrants, are often denied admission to magnet schools in Los Angeles. A de facto quota system effectively denies white males the opportunity to compete for faculty positions at certain state colleges. And, incredibly enough, the state legislature passed a bill calling for ethnic "guidelines" not only for admission to the state-university system but for graduation as well. The bill was vetoed by Governor Pete Wilson; had a Democrat been governor, it would almost certainly have become law.

The true impact of the CCRI can be gauged by the degree of fear it has generated among supporters of affirmative action. So long as the debate could be limited to the courts, the agencies of race regulation, and, when unavoidable, the legislative arena, affirmative action was secure. The mere threat of taking the issue directly to the voters, as the CCRI's sponsors propose to do through the referendum process, has elicited a down-right panicky response— itself a clear indication that the advocates of racial preference understand how unpopular their case is, and how weak.

A Divisive Affair

But a note of caution must be sounded to those who believe that current developments will lead inexorably to the reinstitution of colorblindness as the reigning principle in racial matters. The resilience of affirmative action in the face of widespread popular hostility suggests that even a modest change of course could prove a difficult and highly divisive affair.

There is, to begin with, the fact that affirmative action has been introduced largely by skirting the normal democratic process of debate and legislative action. Affirmative action is by now rooted in literally thousands of presidential directives, court decisions, enforcement-agency guidelines, and regulatory rules. These will not easily be overturned.

There is also the complicating factor of the federal judiciary's central role in overseeing racial policy. Given the emotionally charged character of the racial debate, the critics of racial preference will be tempted to postpone legislative action in the hope that the Supreme Court will resolve the issue once and for all. But while the Court today is less prone to judicial activism than during the Warren and Burger years, and while it may decide to limit the conditions under which a preferential program can be applied, it is unlikely to do away with affirmative action altogether.

The Republicans will face another temptation: to exploit white hostility to racial preference but avoid serious political action to eliminate it. A powerful political logic lies behind this temptation, since getting rid of affirmative action would also deprive the Republicans of a potent wedge issue. Yet one can hardly imagine a less desirable outcome than a prolonged and angry political confrontation over race. Moreover, if responsible politicians who share a principled opposition to preference decline to take the initiative, the door will be opened to racists and unscrupulous demagogues.

An additional obstacle to change is the fact that eliminating affirmative action does not offer much of a financial payoff. Affirmative action is not expensive; its only direct cost to the taxpayer is the expense of maintaining civil-rights agencies like the EEOC.

Claims have been made that affirmative action does represent a major cost to the American economy, but the facts are unclear since neither the media nor scholarly researchers nor the corporations themselves have shown an interest in undertaking an investigation of its economic impact. Indeed, though affirmative action is one of the most intensely discussed social issues of the day, it is probably the least researched. Press coverage is generally limited to the political debate; seldom are stories done about the actual functioning of affirmative-action programs. Nor is there much serious scholarly investigation of such questions as affirmative action's impact on employee morale, the performance of students admitted to college on an affirmative-action track, or the degree to which contract set-asides have contributed to the establishment of stable minority businesses.

Given the truly massive amount of research devoted to racial issues over the years, the lack of attention to preferential policies raises the suspicion that what has been operating here is a deliberate decision to avoid knowing the details of affirmative action's inner workings out of fear of the public reaction.

The Diversity Principle

Opponents of racial preference must also contend with the widespread acceptance of the "diversity" principle within certain key institutions. Here the American university stands out for its uncritical embrace of the notion that, as one recent cliché has it, "diversity is part of excellence." When Francis Lawrence, the president of Rutgers University, came under fire for uttering the now-famous phrase [in which he referred to African American students as lacking "that genetic, heredity background" needed to score well on college entrance exams] which seemed to question the genetic capabilities of black students, his principal defense—indeed practically his only defense—was that he had increased minority enrollment at Rutgers and during a previous administrative stint at Tulane. True to form, no one bothered to ask how black students recruited under Lawrence's diversity initiatives had fared academically or psychologically, or how the campus racial atmosphere had been affected, or how much standards had been adjusted to achieve the quota. The body count, and the body count alone, was what mattered for Lawrence, and, it would seem, for administrators at many campuses.

The diversity principle is also firmly entrenched throughout government service. Most agencies include a diversity or affirmative-action department, headed by an official with deputy-level status, with intrusive authority to promote staff "balance" and minority participation in contract bidding. So, too, private corporations have accepted affirmative action as part of the price of doing business. large corporations, in fact, can usually be counted on to oppose anti-quota legislation, preferring the simplicity of hiring by the numbers to the uncertainty of more flexible systems and the increased possibilities of anti-discrimination litigation brought by minorities or by whites claiming reverse bias.

But of course the most serious obstacle to change is black America's strong attachment to affirmative action. Race-conscious policies have had no demonstrable effect at all on the black poor, but they are widely perceived as having played a crucial role in creating the first mass black middle class in American history. The claim here is wildly exaggerated—to repeat, the trend was already well advanced before affirmative action got going. Nevertheless, to many blacks, affirmative action has become not a series of temporary benefits but a basic civil right, almost as fundamental as the right to eat at a restaurant or live in the neighborhood of one's choice, and certainly more important than welfare.

Accordingly, black leaders, who are always quick to condemn even the most modest changes as "turning back the clock" or as a threat to the gains of the civil-rights movement, have now escalated the counterattack in response to the more sweeping recent challenge to affirmative action. When Governor Pete Wilson made some favorable comments about the CCRI, Jesse Jackson compared him to George Wallace [former governor famous for his opposition to desegregation] blocking the schoolhouse door in Jim Crow Alabama. And when congressional Republicans moved to rescind a set-aside program in the communications industry, Representative Charles Rangel, a Democrat from Harlem, declared that the move reflected a Nazi-like mindset.

It is true that many blacks are ambivalent about preferences, or even critical of them. At the same time, however, they are highly sensitive to perceptions of white assaults on civil rights, and they may well find polemics of the Jackson and Rangel variety persuasive.

Eliminating Preference Programs

Confronted with all these obstacles, some opponents of affirmative action are leaning toward a compromise strategy involving a program-by-program review. This would be a serious mistake; the most desirable and politically effective course would be federal legislation modeled on the CCRI. Such a measure would leave in place the old laws against discrimination but would eliminate all federal programs which extend preference on the basis of race (as well as ethnicity or gender).

The measure could conceivably take the form of a reaffirmation of the sections of the 1964 Civil Rights Act dealing with the workplace, with special emphasis on the clauses explicitly prohibiting reverse discrimination. But whatever the specific shape of the new legislation, absolute clarity would be required on the principal issue: there would be no room for fudging, vagueness, or loopholes on the question of bringing the era of race-conscious social policy to a close. The legislation would therefore also have to include an explicit disavowal of the disparate-impact doctrine, under which the disproportionate representation of the races (or sexes) is often regarded as evidence in itself of discrimination, and which has often led to the imposition of the de facto quota systems.

The political struggle over this kind of sweeping legislation would be angry and unpleasant. But eliminating both the practice of racial preference and the controversy surrounding it would set the stage for an ultimate improvement in the racial environment throughout American society. On the other hand, an approach focusing on a program-by-program review of the multitude of preference initiatives in an ephemeral search for compromise only guarantees the permanence both of affirmative action itself and of the affirmative-action controversy.

A less sweeping but nevertheless useful approach would be a presidential decree revoking the executive order issued by president Johnson which opened the way to federally mandated quotas. Though (as we have seen)Johnson did not necessarily intend this to happen, the fact is that his directive became a crucial pillar of the affirmative-action structure. With the stroke of a pen it could be rescinded.

Restoring Fixed Academic Standards

So far as the universities are concerned, the elimination of affirmative action would mean an end to lowering standards in order to fill racial quotas. No doubt this would also mean a smaller number of blacks at the elite universities, but there are perfectly decent state colleges and private institutions for every promising student whose qualifications do not meet the standards of Yale or Stanford. The notion that a degree from one of these institutions consigns the graduate to a second-class career is based on sheer prejudice and myth; for evidence to the contrary, one need look no further than the new Republican congressional delegation, which includes a number of graduates from what would be considered second- or third-tier colleges.

It hardly needs to be added that directing a student to a university for which he is educationally and culturally unprepared benefits neither the student nor the university nor the goal of integration. The results are already clear to see in the sorry state of race relations on campus. Many colleges are dominated by an environment of racial balkanization, with blacks increasingly retreating into segregated dormitories and black student unions, rejecting contacts with white students out of fear of ostracism by other blacks, and then complaining of the loneliness and isolation of campus life. Drop-out rates for those admitted on affirmative-action tracks are high, adding to black student frustration. These problems are invariably exacerbated by college administrators who respond to racial discontent with speech codes, sensitivity training, multicultural seminars, curriculum changes, and other aggressively prosecuted diversity initiatives.

Some have proposed basing affirmative action in university admissions on social class—that is, extending preferences to promising students from impoverished backgrounds, broken homes, and similar circumstances. On a superficial level, this would seem a sensible idea. Blacks would profit because they suffer disproportionately from poverty. Universities would gain from the high motivation of the students selected for the program. And real diversity would be enhanced by the presence of students whose backgrounds differed radically from the middle- and upper-class majority, and whose opinions could not be so predictably categorized along the conformist race (and gender) lines which dominate campus discussion today.

One major caveat is that college administrators, who give every indication of total commitment to the present race-based arrangements, would discover ways to circumvent a program based on color-blind standards. Indeed, they have already done so. Under the terms of the *Bakke* case (1978), which established the guidelines for affirmative action in university admissions, race could be counted as one of several factors, including social class; affirmative action based on race alone, the Supreme Court said, could not pass muster. As matters have evolved, affirmative action on many state campuses, most notably those in California, is based almost exclusively on race and ethnicity.

A similar class-based formula is difficult to envision outside the realm of university admissions. Yet there is no reason to assume that private businesses would respond to the elimination of government-enforced affirmative action by refusing to hire and promote qualified blacks. A return to race-neutral government policies would also enable black executives and professionals to shed the affirmative-action stigma, since no one would suspect that they were in their positions only as the result of pressure by a federal agency. The supporters of preferential policies may dismiss affirmative action's psychological effects on the beneficiaries as unimportant. But the evidence indicates that the image of a black professional class having risen up the career ladder through a special racial track is a source of serious workplace demoralization for members of the black middle-class.

Disproportionate Numbers

The arguments which have lately been advanced in favor of retaining affirmative action are by and large the same arguments that were made more than twenty years ago, when the intellectual debate over preference began.

Probably the least compelling of these is the contention that the advantages extended by university admissions offices to athletes, the children of alumni, and applicants from certain regions of the country justify extending similar advantages on the basis of race. The answer to this contention is simple: race is different from other criteria. America acknowledged the unique nature of racial discrimination when it enacted the landmark civil-rights laws of the 1960s. Moreover, the suggestion cannot be sustained that outlawing preference based on race while permitting preference based on nonracial standards would leave blacks even farther behind. Blacks, in fact, benefit disproportionately from admissions preferences for athletes or those with talents in music and art. No one objects, or thinks it unusual or wrong for some groups to be overrepresented and others to be underrepresented on the basis of such criteria.

A similar, but even weaker, argument (already alluded to above) holds that America has never functioned as a strict meritocracy, and that white males have maintained their economic dominance through connections, pull, and family. Affirmative action, this theory goes, simply levels the playing field and actually strengthens meritocracy by expanding the pool of talent from which an employer draws. The problem is that those who advance this argument seem to assume that only white males rely on personal relationships or kinship. Yet as we have learned from the experience of immigrants throughout American history, every racial and ethnic group values family and group ties. Korean-American shop-owners enlist their families, Haitian-American taxi fleets hire their friends.

What about the claim that affirmative action has improved the racial climate by hastening the integration of the workplace and classroom? While the integration process has often been painful and disruptive, there is no question that more contact between the races at school and at work has made America a better society. But integration has not always succeeded, and the most signal failures have occurred under conditions of government coercion, whether through busing schemes or the imposition of workplace quotas. In case after case, the source of failed integration can be traced to white resentment over racial preference or the fears of blacks that they will be perceived as having attained their positions through the preferential track.[2]

There is, finally, the argument that, since black children suffer disproportionately from poor nutrition, crack-addicted parents, wrenching poverty, and outright discrimination, affirmative action rightly compensates for the burden of being born black in America. Yet affirmative action has been almost entirely irrelevant to these children, who rarely attend college or see a professional career. The new breed of Republican conservatives may sometimes betray a disturbing ignorance of the history of racial discrimination in America. But on one crucial issue they are most certainly right: the march toward equality begins at birth, with the structure, discipline, and love of a family. The wide array of government-sponsored compensatory programs, including affirmative action, has proved uniformly ineffective in meeting the awesome challenge of inner-city family deterioration.

The End of an Era

To advocate a policy of strict race neutrality is not to ignore the persistence of race consciousness, racial fears, racial solidarity, racial envy, or racial prejudice. It is, rather, to declare that government should not be in the business of preferring certain groups over others. Because it got into this business, the United States has been moved dangerously close to a country with an officially sanctioned racial spoils system. Even Justice Blackmun was concerned about this kind of thing. In his *Bakke* opinion, Blackmun made it clear that preferential remedies should be regarded as temporary, and he speculated that race-conscious policies could be eliminated in ten years—that is, by the end of the 1980s.

Affirmative action's supporters grow uncomfortable when reminded of Blackmun's stipulation, which clashes with their secret conviction that preferences will be needed forever. Despite considerable evidence to the contrary, they believe that racism (and sexism) pervade American life, and they can always find a study, a statistic, or an anecdote to justify their prejudice.

If racial preference is not eliminated now, when a powerful national momentum favors resolving the issue once and for all, the result may well be the permanent institutionalization of affirmative action, though probably at a somewhat less expansive level than is the case right now. Alternatively, a cosmetic solution, which eliminates a few minor policies while leaving the foundation of racial preference in place, could trigger a permanent and much more divisive racial debate, with a mushrooming of state referenda on preference and the growing influence of extremists of both races.

It is clear that a bipartisan majority believes that the era of racial preference should be brought to a close. It will take an unusual amount of political determination and courage to act decisively on this belief. But the consequences of a failure to act could haunt American political life for years to come.

Notes

1. Affirmative action has, of course, been extended to women and certain other groups, but I will confine the discussion here to race. Affirmative action was devised primarily to promote the economic status of blacks, and the racial implications of the debate over this policy are far more significant than questions arising from preferences for women or other ethnic minorities. I should add that if preference for black Americans is unjustified, there is even less to be said for it when applied to women or to such immigrant groups as Hispanics and Asians.

2. An important exception is the military, where affirmative action is applied to promotions but where standards have not been lowered to enlarge the pool of qualified black applicants.

Article 10.3

Mend It, Don't End It

Bill Clinton

The purpose of affirmative action is to give our nation a way to finally address the systematic exclusion of individuals of talent on the basis of their gender or race from opportunities to develop, perform, achieve, and contribute. Affirmative action is an effort to develop a systematic approach to open the doors of educational, employment, and business development opportunities to qualified individuals who happen to be members of groups that have experienced long-standing and persistent discrimination.

It is a policy that grew out of many years of trying to navigate between two unacceptable paths. One was to say simply that we have declared discrimination illegal, and that's enough. We saw that that way still relegated blacks with college degrees to jobs as railroad porters, and kept women with degrees under a glass ceiling, with lower paychecks. The other path was simply to try to impose change by leveling draconian penalties at employer who didn't meet certain imposed, ultimately arbitrary, and sometimes unachievable quotas. That approach too was rejected out of a sense of fairness.

So a middle ground was developed that would change an inequitable status quo gradually but firmly by building the pool of qualified applicants for college, for contracts, for jobs, and giving more people the chance to learn, work, and earn. When affirmative action is done right it is flexible, it is fair, and it works.

I know some people are honestly concerned about the times affirmative action doesn't work, when it's done in the wrong way. And I know there are times when some employers don't use it in the right way. They may cut corners and treat a flexible goal as a quota. They may give opportunities to people who are unqualified instead of those who deserve them. They may, in so doing, allow a different kind of discrimination. When this happens, it is also wrong. But it isn't affirmative action, and it is not legal.

So when our administration finds cases of that sort, we will enforce the law aggressively. The Justice Department files hundreds of cases every year attacking discrimination in employment, including suits on behalf of white men. Most of these suits, however, affect women and minorities, for a simple reason: because the vast majority of discrimination in America is still discrimination against them. But the law does require fairness for everyone, and we are determined to see that that is exactly what the law delivers.

Let me be clear about what affirmative action must not mean and what I won't allow it to be. It does not mean—and I don't favor—the unjustified preference of the unqualified over the qualified of any race or either gender. It doesn't mean—and I don't favor—numerical quotas. It doesn't mean—and I don't favor—selection or rejection of any employee or student solely on the basis of race or gender without regard to merit.

Like many business executives and public servants, I owe it to you to say that my views on this subject are, more than anything else, the product of my personal experience. I have had experience with affirmative action, nearly twenty years of it now, and I know it works. When I was attorney general of my home state, I hired a record number of women and African-American lawyers—every one clearly qualified and exceptionally hardworking. As governor, I appointed more women to my cabinet and state boards than any other governor in the state's history, and more African-Americans than all the governors in the state's history combined. No one ever questioned their qualifications or performance. And our state was better and stronger because of their service.

As president, I am proud to have the most diverse administration in our history in my cabinet, my agencies, and my staff. And I must say, I have been surprised at the criticism I have received from some quarters in my determination to achieve this. In the last two and a half years, the most outstanding example of affirmative action in the United States, the Pentagon, has opened 260,000 positions for women who serve in our armed forces. I have appointed more women and minorities to the federal bench than any other president, more than the last two combined. At the same time, far more of our judicial appointments have received the highest rating from the American Bar Association than any other administration since those ratings have been given.

In our administration, many government agencies are doing more business than ever before with qualified firms run by minorities and women. The Small Business Administration has reduced its budget by 40%, doubled its load outputs, and dramatically increased the number of loans to women and minority small business people—all without reducing the number of loans to white business owners who happen to be male, and without changing the loan standards for a single, solitary application. Quality and diversity can go hand in hand, and they must.

Let me say that affirmative action has also done more than just open the doors of opportunity to individual Americans. Most economists who have studied this issue agree that affirmative action has also been important in closing gaps in economic opportunity in our society, thereby strengthening the entire economy.

A group of distinguished business leaders told me just a couple of days ago that their companies are stronger and their profits larger because of the diversity and the excellence of their workforce, achieved through intelligent and fair affirmative action programs. And they said, We have gone far beyond anything the government might require us to do, because managing diversity and individual opportunity and being fair to everybody is the key to our future economic success in the global marketplace.

Now there are those who say, my fellow Americans, that even good affirmative action programs are no longer needed; that it should be enough to resort to the courts or the Equal Employment Opportunity Commission in cases of actual, provable individual discrimination because there is no longer any systematic discrimination in our society. In deciding how to answer that, let us consider the facts.

The unemployment rate for African-Americans remains about twice that of whites. The Hispanic rate is still higher. Women have narrowed the earnings gap, but they still make only 72% as much as men do for comparable jobs. The average income for a Hispanic woman with a college degree is still less than the average income of a white man with a high school diploma.

According to the recently completed report of the Glass Ceiling Commission, sponsored by Republican members of Congress, in the nation's largest companies only 0.6% of senior management positions are held by African-Americans, 0.4% by Hispanic Americans, and 0.3% by Asian-Americans; women hold between 3 and 5% of these positions. White men make up 43% of our workforce, but they hold 95% of these jobs.

Just last week, the Chicago Federal Reserve Bank reported that black home loan applicants are more than twice as likely to be denied credit as whites with the same qualifications, and that Hispanic applicants are more than one and a half times as likely to be denied loans as whites with the same qualifications.

Last year alone, the federal government received more than ninety thousand complaints of employment discrimination based on race, ethnicity, or gender. Less than 3% were for reverse discrimination.

Evidence abounds in other ways of the persistence of the kind of bigotry that can affect the way we think even if we're not conscious of it, in hiring and promotion and business and educational decisions.

Crimes and violence based on hate against Asians, Hispanics, African Americans, and other minorities are still with us. And, I'm sorry to say, the worst and most recent evidence of this involves a report of federal law enforcement officials in Tennessee attending an event literally overflowing with racism—a sickening reminder of just how pervasive these kinds of attitudes still are.

By the way, I want to tell you that I am committed to finding the truth about what happened there and to taking appropriate action. And I want to say that if anybody who works in federal law enforcement thinks that that kind of behavior is acceptable, he or she ought to think about working someplace else.

Now, let's get to the other side of the argument. If affirmative action has worked and yet there is evidence that discrimination still exists on a wide scale, in ways that are both conscious and unconscious, then why should we get rid of it, as many people are urging? Some question the effectiveness or the fairness of particular affirmative action programs. I say to all of you, those are fair questions, and they prompted the review of our affirmative action programs, about which I will talk in a few moments.

Some question the fundamental purpose of the effort. There are people who honestly believe that affirmative action always amounts to group preferences over individual merit; that affirmative action always leads to reverse discrimination; and that ultimately, therefore, it demeans those who benefit from it and discriminates against those who are not helped by it.

I just have to tell you that all of you have to decide how you feel about that, and all of our fellow countrymen and women have to decide as well. But I believe that if there are no quotas—if we give no opportunities to unqualified people—if we have no reverse discrimination—and if, when the problem ends, the program ends—then that criticism is wrong. That's what I believe. But we should have this debate, and everyone should ask the question.

Now let's deal with what I think is really behind so much of the current debate. There are a lot of people who oppose affirmative action today who supported it for a very long time. I believe they are responding to the sea change in the experiences that most Americans have in the world in which we live.

If you say you're now against affirmative action because the government or the private sector is using its power to help minorities at the expense of the majority, that gives you a way of explaining away the economic distress that a majority of Americans honestly feel. It gives you a way of turning resentment against minorities or against a particular government program, instead of having an honest debate about how we all got into the fix we're in and what we're all going to do together to get out of it.

That explanation, the affirmative action explanation for the fix we're in, is just wrong. It is just wrong. Affirmative action did not cause the great economic problems of the American middle class. And because most minorities and women are either members of the middle class or poor people who are struggling to get into it, we must also admit that affirmative action alone won't solve the problems of minorities and women who seek to be a part of the American Dream. To do that, we have to have an economic strategy that reverses the decline in wages and the growth of poverty among working people. Without that, women, minorities, and white men will all be in trouble in the future.

But it is wrong to use the anxieties of the middle class to divert the American people from the real causes of their economic distress—the sweeping historic changes that are taking all the globe in their path, and the specific policies, or lack of them, in our own country which have aggravated those challenges. It is simply wrong to play politics with the issue of affirmative action and divide our country at a time when, if we're really going to change things, we have to be united.

I must say, I think it is ironic that some—not all, but some—of those who call for an end to affirmative action also advocate policies that will make the real economic problems of the anxious middle class even worse. They talk about being for equal opportunity for everyone, and then they reduce investment in equal opportunity on an evenhanded basis. For example, if our goal is economic opportunity for all Americans, why in the world would we reduce our investment in education, from Head Start to affordable college loans? Why don't we make college loans available to every American instead?

If the real goal is empowering all middle-class Americans and empowering poor people to work their way into the middle class without regard to race or gender, why in the world would the people who advocate that turn around and raise taxes on our poorest working families, or reduce the money available for education and training when workers lose their jobs or they're living on poverty wages, or increase the cost of housing for lower-income working people with children?

Why would we do that? If we're going to empower Americans, we have to do more than talk about it; we have to do it. And surely we have learned that we cannot empower all Americans by a simple strategy of taking opportunity away from some Americans.

So to those who use this as a political strategy to divide us, we must say no. We must say no. But to those who raise legitimate questions about the way affirmative action works, or who raise the larger question about the genuine problems and anxieties of all the American people and their sense of being left behind and treated unfairly, we must say, yes, you are entitled to answers to your questions. We must say yes to that.

Now, that's why I ordered this review of all our affirmative action programs—a review to look at the facts, not the politics, of affirmative action. This review concluded that affirmative action remains a useful tool for widening economic and educational opportunity. The model used by the military, the army in particular—and I'm delighted to have the commanding general of the army here today, because he set such a fine example—that model has been especially successful because it emphasizes education and training, ensuring that it has a wide pool of qualified candidates for every level of promotion. That approach has given us the most racially diverse and the best-qualified military in our history. There are more opportunities for women and minorities there than ever before. And now there are over fifty generals and admirals who are Hispanic, Asian-, or African-American.

We found that the Education Department had programs targeted at underrepresented minorities that do a great deal of good with the tiniest of investments. We found that these programs comprised forty cents of every $1,000 in the Education Department's budget. Now, college presidents will tell you that the education their schools offer actually benefits from diversity—colleges where young people get the education and make the personal and professional contacts that will shape their lives. If their colleges look like the world they're going to live and work in, and they learn from all different kinds of people things that they can't learn in books, our system of higher education becomes stronger.

I believe that every child must have the chance to go to college. Every child. That means that every child has to have a chance to get affordable, repayable college loans—Pell Grants for poor kids—and a chance to do things like joining AmeriCorps and work his or her way through school. Every child is entitled to that. That is not an argument against affirmative action; it's an argument for more opportunity for more Americans, until everyone is reached.

As I said a moment ago, the review found that the Small Business Administration last year increased loans to minorities by over two-thirds, loans to women by over 80%, did not decrease loans to white men, and not a single loan went to an unqualified person. People who never had a chance before to be part of the American system of free enterprise now have it. No one was hurt in the process. That made America stronger.

This review also found that the executive order on employment practices of large federal contractors has also helped to bring more fairness and inclusion into the work force. Since President Nixon was here in my job, America has used goals and timetables to preserve opportunity and to prevent discrimination, to urge businesses to set higher expectations for themselves and to realize those expectations. But we did not and we will not use rigid quotas to mandate outcomes.

We also looked at the way we award procurement contracts under the programs known as set-asides. There's no question that these programs have helped to build up firms owned by minorities and women, who historically had been excluded from the old-boy networks in these areas. They have helped a new generation of entrepreneurs to flourish, opening new paths to self-reliance and economic growth in which all of us ultimately share. Because of the set-asides, businesses ready to compete have had the chance to compete—a chance they would not have had otherwise.

But as with any government program, set-asides can be misapplied, misused, even intentionally abused. There are critics who exploit that fact as an excuse to abolish all these programs, regardless of their effects. I believe these critics are wrong, but I also believe that, based on our factual review, we clearly need some reform. So first, we should crack down on those who take advantage of everyone else through fraud and abuse. We must crack down on fronts and pass-throughs, people who pretend to be eligible for these programs but aren't. That is wrong.

In offering new businesses a leg up, we must also make sure that the set-asides go to those businesses that need them most. We must really look and make sure that our standard for eligibility is fair and defensible. We have to tighten the requirement to move businesses out of programs once they've had a fair opportunity to compete. The graduation requirement must mean something—it must mean *graduation*. There should be no permanent set-aside for any company.

Second, we must and we will comply with the Supreme Court's *Adarand* decision of last month. Now, in particular, that means focusing set-aside programs on particular regions and business sectors where the problems of discrimination or exclusion are provable and clearly require affirmative action. I have directed the attorney general and the agencies to move forward with compliance with *Adarand* expeditiously. But I also want to emphasize that the *Adarand* decision did not dismantle affirmative action and did not dismantle set-asides. In fact, while setting stricter standards to mandate reform of affirmative action, it actually reaffirmed the continuing existence of systematic discrimination in the United States, and reaffirmed the need for affirmative action. What the Supreme Court ordered the federal government to do was to meet the same, more rigorous standard for affirmative action programs that state and local governments were ordered to meet several years ago. The best set-aside programs under that standard have been challenged and have survived.

Third, beyond eliminating discrimination, we need to do more to help disadvantaged people and those in distressed communities, no matter what their race or gender. There are places in our country where the chances for growth offered by our free enterprise system simply don't reach. In some places, our economic system simply isn't working to provide jobs and opportunities. Disproportionately, these areas in both urban and rural America are highly populated by racial minorities, but not entirely. To make this initiative work, I believe the government must become a better partner for people in places in urban and rural America who are caught in a cycle of poverty. And I believe we have to find ways to get the private sector to assume its rightful role as a driver of economic growth.

We have given incentives to our businesspeople to help develop poor economies in other parts of the world, our neighbors in the Caribbean and elsewhere—and I have supported this aid when not subject to abuse. But it has always amazed me that we ignore the biggest source of economic growth available to the American economy: the poor economies isolated within the United States of America.

There are those who say, Well, even if we made jobs available, people wouldn't work—they haven't tried. But most people in disadvantaged communities work, and most of those who don't work have a very strong desire to do so. In central Harlem, fourteen people apply for every single minimum-wage job opening. Think how many more would apply if there were good jobs with good futures. Our challenge is to connect disadvantaged people and disadvantaged communities with economic opportunity so that everybody who wants to work can do so.

We've been working at this through our empowerment zones and community development banks, through the initiatives of Secretary Cisneros of the Housing and Urban Development Department, and many other things that we have tried to do to put capital where it is needed. And now I have asked Vice President Gore to develop a proposal to use federal contracting to support businesses that locate themselves in these distressed areas or that hire a large percentage of their workers from these areas—not to substitute for what we're doing in affirmative action but to supplement it, to go beyond it, to do something that will help to deal with the economic crisis of America. We want to make our procurement system more responsive to people in these areas who need help.

My fellow Americans, affirmative action has to be made consistent with our highest ideals of personal responsibility and merit, and our urgent need to find common ground, in order to prepare all Americans to compete in the global economy of the next century. Today I am directing all federal agencies to comply with the Supreme Court's *Adarand* decision, and also to apply the four standards of fairness that I have already articulated to all our affirmative action programs; no quotas, in theory or in practice; no illegal discrimination of any kind, including reverse discrimination; no preference for people who are not qualified for jobs or other opportunities; and as soon as a programs has succeeded, it must be retired. Any program that doesn't meet these four principles must be eliminated or reformed to meet them.

But let me be clear: affirmative action has been good for America.

Affirmative action has not always been perfect, and affirmative action should not go on forever. It should be changed now to take care of those things that are wrong, and it should be retired when its job is done. I am resolved that that day will come. But the evidence suggests—indeed, screams—that that day has not yet come.

The job of ending discrimination in this country is not over. That should not be surprising. We had slavery for centuries before the passage of the Thirteenth, Fourteenth, and Fifteenth Amendments. We waited another hundred years for our civil rights legislation. Women have had the vote less than a hundred years. We have always had difficulty with these things, as most societies do. But we are making more progress than are many other countries.

Based on the evidence, the job is not done. So here is what I think we should do. We should reaffirm the principle of affirmative action and fix the practices. We should have a simple slogan: Mend it, but don't end it.

Let me ask all Americans, whether they agree or disagree with what I have said today, to see this issue in the larger context of our times. President Lincoln said that we cannot escape our history. We cannot escape our future, either. And that future must be one in which every American has the chance to live up to his or her God-given capacities.

New technology, instant communications, the explosion of global commerce—all these have created both enormous opportunities and enormous anxieties for Americans. In the last two and a half years we have seen seven million new jobs, more millionaires and new businesses than ever before, high corporate profits, and a booming stock market. Yet most Americans are working harder for the same or lower pay. And they feel more insecure about their jobs, their retirement, their health care, and their children's education. Too many of our children are being exposed to poverty, violence, and drugs.

These are the great challenges for our whole country on the home front at the dawn of the twenty-first century. We've got to find the wisdom and the will to create family-wage jobs for everyone who wants to work; to open the door of college to all Americans; to strengthen families and reduce the awful problems to which our children are exposed; to move poor Americans from welfare to work.

This is the work of our administration—to give people the tools they need to make the most of their own lives, to give families and communities the tools they need to solve their own problems. But let us not forget: affirmative action didn't cause these problems. It won't solve them. And getting rid of affirmative action certainly won't solve them.

If properly done, affirmative action can help us come together, go forward and grow together. It is in our moral, legal, and practical interest to see that every person can make the most of his or her life. In the fight for the future, we need all hands on deck, and some of those hands still need a helping hand.

In our national community we're all different, yet we're all the same. We want liberty and freedom. We want the embrace of family and community. We want to make the most of our own lives, and we're determined to give our children a better one. Today there are voices of division who would say, Forget all that. But don't you dare. Remember that we're still closing the gap between our founders' ideals and our reality. But every step along the way has made us richer, stronger, and better. And the best is yet to come.

Article 10.4

Bashing Illegals in California

Elizabeth Kadetsky

In the November 1994 election, Californians passed a ballot measure (Proposition 187) that would deny educational, non-emergency medical, and welfare services to illegal immigrants, and several other states have considered or are considering similar measures. Because such federally mandated benefits have been upheld in previous legal decisions, the measure was immediately suspended by state and federal courts. In the following viewpoint, Elizabeth Kadetsky argues that Proposition 187 was promoted by racists who capitalized on a popular sentiment that erroneously blames illegal immigrants for the economic problems of California. Kadetsky is a freelance writer in Los Angeles.

Parrish Goodman had just saved a burdened shopper the trouble of returning her grocery cart and was back at the expanse of sidewalk outside Ralph's supermarket in West Los Angeles competing with the whoosh of the electric doors. Goodman greeted all who passed in such a friendly way that they tended to thank him for his cryptic millionth-generation photocopies that were equal parts longhand and typewriter script. "You'll be voting on this in November," he'd say, winking, all courtesy and ambiguity.

California's Proposition 187

Goodman was campaigning for Proposition 187, the grandiosely titled "Save Our State" (S.O.S.) ballot initiative that, if...validated by the courts, will use strict verification requirements to prevent California's estimated 1.7 million undocumented immigrants from partaking of every form of public welfare including non-emergency medical care, prenatal clinics and public schools. The measure would require employees at public health facilities, welfare offices, police departments and schools to demand proof of legal residency and to report those who can't produce it to the Immigration and Naturalization Service (I.N.S.); it also calls for stiff penalties for creating or using false documents. While conceding that the measure actually does nothing to deter immigration at its source—at the border and with the employers who encourage workers to cross it—advocates say S.O.S. responds to California's economic downturn by making life so difficult for the undocumented that they will either go home or never show up to begin with.

The opposition runs the gamut from those who dispute the premise that immigrants contribute to hard times to those who argue that the initiative scapegoats children, lets employ-

"Bashing Illegals in California" by Elizabeth Kadetsky. Reprinted with permission from the October 17, 1994 issue of *The Nation*.

ers off the hook, inefficiently enlists public employees to do the work of the I.N.S. and violates several federal mandates as well as a Supreme Court decision granting all children the right to free education. That several of the state's major newspapers and a cross section of city governments, school districts, health associations and law-enforcement officials have opposed Save Our State as racist, xenophobic, ineffectual, costly—and just meanspirited—would seem enough to disqualify the avuncular Goodman from its sponsor's ranks.

But Goodman is not alone among Californians, who have responded to the plummeting indicators in almost every measure of quality of life by turning their bitter gaze toward the nation's undocumented immigrants, 43 percent of whom land in California. It's no news that California—strapped by the country's second weakest economy, years of budget shortfalls, the most crowded classrooms in the nation and pockets of the worst smog and traffic—is no longer the "golden door" the Grateful Dead still sometimes sing about.

Blaming Immigrants

Discontent at the condition of the Golden State has exploded in the faces of immigrants, particularly those from Latin America. The American Friends Service Committee border monitoring project investigates two or three incidents of anti-immigrant violence per month. This atmosphere of panic owes its fire to a network of several dozen mostly new grass-roots organizations whose work, fanned by the goading rhetoric or politicians like Governor Pete Wilson, has culminated with S.O.S. The authors of S.O.S. so successfully tapped into a popular sentiment and movement that the group's P.O. Box collected as many as 1,000 pieces of mail a day. S.O.S. had no trouble recruiting volunteers, and those volunteers had an equally easy ride gathering 400,000 of the signatures needed to qualify the initiative for the ballot....

S.O.S.'s core supporters are a ragtag movement replete with registered Greens, Democrats, Perotists, distributors of New Age healing products and leaders of the Republican Party. The participants have little in common, but their rhetoric of invasion—a kaffeeklatsch in the Southern California town of Bellflower calls itself We Stand Ready—and the virulence of their wrath. One S.O.S. organizer, Bette Hannond, drove me through her town's immigrant quarter ranting about an imagined "stench of urine" and pointing to clusters of streetside day laborers who, she asserted, surely defecated in the nearby bushes. "Impacted, impacted, impacted," Hammond spit out as she glanced toward apartment complexes in various states of disrepair. "They come here, they have their babies, and after that they become citizens and all those children use those social services." Barbara Kiley, a Prop 187 backer who is also mayor of the Orange County town of Yorba Linda, described such children to one reporter as "those little fuckers."...

The Proposition's Supporters

Richard Mountjoy, a finger-jabbing right-wing Republican State assemblyman from east L.A. County, took up the anti-immigrant torch when, he told me, he foresaw "a heated campaign" for re-election in 1992. He has since become the movement's most tenacious government spokesman, introducing ten mostly unsuccessful bills in the state legislature that foreshadowed Prop 187 (one would make it a felony to use a false ID). Mountjoy one-upped

even Prop 187 with a pending bill that would disqualify native-born children of undocumented mothers from their Fourteenth Amendment right to U.S. citizenship. A self-proclaimed
"expert" on immigration, Mountjoy told me he wanted a crackdown on illegal immigration
from countries other than Mexico, such as Puerto Rico, where, unbeknownst to the assemblyman, everyone is a U.S. citizen. Mountjoy, who has contributed $43,000 to S.O.S., has cyni-
cally blamed immigrants for the state's budget crisis after having built his own career
campaigning for Proposition 13, the 1978 antitax initiative that is now acknowledged by experts on all sides as the *actual* cause of that crisis. Other top backers include Don Rogers, a
state senator from outside Palm Springs who kicked in $20,000 and is perhaps best known
for his association with the white supremacist Christian Identity movement.

Mountjoy and Rogers are not alone in lending the movement for S.O.S. a racist patina.
The measure is backed by the Federation for American Immigration Reform (FAIR), an outgrowth of the environmentally leaning Zero Population Growth that has received at least
$800,000 from the Pioneer Fund, a notorious right-wing philanthropy that sponsors studies
on topics like race and I.Q....

If S.O.S.'s visible advocates personify either fringe populism or cynical manipulation of
public sentiment for political gain, their movement has crossed over to the mainstream.
Sixty-two percent of Californians supported S.O.S. in a September 1994 *Los Angeles Times*
poll; however, voters' visceral reaction fades when asked in other polls about the particulars
of the proposition, such as yanking children from public schools or denying medical care,
which are opposed by 54 percent and 74percent, respectively. Still, the initiative passed.

Despite the verbiage about immigrants' economic impact, polls show supporters span the
political and economic spectrums and are not more likely to have been adversely affected by
the recession. Most of S.O.S.'s support, as well as its most vocal advocates, is actually concentrated in areas least affected by the recession or by the state's shifting multicultural composition.

S.O.S. is most popular in Orange County, the sterile midzone of low-slung shopping
malls between border San Diego and multicultural Los Angeles. It's the region that brought
us Richard Nixon, Disneyland and S.O.S.'s ten authors. Here, only 7 percent live in poverty,
as opposed to 17.5 percent in Los Angeles.

Bette Hammond lives in San Rafael, where she moved from a Boston suburb in 1981,
bought a motorcycle and planned "to get the freedom that one hears about from California."
For her the dream is this Marin Country enclave that is 84 percent white, enjoys the well-
above-average median family income of $54,000, the well-below-average unemployment
rate of 6% percent—and probably has more hot tubs per capita than any place in the world.

These demographics suggest that Ron Prince, the vampirishly charming chairman of the
Save Our State Committee, was disingenuous in recommending as a representative volunteer Parrish Goodman, who is African-American. Goodman likewise planned to illustrate
"how the African-American community is organizing around S.O.S."—though he was unable to conjure up one other African-American S.O.S. volunteer besides himself. In fact,
anti-immigrant sentiment is concentrated among whites: 59 percent of white people in
California believe that children of undocumented immigrants should be turned away from

the schools. This contrasts with 41 percent of African-Americans and Asians, and 22 percent of Latinos, according to a Field Institute poll.

A former Black Panther who hails from New York City and is now a union computer technician for the telephone company, Goodman nevertheless exploits black/Latino tensions by harping on a "fight over jobs" in the ethnically volatile African-American and Latino South Central district. Cruising down Venice Boulevard in his white Camaro, Goodman speed-surfed the AM talk-radio channels as his placid surface cracked into little slivers of invective: "These people want you to be like them, poor and mumbling in half-Spanish and half-English." Then Goodman, who came to California in 1980 in search of a "change of attitude," turned calm, almost wistful. "I thought California was supposed to be palm trees and beautiful girls on the beach. Instead we got a gang war. You almost have an enemy presence in your midst."...

Costs and Benefits of Immigration

As the rhetoric flies, California does wrestle with the confounding fact that immigrants strain a social and physical infra-structure already burdened by slow economic expansion and a growing population. None of the dozens of wildly contradictory studies circulating among participants in the immigration debate can adequately estimate the real numbers and costs of undocumented immigrants in California, but several concur that while low-wage immigrants contribute to and are even crucial to the state's long-term economic vitality, those immigrants are a short-term burden on state and city governments that cannot, as one study from the RAND Corporation puts it, "borrow against their future." The most resonant of several studies, by Los Angeles County, reported that immigrants (legal and illegal) and their children cost the county $954 million a year in public services but give back far more, $4.3 billion—albeit in taxes paid to the federal government. That discrepancy has led to bi-partisan railing against federal mandates—the same mandates that S.O.S. violates—that require states to provide social services without the federal dollars to pay for them. In any case, while S.O.S. ostensibly un-does that burden to the state, the state's legislative analysis has calculated that the measure would actually cost billions in the long run.

Even the cost-benefit equation, however, fails to address the fact that immigration from Mexico is a logical outgrowth of the economic interdependency of Mexico and the United States. State Assembly Speaker Willie Brown did, however, call for seizing the assets of employers such as hoteliers who are found to depend on underpaid and poorly treated undocumented immigrants. This proposal elicited an amusing silence from Republican fist-thumpers like Governor Wilson, who have done everything in their power to see that employer-sanction provisions in the 1986 Immigration Reform and Control Act remain unenforced. After eight years, Los Angeles saw the first major criminal employer sanction doled out in the fall of 1994.

That a poorly conceived initiative sponsored by fringe activists with a persecution complex won the support of a majority of voters in November 1994 points to the willingness of politicians to play the immigration card in a volatile social climate.

Article 10.5

Securing Our Nation's Borders

Pete Wilson

In 1994, several states—including California, Florida, Arizona, and Texas—filed lawsuits against the federal government to recover the costs of illegal immigration (though none of the law-suits has succeeded to date). In the following viewpoint, Pete Wilson, governor of California, argues that the costs of providing federally mandated services and benefits to illegal immigrants hurt the economy of California and limit its ability to provide services to its legal residents. He believes that forcing the federal government to reimburse the states for these costs will compel the government to stem illegal immigration. Wilson won reelection as governor of California in November 1994.

The federal government's immigration policy is broken and the time to fix it is now.

It's hard to blame people who day after day pour across our borders. They're coming to find a better life for themselves and their families. It's easy to sympathize with them and even admire their gumption. It is those in Washington that we should condemn—those who encourage the illegals to break the law by rewarding them for their illegal entry.

A Nation of Legal Immigrants

We are a state and a nation of immigrants, proud of our immigrant traditions. Like many of you, I'm the grandchild of immigrants. My grandmother came to this country in steerage from Ireland at age sixteen. She came for the same reason any immigrant comes—for a better future than she could hope for in the old country. And America benefited from her and millions like her.

But we, as a sovereign nation, have a right and an obligation to determine how and when people come into our country. We are a nation of laws, and people who seek to be a part of this great nation must do so according to the law.

The United States already accepts more legal immigrants into our country than the rest of the world combined—1.8 million in 1991 alone.

We are a generous people. But there is a limit to what we can absorb and illegal immigration is now taxing us past that limit.

Thousands come here illegally every day. In fact, the gaping holes in federal policy have made our borders a sieve. President Clinton has used that very word to describe their porous condition.

The results are, in Los Angeles, there's now a community of illegal residents numbering a million people. That's a city the size of San Diego. Alone, it would be the seventh largest city in the nation—half again the population of our nation's capital, Washington, D.C.

Two thirds of all babies born in Los Angeles public hospitals are born to illegal immigrants.

Paying for Illegal Immigration

As we struggle to keep dangerous criminals off our streets, we find that 14 percent of California's prison population are illegal immigrants—enough to fill eight state prisons to design-capacity.

And through a recession that has caused the loss of one-third the revenues previously received by state government, as we have struggled to maintain per-pupil spending and to cover fully enrollment growth with classrooms around the state bursting at the seams, we're forced to spend $1.7 billion each year to educate students who are acknowledged to be in the country illegally.

In total, California taxpayers are compelled *by federal law* to spend more than $3 billion to provide services to illegal immigrants—it's approaching 10 percent of our state budget.

To ignore this crisis of illegal immigration—as some would have us do—is not only irresponsible, but makes a mockery of our laws. It is a slap in the face to the tens of thousands who play by the rules and endure the arduous process of legally immigrating to our country.

It's time to restore reason, integrity and fairness to our nation's immigration policy. And we need to do it now. California can't afford to wait.

First, the federal government must secure our border. That's the first step in securing our future. They must devote the manpower and the technology necessary to prevent people from crossing the border in the first place.

Second, the federal government should turn off the magnetic lure that now rewards people who successfully evade the border patrol and cross the border illegally.

And finally, until our representatives in Washington do act, until they secure the border and turn off the magnetic lure, they should pay the full bill for illegal immigration. The states shouldn't be forced to bear the cost for a failed federal policy that gives a free pass to those who breach our borders, then passes the buck to us.

Those who oppose reform invariably cry racism. They want to stifle even any discussion of the issue.

But this debate isn't about race, it's about responsibility and resources. Washington must accept responsibility for this strictly federal issue, and California must be allowed to devote our limited resources to those people who have come to our country through the legal process.

Holding Washington Accountable

This isn't a partisan issue, or even simply a California issue. Washington's failure to bear responsibility for illegal immigration is forcing states around the nation to bear enormous costs....

Immigration and control of our nation's border are, by virtue of the Constitution, a strictly federal responsibility. But today, there is no fiscal accountability for that policy.

The Congress is writing blank checks on other people's bank accounts—and one of those accounts belongs to the taxpayers of California.

Congress must be forced to bear the fiscal consequences for its immigration policy. If they have to pay the bill for that policy, if they feel the pinch in the federal budget for which they alone are accountable to the voters, then and only then will they have the incentive to fix this policy that simply doesn't work.

President Clinton has acknowledged as much himself. In summer 1993 he said, "One of the reasons the federal government has not been forced to confront this...is that the states of California, Texas and Florida have had to bear a huge portion of the costs for the failure of federal policy."

It's a fundamental element of democracy—a government must be held accountable for its actions.

And if the federal government were held accountable, they would quickly discover that the cost of ignoring the real and explosively growing problem of illegal immigration is far greater than the cost of fixing it.

They would see that the federal resources necessary to secure our nation's border are dwarfed by the billions that California and other states spend today in making massive illegal immigration to America a safety-net for the world. What's more, by compelling California to provide this safety-net for illegals, the feds are tearing gaping holes in the safety-net we seek to provide for our own needy legal residents.

For 1995, the Clinton Administration proposed increasing spending on border enforcement across the country by just $180 million a year. We'll spend nearly ten times that amount just educating illegal immigrants in California schools....

Our goal, though, is larger than simply seeking reimbursement—as important and as urgently needed as it is.

Our goal is to force the federal government to accept responsibility for the crisis of illegal immigration. Only when they accept responsibility will Congress finally adopt the reforms necessary to restore integrity and fairness to our immigration laws.

Once Congress is forced to confront this problem, I'm sure it will waste no time in doing what's necessary to secure our nation's borders.

Article 10.6

Text of Proposition 187— The Save Our State Initiative

This initiative measure is submitted to the people in accordance with the provisions of Article II, Section 8 of the Constitution.

This initiative measure adds sections to various codes; therefore, new provisions proposed to be added are printed in *italic type* to indicate that they are new.

PROPOSED LAW

SECTION 1. Findings and Declaration.

The People of California find and declare as follows:

That they have suffered and are suffering economic hardship caused by the presence of illegal aliens in this state.

That they have suffered and are suffering personal injury and damage caused by the criminal conduct of illegal aliens in this state.

That they have a right to the protection of their government from any person or persons entering this country unlawfully.

Therefore, the People of California declare their intention to provide for cooperation between their agencies of state and local government with the federal government, and to establish a system of required notification by and between such agencies to prevent illegal aliens in the United States from receiving benefits or public services in the State of California.

SECTION 2. Manufacture, Distribution or Sale of False Citizenship or Resident Alien Documents: Crime and Punishment.

Section 113 is added to the Penal Code, to read:

113. Any person who manufactures, distributes or sells false documents to conceal the true citizenship or resident alien status of another person is guilty of a felony, and shall be punished by imprisonment in the state prison for five years or by a fine of seventy-five thousand dollars ($75,000).

SECTION 3. Use of False Citizenship or Resident Alien documents: Crime and Punishment.

From Proposition 187, California State Government.

Section 114 is added to the Penal Code, to read:

114. Any person who uses false documents to conceal his or her true citizenship or resident alien status is guilty of a felony, and shall be punished by imprisonment in the state prison for five years or by a fine of twenty-five thousand dollars ($25,000).

SECTION 4. Law Enforcement Cooperation with INS.

Section 834b is added to the Penal Code, to read:

834b.(a) Every law enforcement agency in California shall fully cooperate with the United States Immigration and Naturalization Service regarding any person who is arrested if he or she is suspected of being present in the United States in violation of federal immigration laws.

(b) With respect to any such person who is arrested, and suspected of being present in the United States in violation of federal immigration laws, every law enforcement agency shall do the following:

(1) Attempt to verify the legal status of such person as a citizen of the United States, an alien lawfully admitted as a permanent resident, an alien lawfully admitted for a temporary period of time or as an alien who is present in the United States in violation of immigration laws. The verification process may include, but shall not be limited to, questioning the person regarding his or her date and place of birth, and entry into the United States, and demanding documentation to indicate his or her legal status.

(2) Notify the person of his or her apparent status as an alien who is present in the United States in violation of federal immigration laws and inform him or her that, apart from any criminal justice proceedings, he or she must either obtain legal status or leave the United States.

(3) Notify the Attorney General of California and the United States Immigration and Naturalization Service of the apparent illegal status and provide any additional information that may be requested by any other public entity.

(c) Any legislative, administrative, or other action by a city, county, or other legally authorized local governmental entity with jurisdictional boundaries, or by a law enforcement agency, to prevent or limit the cooperation required by subdivision (a) is expressly prohibited.

SECTION 5. Exclusion of Illegal Aliens from Public Social Services.

Section 10001.5 is added to the Welfare and Institutions Code, to read:

10001.5. (a) In order to carry out the intention of the People of California that only citizens of the United States and aliens lawfully admitted to the United States may receive the benefits of public social services and to ensure that all persons employed in the providing of those services shall diligently protect public funds from misuse, the provisions of this section are adopted.

(b) A person shall not receive any public social services to which he or she may be otherwise entitled until the legal status of that person has been verified as one of the following:

(1) A citizen of the United States.

(2) An alien lawfully admitted as a permanent resident.

(3) An alien lawfully admitted for a temporary period of time.

(c) If any public entity in this state to whom a person has applied for public social services determines or reasonably suspects, based upon the information provided to it, that the person is an alien in the United States in violation of federal law, the following procedures shall be followed by the public entity:

(1) The entity shall not provide the person with benefits or services.

(2) The entity shall, in writing, notify the person of his or her apparent illegal immigration status, and that the person must either obtain legal status or leave the United States.

(3) The entity shall also notify the State Director of Social Services, the Attorney General of California, and the United States Immigration and Naturalization Service of the apparent illegal status, and shall provide any additional information that may be requested by any other public entity.

SECTION 6. Exclusion of Illegal Aliens from Publicly Funded Health Care.

Chapter 1.3 (commencing with Section 130) is added to Part 1 of Division 1 of the Health and Safety Code, to read:

Chapter 1.3. Publicly-Funded Health Care Services

130. (a) In order to carry out the intention of the People of California that, excepting emergency medical care as required by federal law, only citizens of the United States and aliens lawfully admitted to the United States may receive the benefits of publicly-funded health care, and to ensure that all persons employed in the providing of those services shall diligently protect public funds from misuse, the provisions of this section are adopted.

(b) A person shall not receive any health care services from a publicly-funded health care facility, to which he or she is otherwise entitled until the legal status of that person has been verified as one of the following:

(1) A citizen of the United States.

(2) An alien lawfully admitted as a permanent resident.

(3) An alien lawfully admitted for a temporary period of time.

(c) If any publicly-funded health care facility in this state from whom a person seeks health care services, other than emergency medical care as required by federal law, determines or reasonably suspects, based upon the information provided to it, that the person is an alien in the United States in violation of federal law, the following procedures shall be followed by the facility:

(1) The facility shall not provide the person with services.

(2) The facility shall, in writing, notify the person of his or her apparent illegal immigration status, and that the person must either obtain legal status or leave the United States.

(3) The facility shall also notify the State Director of Health Services, the Attorney General of California, and the United States Immigration and Naturalization Service of the apparent illegal status, and shall provide any additional information that may be requested by any other public entity.

(d) For purposes of this section "publicly-funded health care facility" shall be defined as specified in Sections 1200 and 1250 of this code as of January 1, 1993.

SECTION 7. Exclusion of Illegal Aliens from Public Elementary and Secondary Schools.

Section 48215 is added to the Education code, to read:

48215. (a) No public elementary or secondary school shall admit, or permit the attendance of, any child who is not a citizen of the United States, an alien lawfully admitted as a permanent resident, or a person who is otherwise authorized under federal law to be present in the United States.

(b) Commencing January 1, 1995, each school district shall verify the legal status of each child enrolling in the school district for the first time in order to ensure the enrollment or attendance only of citizens, aliens lawfully admitted as permanent residents, or persons who are otherwise authorized to be present in the United States.

(c) By January 1, 1996, each school district shall have verified the legal status of each child already enrolled and in attendance in the school district in order to ensure the enrollment or attendance only of citizens, aliens lawfully admitted as permanent residents, or persons who are otherwise authorized under federal law to be present in the United States.

(d) By January 1, 1996, each school district shall also have verified the legal status of each parent or guardian of each child referred to in subdivisions (b) and (c), to determine whether such parent or guardian is one of the following:

(1) A citizen of the United States.

(2) An alien lawfully admitted as a permanent resident.

(3) An alien admitted lawfully for a temporary period of time.

(e) Each school district shall provide information to the State Superintendent of Public Instruction, the Attorney General of California, and the United States Immigration and Naturalization Service regarding any enrollee or pupil, or parent or guardian, attending a public elementary or secondary school in the school district determined or reasonably suspected to be in violation of federal immigration laws within forty-five days after becoming aware of an apparent violation. The notice shall also be provided to the parent or legal guardian of the enrollee or pupil, and shall state that an existing pupil may not continue to

attend the school after ninety calendar days from the date of the notice, unless legal status is established.

(f) For each child who cannot establish legal status in the United States, each school district shall continue to provide education for a period of ninety days from the date of the notice. Such ninety day period shall be utilized to accomplish an orderly transition to a school in the child's country of origin. Each school district shall fully cooperate in this transition effort to ensure that the educational needs of the child are best served for that period of time.

SECTION 8. Exclusion of Illegal Aliens from Public Postsecondary Educational Institutions.

Section 66010.8 is added to the Education Code, to read:

66010.8 (a) No public institution of postsecondary education shall admit, enroll, or permit the attendance of any person who is not a citizen of the United States, an alien lawfully admitted as a permanent resident in the United States, or a person who is otherwise authorized under federal law to be present in the United States.

(b) Commencing with the first term or semester that begins after January 1, 1995, and at the commencement of each turn or semester thereafter, each public postsecondary educational institution shall verify the status of each person enrolled or in attendance at that institution in order to ensure the enrollment or attendance only of United States citizens, aliens lawfully admitted as permanent residents in the United States, and persons who are otherwise authorized under federal law to be present in the United States.

(c) No later than 45 days after the admissions officer of a public postsecondary educational institution becomes aware of the application, enrollment, or attendance of a person determined to be, or who is under reasonable suspicion of being, in the United States in violation of federal immigration laws, that officer shall provide that information to the State Superintendent of Public Instruction, the Attorney General of California, and the United States Immigration and Naturalization Service. The information shall also be provided to the applicant, enrollee, or person admitted.

SECTION 9. Attorney General Cooperation with the INS.

Section 53069.65 is added to the Government Code, to read:

53069.65. Whenever the state or a city, or a county, or any other legally authorized local governmental entity with jurisdictional boundaries reports the presence of a person who is suspected of being present in the United States in violation of federal immigration laws to the Attorney General of California, that report shall be transmitted to the United States immigration and Naturalization Service. The Attorney General shall be responsible for maintaining on-going and accurate records of such reports, and shall provide any additional information that may be requested by any other government entity.

SECTION 10. Amendment and Severability.

The statutory provisions contained in this measure may not be amended by the Legislature except to further its purposes by statute passed in each house by rollcall vote entered in the journal, two-thirds of the membership concurring, or by a statute that becomes effective only when approved by the voters.

In the event that any portion of this act or the application thereof to any person or circumstance is held invalid, that invalidity shall not affect any other provision or application of the act, which can be given effect without the invalid provision or application, and to that end the provisions of this act are severable.

Article 10.7

Text of Proposition 209— The California Civil Rights Initiative

(a) The state shall not discriminate against, or grant preferential treatment to, any individual or group on the basis of race, sex, color, ethnicity, or national origin in the operation of public employment, public education, or public contracting.

(b) This section shall apply only to action taken after the section's effective date.

(c) Nothing in this section shall be interpreted as prohibiting bona fide qualifications based on sex which are reasonably necessary to the normal operation of public employment, public education or public contracting.

(d) Nothing in this section shall be interpreted as invalidating any court order or consent decree which is in force as of the effective date of this section.

(e) Nothing in this section shall be interpreted as prohibiting action which must be taken to establish or maintain eligibility for any federal program, where ineligibility would result in a loss of federal funds to the state.

(f) For the purposes of this section, "state" shall include, but not necessarily be limited to, the state itself, any city, county, city and county, public university system, including the University of California, community college district, school district, special district, or any other political subdivision or governmental instrumentality of or within the state.

(g) The remedies available for violations of this section shall be the same, regardless of the injured party's race, sex, color, ethnicity, or national origin, as are otherwise available for violations of then-existing California anti-discrimination law.

(h) This section shall be self-executing. If any part or parts of this section are found to be in conflict with federal law or the United States Constitution, the section shall be implemented to the maximum extent that federal law and the United States Constitution permit. Any provision held invalid shall be severable from the remaining portions of this section.

From Proposition 209, California State Government.

Article 10.8

Text of Proposition 227— The English Language Education for Children in Public Schools Initiative

SECTION 1. Chapter 3 (commencing with Section 300) is added to Part 1 of the Educational Code, to read:

CHAPTER 3. ENGLISH LANGUAGE EDUCATION FOR IMMIGRANT CHILDREN

ARTICLE 1. Findings and Declarations

300. The people of California find and declare as follows:

(a) WHEREAS the English language is the national public language of the United States of America and of the State of California, is spoken by the vast majority of California residents, and is also the leading world language for science, technology, and international business, thereby being the language of economic opportunity; and

(b) WHEREAS immigrant parents are eager to have their children acquire a good knowledge of English, thereby allowing them to fully participate in the American Dream of economic and social advancement; and

(c) WHEREAS the government and the public schools of California have a moral obligation and a constitutional duty to provide all of California's children, regardless of their ethnicity or national origins, with the skills necessary to become productive members of our society, and of these skills, literacy in the English language is among the most important; and

(d) WHEREAS the public schools of California currently do a poor job of educating immigrant children, wasting financial resources on costly experimental language programs whose failure over the past two decades is demonstrated by the current high drop-out rates and low English literacy levels of many immigrant children; and

(e) WHEREAS young immigrant children can easily acquire full fluency in a new language, such as English, if they are heavily exposed to that language in the classroom at an early age.

From Proposition 227, California State Government.

(f) THEREFORE it is resolved that: all children in California public schools shall be taught English as rapidly and effectively as possible.

ARTICLE 2. English Language Education

305. Subject to the exceptions provided in Article 3 (commencing with Section 310), all children in California public schools shall be taught English by being taught in English. In particular, this shall require that all children be placed in English language classrooms. Children who are English learners shall be educated through sheltered English immersion during a temporary transition period not normally intended to exceed one year.

Local schools shall be permitted to place in the same classroom English learners of different ages but whose degree of English proficiency is similar.

Local schools shall be encouraged to mix together in the same classroom English learners from different native-language groups but with the same degree of English fluency. Once English learners have acquired a good working knowledge of English, they shall be transferred to English language mainstream classrooms. As much as possible, current supplemental funding for English learners shall be maintained, subject to possible modification under Article 8 (commencing with Section 335) below.

306. The definitions of the terms used in this article and in Article 3 (commencing with Section 310) are as follows:

(a) "English learner" means a child who does not speak English or whose native language is not English and who is not currently able to perform ordinary classroom work in English, also known as a Limited English Proficiency or LEP child.

(b) "English language classroom" means a classroom in which the language of instruction used by the teaching personnel is overwhelmingly the English language, and in which such teaching personnel possess a good knowledge of the English language.

(c) "English language mainstream classroom" means a classroom in which the students either are native English language speakers or already have acquired reasonable fluency in English.

(d) "Sheltered English immersion" or "structured English immersion" means an English language acquisition process for young children in which nearly all classroom instruction is in English but with the curriculum and presentation designed for children who are learning the language.

(e) "Bilingual education/native language instruction" means a language acquisition process for students in which much or all instruction, textbooks, and teaching materials are in the child's native language.

ARTICLE 3. Parental Exceptions

310. The requirements of Section 305 may be waived with the prior written informed consent, to be provided annually, of the child's parents or legal guardian under the circum-

stances specified below and in Section 311. Such informed consent shall require that said parents or legal guardian personally visit the school to apply for the waiver and that they there be provided a full description of the educational materials to be used in the different educational program choices and all the educational opportunities available to the child. Under such parental waiver conditions, children may be transferred to classes where they are taught English and other subjects through bilingual education techniques or other generally recognized educational methodologies permitted by law. Individual schools in which 20 students or more of a given grade level receive a waiver shall be required to offer such a class; otherwise, they must allow the students to transfer to a public school in which such a class is offered.

311. The circumstances in which a parental exception waiver may be granted under Section 310 are as follows:

(a) Children who already know English: the child already possesses good English language skills, as measured by standardized tests of English vocabulary comprehension, reading, and writing, in which the child scores at or above the state average for his grade level or at or above the 5th grade average, whichever is lower; or

(b) Older children: the child is age 10 years or older, and it is the informed belief of the school principal and educational staff that an alternate course of educational study would be better suited to the child's rapid acquisition of basic English language skills; or

(c) Children with special needs: the child already has been placed for a period of not less than thirty days during that school year in an English language classroom and it is subsequently the informed belief of the school principal and educational staff that the child has such special physical, emotional, psychological, or educational needs that an alternate course of educational study would be better suited to the child's overall educational development. A written description of these special needs must be provided and any such decision is to be made subject to the examination and approval of the local school superintendent, under guidelines established by and subject to the review of the local Board of Education and ultimately the State Board of Education. The existence of such special needs shall not compel issuance of a waiver, and the parents shall be fully informed of their right to refuse to agree to a waiver.

ARTICLE 4. Community-Based English Tutoring

315. In furtherance of its constitutional and legal requirement to offer special language assistance to children coming from backgrounds of limited English proficiency, the state shall encourage family members and others to provide personal English language tutoring to such children, and support these efforts by raising the general level of English language knowledge in the community. Commencing with the fiscal year in which this initiative is enacted and for each of the nine fiscal years following thereafter, a sum of fifty million dollars ($50,000,00) per year is hereby appropriated from the General Fund for the purpose of providing additional funding for free or subsidized programs of adult English language instruc-

tion to parents or other members of the community who pledge to provide personal English language tutoring to California school children with limited English proficiency.

316. Programs funded pursuant to this section shall be provided through schools or community organizations. Funding for these programs shall be administered by the Office of the Superintendent of Public Instruction, and shall be disbursed at the discretion of the local school boards, under reasonable guidelines established by, and subject to the review of, the State Board of Education.

ARTICLE 5. Legal Standing and Parental Enforcement

320. As detailed in Article 2 (commencing with Section 305) and Article 3 (commencing with Section 310), all California school children have the right to be provided with an English language public education. If a California school child has been denied the option of an English language instructional curriculum in public school, the child's parent or legal guardian shall have legal standing to sue for enforcement of the provisions of this statute, and if successful shall be awarded normal and customary attorney's fees and actual damages, but not punitive or consequential damages. Any school board member or other elected official or public school teacher or administrator who willfully and repeatedly refuses to implement the terms of this statute by providing such an English language educational option at an available public school to a California school child may be held personally liable for fees and actual damages by the child's parents or legal guardian.

ARTICLE 6. Severability

325. If any part or parts of this statute are found to be in conflict with federal law or the United States or the California State Constitution, the statute shall be implemented to the maximum extent that federal law, and the United States and the California State Constitution permit. Any provision held invalid shall be severed from the remaining portions of this statute.

ARTICLE 7. Operative Date

330. This initiative shall become operative for all school terms which begin more than sixty days following the date at which it becomes effective.

ARTICLE 8. Amendment.

335. The provisions of this act may be amended by a statute that becomes effective upon approval by the electorate or by a statute to further the act's purpose passed by a two-thirds vote of each house of the legislature and signed by the Governor.

ARTICLE 9. Interpretation

340. Under circumstances in which portions of this statute are subject to conflicting interpretations, Section 300 shall be assumed to contain the governing intent of the statute.